A History of England in 25 Poems

A History of England in 25 Poems

CATHERINE CLARKE

With illustrations by Edward Bettison

ALLEN LANE
an imprint of
PENGUIN BOOKS

ALLEN LANE

UK | USA | Canada | Ireland | Australia
India | New Zealand | South Africa

Allen Lane is part of the Penguin Random House group of companies
whose addresses can be found at global.penguinrandomhouse.com.

Penguin Random House UK
One Embassy Gardens, 8 Viaduct Gardens, London SW11 7BW

penguin.co.uk

Penguin
Random House
UK

First published in Great Britain by Allen Lane 2025
002

Text copyright © Catherine Clarke, 2025
Illustrations © Edward Bettison, 2025

Pages 365–7 constitute an extension of this copyright page

Set in 12/14.75pts Dante MT Std
Typeset by Jouve (UK), Milton Keynes
Printed and bound in Great Britain by Clays Ltd, Elcograf S.p.A.

The authorized representative in the EEA is Penguin Random House Ireland,
Morrison Chambers, 32 Nassau Street, Dublin D02 YH68

A CIP catalogue record for this book is available from the British Library

ISBN: 978–0–241–76598–2

Contents

Contents

Introduction

I'm sitting in the Rare Books room of the Library at Senate House, University of London, where I've handled so many remarkable materials during my research for this book. Today, I'm reading *Rump Songs*, an original 1662 collection of Royalist satirical poems against the short-lived English Republic, including the memorably scatological ballad 'Bum-fodder' (skim on to Chapter 12 if you're curious). It's a decorative little volume, bound in gilt calf-skin, with a handsome engraved title page. And then, as I turn to the last pages of the book, there's a tiny, twisty hole burrowed through.

Pasted inside the front cover, there's a label from Maggs Bros. of London – one of the oldest antiquarian booksellers in the world, established in 1853 – noting 'a wormhole through some leaves at the end'. It's a rambling, sinuous tunnel, where the larva of some insect (not technically a worm at all) has munched its way. I hold it up to the light (avoiding eye contact with the Special Collections librarian) and can see straight through from page 183 to the endpapers. It reminds me of Eric Carle's *The Very Hungry Caterpillar*, on my children's bookshelves at home. And I think of the earliest reference to a 'bookworm' in English poetry: a riddle written down in the tenth century, which castigates those greedy readers who devour endless words but remain 'no whit the wiser'. I hope I'm faring better. Most of all, though, I think of pages and wormholes – in the science-fiction sense – and how books have that unique power to transport us, instantly, to other places and points far distant in time.

Poems, most especially, have the power to open a direct portal between us and moments in the past. Poems aren't just a bridge to the events of history, but into the experiences, emotions and imaginations of those people living and breathing through it. It's an astonishing fact – as audacious and thrilling as any interstellar fantasy. Poetry can shortcut time and distance, connecting us immediately, intimately, with individuals, their feelings and their worlds.

This is a history book with a difference. Twenty-five poems, written between the eighth century and today, take us with them on time travel into England's past. They take us inside history. The poem Queen Victoria read after the death of Albert, which tries to make sense of new scientific knowledge alongside religious faith and consolation. Guerrilla poetry written in English after 1066, holding William the Conqueror to account. Verse which takes us 'below stairs' in an eighteenth-century country house – penned by a housemaid dismissed for scribbling when she should have been turning the spit. Summer birdsong at a deserted railway station and the ghosts of the Great War. The wheels of Victorian industry and a tragedy in a coalmine. Voices from inside a medieval pandemic and the lived experience of the Black Death. A box of matches and the 1984–5 miners' strike. Each poem opens a doorway into the past, revealing England's history in new and often surprising ways.

From major historical events to individual lives in times of great change and turmoil; from familiar and well-loved poems to little-known texts from the archive, each chapter takes us into a particular historical moment: the events, ideas, emotions and everything that's at stake. You can dip in, finding poems which catch your eye or historical periods that appeal to you. Or start now, with the present day and the lush high-summer cricket field of Zaffar Kunial's 'The Groundsman', and read backwards, peeling away layers of history. Better still, read the chapters in sequence, making your way from the Saxons through to post-Brexit Britain: follow stories of Englishness as they are gradually crafted and reshaped, and listen in on conversations between poems which unfold over centuries. Each chapter is an immersive exploration of a specific point in time.

Poems are never just neutral observers. They are involved, engaged, partisan – they have skin in the game. Poems can be rebels, provocateurs and double agents. They leave us one half of a dynamic dialogue with their own rich and complex present: the impression of a vanished moment in words on a page.

Why the history of *England*? Why focus on just this one national narrative from the many identities and stories of our north Atlantic archipelago? I'm wary of complicity with practices of writing 'British' history which, all too often, erase and elide the cultural diversity and complexity of the many nations and communities within these islands. They have their own rich heritages and poetic traditions. And, above all, the poems I've chosen for this collection make their own compelling case for a legible history of England in verse.

From the very earliest writing to the present day, we can trace poetic traditions and images which shape a distinctive imaginary of 'England' and 'Englishness'. Think of the words of the verses known as 'Jerusalem' by William Blake, most familiar today in the hymn setting by Sir Hubert Parry. The poem's vision of 'England's green and pleasant land' has resonated through two centuries: an idealised English pastoral, fusing the character of the nation with its landscape, those 'mountains green' and 'pleasant pastures'. Sung annually at the Last Night of the Proms, adopted by various English sports as an unofficial anthem, featured in the opening ceremony of the 2012 London Olympics, and invoked regularly by politicians of all persuasions, the 'green and pleasant land' has become a powerful emblem for England. But, as we'll see, that imagery doesn't begin with Blake. He's drawing on a poetic tradition going back a further thousand years and more, cultivating narratives of national identity out of the green hills and fields of the land itself.

England's green radiates through the 1300 years of poetry and history in this book. But there are other patterns in this poetry of Englishness, too, stretching back to some of our very first surviving instances of the English language. Uses of nostalgia, mythologies of greatness, burnished images of honour, fair play and 'stiff upper lip', expressions of whimsy and playfulness. Poetry has always been intimately involved in forming ideas of English identity – and in troubling it, too. Over a thousand years, we can see how images and stories of England are shaped and deployed: ambitions, dreams and monsterings; lines of dissent and resistance.

Often strikingly self-conscious about their place in this tradition, poems speak back and forwards to each other over the centuries. While the poems in this book are set out in chronological order, a history of England through poetry disrupts a strict linear timeline. As well as twenty-five specific historical moments, these poems represent texts and conversations entangled across time. We'll witness how people can make poems do what they wish: how lines can be used to speak and signify in different historical moments and for different purposes. Authors don't have the monopoly on meaning; that's something interpreted – and often contested – between readers within and across time.

We'll encounter imagery of England as the 'island nation' or 'sceptred isle', stealthily conflating geography with destiny and erasing other countries and communities within Britain. Reading poems with political agendas and ambitions, we'll be alert to the ways they can make words – and geography – work to their own ends. But, of course, we read these poems with an understanding that the stories of England and its nearest neighbours have always been interwoven. It's not always possible – or desirable – to untwine a completely separate, uniquely 'English' history.

You certainly don't have to be a poetry expert – or even an avid reader of poems – to enjoy this book. Absolutely no prior knowledge of these poems, or their historical periods, is required. Poetry sceptics are especially welcome: I hope you'll discover the many surprising and enthralling things we can do with poems, and how a few lines of verse can open up a whole historical world. In this book, I want to invite you to explore new encounters and unexpected adventures.

With the right tools, we can unlock the coded and covert messages of these poems in their historical moments: the loaded words and charged language which speak to contemporary factions or controversies, or, even, the gaps and silences which point to something so significant or dangerous it can't be written. Careful, forensic analysis can reveal a diverse range of voices and perspectives: from power and propaganda to the marginalised and disenfranchised, and those speaking from the very edge of society.

Is it possible to tell the history of England – all those crowded, colourful, messy and eventful centuries – in just twenty-five poems? It's been a daunting, exhilarating, thrilling experiment. Following the poems moves us beyond a 'great men and battles' version of history, bringing into focus more varied histories and voices. Individual life records, small stories and emotional intimacies are here, bound up with momentous national events and historical milestones.

Spanning 1300 years, many of the historical moments covered in these chapters are deeply strange, even alien to us, both in the materiality of everyday life and in their mindsets and beliefs. The poems open windows into wholly other ways of seeing the world. But even in these other Englands we can discover intense emotional connection and affinity. We listen in on distant griefs, share laughter, rekindle old anger, draw breath alongside companions from centuries long gone in awe and wonder. The mission of this book, in part, is to take up this call to radical empathy across time, experience and difference. Reading these twenty-five poems, I hope, can challenge us to more ambitious, daring, generous ways of imagining and empathising with the lives of others – past and present.

Of course, twenty-five poems can never offer a comprehensive account of English history, though each of these chapters does reach more widely to draw in other texts and historical details. Not all are my favourite poems – though there are certainly words here to cherish and treasure. Instead, I've chosen poems which work best as time machines, transporting us into their fascinating moments in the past.

The twenty-five poems I've chosen are certainly different from the ones you would have picked if you were writing this book. What are your own landmark poems? Those lines that transport you through a portal into the past? Perhaps they connect with your own personal memories as well as history, taking you instantly to events and experiences in your own life. At the end of the book, there's space for you to make this book your own, by adding in your own choice of poems. I hope this is a book you'll return to and share.

Making my own selection of poems, I've felt a keen sense of what's missing – what's *not* there. I've welcomed this opportunity to think critically about literary value and values, and the notion of an

English 'canon': that literary 'hall of fame' constituted over generations by countless anthologies and student textbooks. How to capture a sense of English poetic tradition in just twenty-five poems? What makes a poem worth including and reading today, perhaps hundreds of years after it was written? Are there poems more worth reading now than, say, a century ago? How has a national canon of 'English Literature' been formed over time – and who has it excluded? How might we start to escape its confines and fray its edges? Who gets to tell England's story?

So, this book is also a kind of manifesto, inviting us to think through and beyond familiar notions of 'English Literature', 'history' and 'England', seeking to enlarge our sense of the ways we might tell and interrogate the stories of this country's past. It shows what can happen when we bring history and literature together into dialogue. And it makes the case for attentive, historically aware, critical reading – an ever more vital tool for navigating the multimedia battlegrounds of our world today.

The most fascinating history is often hidden beneath the surface or between the lines. If we know where to look, there are intriguing, unexpected and powerful stories to be discovered, and extraordinary insights into England's colourful, turbulent, always contested history.

A Note on Texts and Translations

No existing knowledge of any of these poems, or their historical periods, is expected.

For the first eight chapters of this book, with poems in Old English, Middle English and Latin, I have given my own full translations alongside the original texts. These translations can't capture the full style and nuance of the original (as the Venerable Bede says, 'it is not possible to translate a song, however well composed, out of one language and into another without losing some of its grace and dignity'). My primary aim is for them to help readers navigate the original text. For the tricky medieval Latin of Henry of Huntingdon (Chapter 4), I have referred to the excellent translation by Diana Greenway. For later chapters, texts are given in the original language, with some modernised spellings and occasional glosses.

Some of the earliest poems in the book include letter-forms which aren't generally familiar today. In the first three chapters, you'll find the Old English runic letter þ (*thorn*) and ð (*eth*), which both represent *th* sounds. You'll also see the letter æ (*ash*) – a vowel-sound similar to the *a* in *cat*. In Chapter 3, you'll also notice a symbol like a number 7, which is a conventional medieval abbreviation for *and* (medieval scribes got tired hands). You don't need to be able to read the poems aloud or pronounce the words to enjoy them – but it can be fun to try. If you simply 'say what you see', you'll find that familiar words emerge quite readily from the spelling on the page.

I have been fairly broad in my definition of a poem, including songs and an excerpt from a Shakespeare play (blank verse; also a passage regularly anthologised as a 'poem' in its own right). Some are full poems, others are extracts, as indicated in the chapter title. Titles are given in quotation marks for shorter poems and in italics for longer poems or stand-alone works, following standard conventions.

For some medieval sources (such as the Peterborough Chronicle or the Rutland Psalter), I have not used italics, as these are descriptions rather than titles proper.

One of my main aims in this book has been to include diverse voices. But it's more difficult to find, for example, poems written by women or people of colour in the earlier centuries of England's history. Often these sources are simply not or no longer there. As far as possible, I have tried to represent a wide range of perspectives: men and women, people of colour, varied social classes – even the words of children, so often overlooked in broad-sweep histories of England. Discovering less well-represented voices – across England's literary history – is still a work in progress, for me and for other historians and scholars of literature.

All the poems in the book contribute to a history of England, or a poetics of Englishness, in some way. They are not all by English poets and were not all composed in England, as discussed in the individual chapters.

I.

Beginnings

'Cædmon's Hymn' (around 730)

The beginning isn't really a beginning at all. 'Cædmon's Hymn', as modern editors have titled it, is a landmark moment for English history, language and literature. It's there in all the student textbooks and anthologies, selected as the starting-point, the foundation, the bedrock for all the words which follow. Yet what Bede gives us is a brilliant piece of sleight of hand; a beautiful and brilliant illusion, but an illusion nonetheless.

Nu sculon herigean heofonrices weard,	Now we must praise the Guardian of the heaven-kingdom,
meotodes meahte and his modgeþanc,	the power of the Maker and his design,
weorc wuldorfæder, swa he wundra gehwæs,	the work of the glorious Father, as he, eternal Lord, founded the
ece drihten, or onstealde.	beginning of each of the wonders.
He ærest sceop eorðan bearnum	He first created heaven as a roof
heofon to hrofe, halig scyppend;	for the children of earth, holy
þa middangeard moncynnes weard,	Creator; then the middle-earth, the
ece drihten, æfter teode	Guardian of mankind,
firum foldan, frea ælmihtig.	eternal Lord, afterwards ordained the world for people, Lord almighty.

Bede's tale of Cædmon and his 'Hymn' is an origin story, a carefully crafted myth which underpins ideas of English identity through the Middle Ages and far beyond. Bede's account of the poet Cædmon is worked into his *Ecclesiastical History of the English People* (*Historia Ecclesiastica Gentis Anglorum*): a monumental book telling how the peoples he calls 'the Angles, Saxons and Jutes' settle in Britain from the fifth century onwards, and begin to shape a new nation. 'Cædmon's Hymn' conjures the first words sung in English to their new Christian god.

The story of Cædmon is remarkable, putting these precious first words into the mouth of the most humble, lowly figure imaginable. Cædmon, Bede tells us, is a cow-herd, who takes care of the animals at the monastery of Streonæshalch (later known as Whitby Abbey). Cædmon carries a terrible sadness: though he's growing old, he has never learned any songs. In the evenings, when the fire glows in the hall and his people gather together, Cædmon watches the harp being passed from hand to hand, as the old stories are sung and words shared. When he sees the harp nearing him, Cædmon slips away, out of the light and laughter, and into the lonely dark outside.

We can't underestimate this pain; the freighting of Bede's story with the heaviness of loss, shame and exclusion. The mead hall or *meduseld* is at the heart of the early medieval English imaginary of community and belonging. Among the rich vocabulary for this treasured place is the word *seledream* – literally 'hall joys': resonant with all the rituals of fellowship, feasting and story-telling. But Cædmon doesn't have a place by the fire in the mead hall. He's out in the cold.

One night, Bede tells us, Cædmon sees the harp approaching, and hurries out of the hall, back to the stable where his animals are sleeping. The warmth of sleeping oxen, the smells of straw and dung, the faint curls of breath from the animals silvering in the cold night air. If we're reminded of the wintry stable in another familiar story of beginnings and new birth, then perhaps we're not too far astray.

While Cædmon dozes, suddenly, a figure appears to him in his dream and calls to him by name. 'Cædmon, sing me something.' Cædmon immediately protests. 'I don't know how to sing.' He explains that's why he left the feast and has come here, to be alone with the animals. But the figure insists. 'What shall I sing?' Cædmon asks. The reply comes back: 'Sing to me of the first creation.'

So, Cædmon begins to sing words which he has never heard before. And when he wakes, he holds them in his memory, and discovers that he can make more: a flood of beautiful words, woven together in new ways, praising God and remaking all the stories of the Bible in his own tongue. He's taken to the town-reeve or alderman, and then to the abbey, where the abbess, Hild, listens to his songs. All agree that a heavenly gift has been given.

Hild of Whitby is a real historical figure. Born around 614, she lived until 680, and was the founding Abbess of Whitby: a double monastery, where monks and nuns lived separately, but worshipped together as one community. Whitby was renowned as a place of learning. It was also at the centre of early medieval ecclesiastical politics: in 664 it was the venue for the Synod of Whitby, a major council which sought to determine how the date of Easter should be calculated in the emergent English church: using the system practised in Ireland, or following Rome. (Rome won.)

Bede was a monk at Monkwearmouth-Jarrow, not far from Durham in what we now call northern England. A learned and brilliant scholar, writing in Latin, Bede composed works of theology and biblical exegesis, as well as *computus* (texts concerned with calculation of dates and times) and even a treatise on the workings of the cosmos and movements of the tides. *The Ecclesiastical History of the English People* isn't a snappy title, but it's a clear assertion that for Bede, from the start, the nascent 'nation' of the English is bound up with a particular religious identity, church and authority. The *History* is a remarkable and unique source, giving us much of our information about earlier medieval England – though historians in past centuries were sometimes too ready to accept Bede's accounts as self-evident fact. Rather, Bede is shaping an English story: crafting the future mnemonics of a nation.

Cædmon is not attested in any other texts beyond Bede's *Ecclesiastical History*. Cow-herds leave few traces in the historical record. It's been suggested that his name has its origins in a Brittonic language – the ancestor of present-day languages including Welsh and Cornish. His name might hint that his heritage is not English or Saxon, but British: belonging to the people who lived in Britain before the coming of the Saxons, who are displaced, dispossessed and marginalised by the newcomers. The early English name for the Britons – *wealh* – seems to have its origin in the name of a Celtic tribe in the western Roman Empire, the *Volcae*, and became used to refer to peoples perceived to be of Roman descent or culture – like the Romano-British. Later, the meanings of *wealh* creep in darker directions: foreigner, other, slave. Eventually, it becomes the modern English word 'Welsh'. Early English law codes prescribe *wergild* payments – compensation – mandated for violent assault or killing, varying according to the status of the individual. In the Kentish Laws of Ine, probably dating back to the seventh century, the *wergild* of a *wealh* is valued at somewhere around half that of an Englishman of comparable status. English poetry is sung into being by an unlikely, subaltern voice.

The first word of 'Cædmon's Hymn' – 'Now' ('Nu') – isn't a clean start. Instead, it's a hinge, a pivot. It speaks of transformation, silently invoking the 'then' of everything which came before. It defines this moment in relation to the 'before' time, inventing an instant of renewal, new beginning and repurposing.

Bede's *Ecclesiastical History* doesn't start from a blank page, either. In writing his monumental historical work, Bede draws on older Latin texts: history, biblical commentary and exegesis, scripture. His *History* also has a complex, ambivalent relationship with one specific Latin historical text from post-Roman Britain: *On the Ruin and Conquest of Britain (De Excidio et Conquestu Britanniae)* by the sixth-century British cleric Gildas, whose home was in present-day Scotland and Wales and, later, Brittany. But, while Gildas interprets the coming of the Saxons as God punishing the Britons for their internal divisions and conflicts, Bede presents them instead as a new chosen people, and the beautiful, fertile island of Britain as a kind of new Promised Land, ordained for them by God. Janus-like, Bede's *History* looks back to Gildas, while also looking on, ahead, to a vision for a new nation of the English. It's a long way from the historical reality of Bede's own moment: a patchwork of competing kingdoms, often described by later historians as the 'Heptarchy', with their own ambitions, royal dynasties and rivalries. 'England' doesn't exist yet – only in Bede's imagination.

Bede is writing in the eighth century, in his home monastery of Monkwearmouth-Jarrow, during a period known as the Golden Age of Northumbria – the early medieval kingdom covering what is now northern England and southern Scotland. Picture the magnificent interlaced designs and stunning illuminated carpet pages of the Lindisfarne Gospels, or the towering sculpture of the Ruthwell Cross – carved with figures, Mediterranean-style foliate patterns and runic inscriptions. Or perhaps the intricate beauty of the Franks Casket, now on display in the British Museum: a box made from whalebone, decorated with pictures from great and powerful stories. The Roman myth of Romulus and Remus, the Norse legend of Weland the Smith, the biblical Adoration of the Magi: these stories sit, side by side, alongside a runic verse which imagines the sadness of the whale, from whose bone the box is fashioned, as it is beached on the shore.

Archaeological finds and other artefacts continually remind us that early medieval England was connected with the world beyond. The treasures of the Sutton Hoo ship burial – dating to the sixth or seventh century – include silver spoons from Byzantium, as well as materials from what's now Iraq and Syria, possibly brought back by warriors. The sixth-century burial of the 'Prittlewell Prince' in Essex includes a copper flagon depicting St Sergius in the decorative style of the Sasanian Empire – the last Persian imperial dynasty before the early Muslim conquests of the seventh to eighth centuries. Bede's homeland might be almost on the edge of the early medieval known world, but it's embedded in vital networks of trade, travel and cultural exchange reaching across Europe and into Africa and Asia.

Bede's *History* is a bold, ambitious work, inventing for the English people a story of their own. No longer a people in the margins of history, Bede's book seeks to give them status, authority – and power. His text also gives us our first example of the slippage between ideas of England and Britain. The St Petersburg manuscript of Bede's *Ecclesiastical History* – so called because it was taken to St Petersburg around the time of the French Revolution – begins with a beautiful historiated initial (a large opening letter), decorated with vine scrolls, leaves and flowers. Cædmon's foundational picture of the world is made in the image of the Saxon mead hall, but here, in this first letter of the manuscript, we see a 'green and pleasant' imaginary burgeoning into life. But that capital letter is a 'B', beginning the word 'Britannia' – Britain. Bede is writing England into existence, but he is captivated by the beauty of the island of Britain. From the very beginning, we glimpse the persistent, poetic, dangerous entanglements of England and the island.

The opening of the *Ecclesiastical History* celebrates the beauty and wonder of the island of Britain – claimed by Bede as the homeland for his 'English Church and People'. This 'island of the ocean' is laden with green – trees, crops, pasture – filigreed with rivers and springs, stocked with natural resources, and gifted with a treasure-store – metal, copper, iron, lead and silver – beneath the ground, as well as fine black jet, perhaps as familiar to Bede as it would have been to Hild and Cædmon from its abundance on the coast near Whitby. Bede describes another marvel, due to Britain's place 'almost under the North Pole'. During its short summer nights, complete darkness never falls, 'so that often in the middle of the night-time it is hard for those who are watching to say whether it is evening twilight which still lingers, or whether morning has come'. The land is full of the wonders of God's creation.

'Cædmon's Hymn' is a song about creation, and it is itself an act of creation. But, unlike the 'first creation' he sings of, this is not an act of making out of nothing. The words of the 'Hymn', praising the new Christian god, are not new inventions. Instead, in Cædmon's song, we see a reappropriation, a repurposing of the language of secular warrior culture, to voice a new belief system. The word 'God' is not used. Instead, the 'Hymn' imagines the Christian deity as 'heaven-kingdom's guardian' ('heofonrices weard') and a powerful worker of 'glory' ('wuldor'). The 'Hymn' uses exactly the same vocabulary for God as the songs of the mead hall used for a mighty ruler or lord: 'drihten' and 'frea'.

The words of 'Cædmon's Hymn' belong to the world of *Beowulf*: a world of heroes, champions, battle and glory. Even the act of creation celebrated by the poem is shaped by a distinctively early medieval English imaginary: the newly shaped world bears 'heaven as a roof' ('heofon to rofe'), built by its generous protector-lord. The world, as Cædmon sings it, is a mead hall. This daring remaking of creation in English words invests the poet with awesome power. And, the 'Hymn' suggests, that's exactly right. God is described as creator or 'scyppend' – a word for 'maker' which closely parallels the Old English for poet: *scop* or shaper.

'Cædmon's Hymn' presents a distinctly English version of God and his creation ('middangeard' – the 'middle earth' which lies between heaven and hell). We can see a similar impulse in other vocabulary associated with Christianity in pre-Conquest England. Rather than, say, the Latin-derived word *ascension*, the Old English is *upastignesse* (literally, 'up-climbing-ness'). The Holy Trinity, from the Latin *trinitas*, is *þrines*: the opening runic letter þ ('thorn') is pronounced *th*, so it sounds exactly like what it means – 'three-ness'.

The audacious recycling of secular heroic language in 'Cædmon's Hymn' is part of wider patterns of reuse and appropriation. This repurposing of words parallels the reuse of other traditions, beliefs and sacred places in Britain, as part of the strategic process of conversion to Christianity. In a famous letter on the mission to bring Christianity to England, Pope Gregory the Great advises that 'the pagan temples of that people should by no means be destroyed, but only the idols within them. Let holy water be made and sprinkled in the temples; let [Christian] altars be built and relics placed within them.' This is not a mindless iconoclastic rampage, but a concerted endeavour to overlay old imaginaries with new meanings.

Bede's good at origin stories. As well as this account of Cædmon and his 'Hymn', he also gives us the story of the two slave boys in the marketplace at Rome. Seeing their fair hair and beauty, Pope Gregory asks who they are. 'Angles', he is told. '*Non angli, sed angeli*', comes his famous reply: 'Not Angles, but angels'. At that moment, their true nature as God's chosen people is revealed: they must be converted, saved, brought into the fold of Christendom. Another myth of identity which has exerted power across the centuries, Bede's story of the slave boys shapes fantasies of racial purity and innate superiority which, later, serve to underpin English (and British) ideologies of power and empire, with all their violence.

Cædmon is a unique figure in English literature and history. Bede's *Ecclesiastical History* brings him in from the cold of the cowshed, and incorporates him into an English canon – in a book otherwise populated with kings, saints and bishops. But Cædmon does have one parallel in early medieval English literature – a strange and unsettling counterpart which opens up troubling questions about identity, community and belonging, right from the start of our journey through English words and history.

In the Old English poem *Beowulf*, the eponymous hero fights a terrible monster, Grendel. Grendel is a 'mearcstapa' – a 'boundary-stepper' or 'edge-walker' – who haunts the wilds beyond the world of the mead hall and treads the margins between the human and the other. He raids the once-splendid hall of Lord Hrothgar and feasts on the men inside. Terrifying and appalling, Grendel does, however, have one striking affinity with Cædmon. Like Cædmon, before his dream, Grendel cannot bear the sounds of music and song which echo from the mead hall. Outside, alone in the shadows, Grendel hears the *scop* sing the story of creation, and how the beauty of the world was shaped for the joy of mankind. And it is agony for him. The Old English uses the verb *geþolian*: he suffered, was harrowed, tormented.

What does it mean that Cædmon and Grendel share this dark, intimate affinity of pain and shame? Is Grendel what Cædmon might have become, but for the shining visitor in his dream? This uncanny parallel invites us to ask questions, from the beginning of our story of English history and poetry, about the arbitrariness of violence or brutality, and about who is included within the community – and who is cast beyond, at the shadowed edges.

There's one last twist to Bede's origin myth. Bede's writing this story as a celebration of Englishness and the English language. He's making a statement and setting out a kind of manifesto: for the ambition, status and authority of this emerging new people of the English and their place in the world. 'Cædmon's Hymn' is an originary moment for that inter-connection of nation, identity and language – sometimes wonderful, sometimes toxic, pernicious and exclusionary, which we'll trace throughout this book.

But, when the first manuscript of the *Ecclesiastical History* is written down, there's no English in this story. Instead, the narrative of 'Cædmon's Hymn' – including the poem itself – is, like the rest of the *History*, given entirely in Latin. Bede is apologetic, noting that 'This is the sense however not the order of the words which he sang while sleeping; for it is not possible to translate a song, however well composed, out of one language and into another without losing some of its grace and dignity'.

The Old English we have here – Bede's point of origin for literature in this country's language, and the purpose of his story – is instead reverse-engineered into the story much later. The earliest surviving manuscript which includes the 'Hymn' in English as part of the main text dates from the tenth century. In other, earlier manuscripts of the *Ecclesiastical History*, the English words of the 'Hymn' are retrofitted into the text: squeezed by later scribes into the margins, translating the Latin. That potent, foundational moment of Englishness imagined by Bede almost slips off the edge of the story: a footnote to its own genesis.

Poems, we see already, can be unreliable witnesses to the past. So much can fall through the cracks between their lines. From the very beginning, poetry is a slippery, ambiguous, disconcerting, exasperating and revealing place to look for history.

2.

Vikings

Extract from The Battle of Maldon
(around 1000)

Just outside Maldon, near where the River Chelmer runs into the Blackwater Estuary, a narrow causeway leads across saltmarsh and water to the tidal island of Northey. Bladderwrack banks the edges of the narrow track; purple laver and gutweed ribbon the ground. Ripples ridge-and-furrow the water. At the ebb of the tide, rivulets and runnels snake through the mud, like the interlaced worms on the golden treasure of a Saxon hoard. Today, in the June sunshine, black-headed gulls are foraging, swifts squeal and swoop, and a little egret steps fastidiously along a channel. There's the tang of salt and seaweed in the air; the rich, oozy stink of the marsh. Along the causeway, if you stop to listen, the mud is ticking and tutting, whispering under its breath. All around, the flat edgelands of Essex: land meeting water, sea touching scoured, empty sky.

Here, in August 991, was the site of the Battle of Maldon: a Viking attack met by English fighters led by Byrhtnoth, Ealdorman of Essex, and recorded in a number of texts, including the Old English poem *The Battle of Maldon*. The Vikings land on Northey Island, while the English army waits across the water, on the mainland, to engage them. The Vikings request passage along the causeway, which Byrhtnoth grants. The ensuing battle is bloody: Byrhtnoth is killed, many of his warriors flee the field, and it is a catastrophic defeat for the English.

But the version of the battle in the Old English poem is something far more complex. Far from the dispassionate, factual account of a modern-day war correspondent, the poem is less interested in what we'd call 'accuracy', and more focused on a particular kind of myth-making. The poem mobilises all the resources of Old English heroic tradition to celebrate the courage of Byrhtnoth's army, to define an emerging nation of England, and to remake a disastrous defeat into a victory for English honour.

And *The Battle of Maldon* does something more, too. Composed not long after the battle itself, it engages actively in a fraught historical moment and fierce contemporary political controversy. What seems, at first, like timeless heroic verse is in fact an excoriating critique of tenth-century English leadership, and a brilliant piece of propaganda, voiced here through the words of Byrhtnoth himself, as he responds scornfully to the Viking messenger and his offer of truce.

Byrhtnoð maþelode,   bord hafenode,
wand wacne æsc,   wordum mælde,
yrre and anræd   ageaf him andsware:
'Gehyrst þu, sælida,   hwæt þis folc segeð?
Hi willað eow to gafole   garas syllan,
ættrynne ord   and ealde swurd,
þa heregeatu   þe eow æt hilde ne deah.
Brimmanna boda,   abeod eft ongean,
sege þinum leodum   miccle laþre spell,
þæt her stynt unforcuð   eorl mid his werode,
þe wile gealgean   eþel þysne,
Æþelredes eard,   ealdres mines,
folc and foldan.   Feallan sceolon
hæþene æt hilde.   To heanlic me þinceð

Byrhtnoth spoke out, raised his shield,
shook his slender ash spear, spoke with these words,
angry and single-minded gave him answer:
'Do you hear, seaman, what this people says?
They intend to give you spears as tribute,
the poisoned tip and ancient sword,
that war-gear which will be no profit to you in battle.
Messenger of the seamen, deliver a message back again,
tell your people much more unpleasant report –
that here stands an unblemished *eorl* with his company,
who wishes to defend this homeland,
the land of Æthelræd, my lord,
people and territory. The heathens

þæt ge mid urum sceattum   to
   scype gangon
unbefohtene,   nu ge þus feor hider
on urne eard   in becomon.
Ne sceole ge swa softe   sinc
   gegangan;
us sceal ord and ecg   ær geseman,
grim guðplega,   ær we gofol
   syllon.'

must die in battle. Too shameful it
   seems to me
that you should go to your ship
   with our coins
unfought, now that you have
   come here
thus far, into our land.
You shall not get treasure so easily!
Point and blade shall first settle
   things between us,
the grim game of battle, before we
   give tribute.'

Bloody and devastating, the attack at Maldon in 991 was, of course, by no means the first Viking raid on pre-Conquest England. Raids by the Vikings – more commonly known, at the time, as 'Danes' – on the English coast began in the late eighth century, recorded in contemporary sources such as the Anglo-Saxon Chronicle. Lindisfarne, off the north-east coast of England, was one of the monasteries to be sacked. The Chronicle entry for 793 gives an account of the 'ferocious robbery and slaughter', prefaced by descriptions of 'dreadful forewarnings' which paint the apocalyptic horror of the event in English eyes: lightning, whirlwinds and famine, and 'fiery dragons' seen flying in the sky over the kingdom of Northumbria.

Over the following centuries, Viking raids and incursions continued – as well as Danish settlement in the midlands and north of England, resulting in the territory under Danish rule known as the 'Danelaw'. By the tenth century, the geography of England was changing. The West Saxon king Æthelstan (ruled 927–939) had conquered the last remaining Viking kingdom, York, and brought the various kingdoms and factions of England together under his rule. But by 991, with King Æthelræd 'The Unready' on the throne, Viking attacks on England's coasts were rising again.

In this extract from the poem, Byrhtnoth is speaking – responding directly to the Viking messenger who has just offered a deal instead of battle. 'Buy off this spear-storm with tribute', the messenger has offered; 'we are willing to fix a truce in exchange for the gold'. Old English poetry is structured around alliteration and rhythm instead of rhyme. Here, the stressed, alliterated syllables underline the exchange being offered: spear-attack ('garræs') bought off with tribute ('gafole'), and gold ('golde') paid for truce ('grið'). It's clearest of all in the final lines of the messenger's ultimatum. The deal is quite simple: 'feoh wið freode' or 'wealth in exchange for peace'. 'We'll go to our ships (scype) with your money (sceattum)', the Viking envoy says. But the whole tone of his speech has been riling, insulting – condescendingly offering the English a way out, on the assumption that they're not up to the fight.

Now, Byrhtnoth answers. The poem tells us that he was an old man at the time of the battle – perhaps over sixty. He's described as a 'har hilderinc' or 'grey-haired battle-warrior'. Other contemporary sources record that he was notably tall – likely over six feet in height. As he raises his voice in speech, he lifts up his weapons, brandishing his shield and ash spear. A conventional motif in heroic poetry and literary depictions of battle speeches, it's a first clue that this isn't reportage but epic and myth-making. The exchange of taunting speeches between the two sides is another traditional feature of battle poetry: known as a *flyting*, these volleys of words anticipate the later exchange of physical blows and violence. Byrhtnoth rejects the insulting Viking offer, calling on a sense of proud English warrior identity. They will not pay tribute.

The historical Battle of Maldon is recorded in a number of contemporary sources, including the Chronicle – the main historical record kept in the English language during the centuries from King Alfred to the Norman Conquest (and, in some cases, beyond), written down in a range of different versions in various places across England. And the entry in the Chronicle for 991 gives us the first clues that the poem *The Battle of Maldon* might be something more loaded and politically driven than a straightforward account of the battle.

The Chronicle for 991 is typically terse and sparing. But there's a significance to the key events it groups together. 'This year was Ipswich plundered; and very soon afterwards was Alderman Byrhtnoth slain at Maldon. In this same year, it was resolved that tribute should be given, for the first time, to the Danes, for the great terror they caused by the sea-coast. That was first 10,000 pounds. The first who advised this measure was Archbishop Siric.' The 'tribute' referred to by the Chronicle is in fact the payment which later came to be known as *Danegeld* or, literally, Dane-money. Levied as an unpopular and controversial tax, this money was paid to the Vikings to buy off attacks – a pragmatic policy nevertheless deeply dissonant with the self-image of the English people as a brave, warrior nation.

If we look again at *The Battle of Maldon*, we can find coded language engaging with the *Danegeld* question throughout Byrhtnoth's speech. On the surface, it's a defiant response to the Viking messenger, in the time-worn traditions of heroic battle poetry. But, if we know what to look for – if we're alive to the fraught political context of late tenth-century England – then we can see it's actually a searing response to English policy, and a charge of failed leadership at the highest levels.

Furious, Byrhtnoth picks up the language of tribute and turns it back on the Vikings. He makes a new offer: to give spears as tribute ('to gafole garas syllan') – an ironic, violent gift which will be less profitable (an arch understatement) to the invaders. 'You shall not get treasure so easily!' he declares. The English army won't capitulate and pay before they've stood their ground and fought.

Placed in a position of extra emphasis, at the beginning of a half line, the words 'To heanlic' ('too shameful') gain extra force and power. 'Too shameful it seems to me,' Byrhtnoth says, 'that you should go to your ship with our coins, unfought'. Again, there's that alliterative pairing of 'sceattum' ('coins') and 'scype' ('ship'). It's deeply unusual for Old English poetry to include this kind of direct reference to money – to coins. Rather, wealth and value in traditional Old English verse are carried symbolically by treasure: by gifts and rings and ancient heirlooms such as the weapons the English carry into battle here. The reference to money – cold hard cash – is a gut punch, a blow which exposes the Vikings' greed and the sordid bargain being driven. And that notion of shamefulness is what resonates loudest – what blazes searingly out of the page. Paying off the Danes would be an act of shame.

Byrhtnoth is unequivocally cast as the moral authority here. He is described as an earl 'unforcuð', or of 'unblemished' reputation. The Old English adjective begins with the negative prefix 'un'-, just like the modern English translation of the word. Why celebrate Byrhtnoth with a negative – something he's *not*? Does the poem hint, stealthily, that others in positions of leadership *are* in fact blemished and compromised? Does it plant the germ of an idea that Byrhtnoth's honour and courage are in contrast to something – or someone – else?

There's an even clearer hint in the first lines here. Byrhtnoth returns his message to the Viking envoy in a righteous rage: 'angry and single-minded' ('yrre and anræd'). That word *anræd* is a compound – that is, formed out of two parts: *an*, or 'single', and *ræd* – 'counsel', 'advice', or in this context, 'mind'. We're left in no doubt that Byrhtnoth is completely resolute and focused on his goal to defeat the Viking army. But 'anræd' rings a bell, and again points to something more than a celebration of Byrthnoth's courage. Someone other than the Vikings, it seems, is in the poem's firing line.

The English king at the time of the Battle of Maldon – and almost certainly at the time of the composition of the poem also – is Æthelræd, known popularly today as 'The Unready'. A contemporary Old English epithet too, the name doesn't mean that he wasn't ready or equipped (though some might argue so). Instead, it's formed similarly to the word we've just seen used to describe Byrhtnoth. But in Æthelræd's case, while *ræd* means 'counsel' or 'advice', the negative prefix *un* means 'no' or 'bad'. 'Æthelræd No-counsel', 'Bad-counsel' or 'Weak-counsel'. It's a satirical byname which denigrates his leadership – an epithet which arose out of perceived failures, including his weak handling of Viking raids and the *Danegeld* policy. While Æthelræd is *unræd*, Byrhtnoth is *anræd* – a pointed contrast, the poem depicting a hero whose uncowed honour and single-mindedness shame the king.

Byrhtnoth's single-minded vow to defend his homeland is striking – especially since the idea of a single English nation is only just coming into being. King Æthelstan's unification of the separate English kingdoms was, in reality, still a work in progress. But Byrhtnoth's speech is emphatic, clear, unwavering in its sense of what he's fighting for. The language is emotive. Byrhtnoth declares his intention to defend 'this homeland, the land of Æthelræd, my lord, people and territory'. The word for homeland, 'eþel', is charged with notions of belonging, devotion – and even baked-in, ready-made nostalgia. The Old English 'folc and foldan' unites the concepts of people and territory in a perfectly linked, seemingly inviolable, alliterative pairing.

There's a sense of violation here: that the Vikings have intruded 'too far' into English land: an insult which must be met with battle. But the Vikings, in fact, play a very useful role in the poem's depiction of a fledgling England. Paradoxically, it's this moment of threat and jeopardy which allows the nascent idea of a unified nation of England to be reinforced and strengthened. England and Englishness – embodied in the poem by Byrhtnoth's courage – are defined against the Vikings, imagined as a foil or opposing 'other'. The poem exploits religious difference to do this, too, when Byrhtnoth asserts that 'the heathens must die in battle'. The poem does energetic, determined work in the invention of an idea of England – an idea which will at times, over the centuries, exclude, dehumanise and monster others in its quest for endurance and power.

So, stripping back the poem's propaganda and its political manoeuvring, who was Byrhtnoth really? He's one of several named characters in the poem, though most are likely an imagined cast of foot soldiers used to paint a picture of an English army unified across geographical regions and across age and social rank. Some names seem more obviously symbolic. Two characters named Godric are on the battlefield: one deserts and flees the battle, while the other fights on, nobly, to a heroic death. Meaning 'good kingdom', their shared name – and contrasting choices – seem to present the stark alternatives facing England as it deals with the Viking threat: to capitulate or to keep its honour.

We do know that Byrhtnoth was a real historical figure. As well as the Chronicle, he's attested in other texts, including the *Liber Eliensis* or *Book of Ely* – a monastic chronicle from the Abbey of Ely, telling the history of the monastery – and the *Life of St Oswald*, an English saint. He's depicted in these texts as a great leader and brave warrior – but also as a figure of piety and devotion; a patron and benefactor of the church. Perhaps that devout Christian is hard to reconcile with the image of Byrhtnoth in *The Battle of Maldon*, apparently relishing the prospect of the 'game of battle' about to unfold. We see conflicting sides to Byrhtnoth in the poem: a fierce warrior who dies saying a prayer; a noble leader defending his homeland who sends his men into what turns out to be a suicide mission.

There are hints of hubris and arrogance even in the noble Byrhtnoth depicted in the poem. After his response to the Viking messenger, it becomes plain that the tide is against them: the Vikings are stranded on Northey Island and can't reach the mainland to engage the English. The watery geography is instantly recognisable from the causeway across the saltmarsh today: the poem tells us that 'then came flowing / the flood after the ebb' – that is, the turn of the tide. The 'sea-streams' ('lagustreamas') are rushing in, and the armies are cut off from each other 'because of the water there'.

Byrhtnoth has a dilemma: to engage the Vikings or leave them stranded. He chooses to offer them safe passage across the causeway (the poem calls it a 'ford') to the mainland – perhaps rather than letting the Vikings sail along the coast to attack an undefended landing point. But the poem deals even Byrhtnoth a word of reckoning here. In the Old English, it tells us that he allows the Vikings to cross because of his 'ofermode'.

Ofermod isn't an easy word to translate. *Mod* means 'spirit' or 'courage' – almost always a virtue in Old English heroic literature. *Ofer* is what it looks like: 'over' or 'excessive'. If a great hero has to have a flaw, then an excess of courage isn't a bad one. But the word can be translated as 'pride', 'arrogance' or 'hubris'. And it's used on another, telling, occasion in Old English poetry: the story of the fall of the angels from heaven. They are cast down from God's presence into the torment of hell due to the 'ofermod' of Satan: his deadly pride and presumption. Intentionally or not, *The Battle of Maldon* ends up calling attention to the complexities and challenges of leadership, suggesting, perhaps, that truly unblemished leadership in a time of war is ultimately impossible.

Indeed, one of the later writers inspired by *The Battle of Maldon* is the great fantasy author – and medievalist scholar – J. R. R. Tolkien, whose verse-play *The Homecoming of Beorhtnoth Beorhthelm's Son* (written in an alliterative style, similar to Old English poetry) imagines two warriors in the aftermath of the battle, recovering the body of Byrhtnoth from the field. The play is accompanied by an important essay on the Old English word *ofermod* and its possible meanings. The play's two characters, Tidwald and Torhthelm, exchange their own different opinions about whether Byrhtnoth was a noble hero or a fool whose error cost the lives of his men. But Tolkien himself is alive to the complexity – the tragedy – of Byrhtnoth's dilemma and the price of heroism. In Tolkien's own flawed heroes – Boromir, Theoden or Isildur, in his world of Middle Earth – we see echoes of the moral ambiguity and complexity to which the Old English poem points.

Today, not far from the causeway to Northey Island, a statue of Byrhtnoth, by the British sculptor John Doubleday, looks out across the Blackwater and the battle site. Doubleday is known for his statues of political leaders, such as Nelson Mandela and Golda Meir, as well as English cultural heroes: The Beatles, Sherlock Holmes, Laurel and Hardy. A plaque set into the ground near the monument states that Byrhtnoth was 'the principal voice in rejecting the policy of appeasement which dominated' in the late tenth century.

'Appeasement': it's an interesting and deliberate choice of word. It casts the Battle of Maldon in the image of more recent resistance against aggression in Europe – most strikingly, of course, the disastrous British policy, in the 1930s, of allowing Hitler's Nazi Germany to expand its ambitions and territory unchecked. The plaque's wording hints at a continuity, a shared identity, across all those centuries: an England (and Britain) which will always wake up to the evils of appeasement and fight on the side of right and justice. The Battle of Maldon has been co-opted into this national mythology of honour and fair play by others, too: Rudyard Kipling's poem 'Danegeld' (published 1911) cautions that it's always better to stand up and fight, as 'once you have paid him the Dane-geld / You never get rid of the Dane'. Stirring words – but far from the more nuanced, poignant awareness of human cost and moral complexity we find in Tolkien, or even in the Old English poem itself.

The Maldon statue reflects how Byrhtnoth is held onto as a hero even now – locally, in Essex, but also more problematically, sometimes, as an emblem of English independence, defiance, nationalism. The rousing words of Byrhtnoth's speech in *The Battle of Maldon* continue to do their work – and it's easy to take them at face value. But the poem's depiction of an army of English heroes, resolute and ready to give their lives in an honourable cause, is part of its propagandist purpose. Its representation of Byrhtnoth and his warriors – carrying their ancient swords into battle against a terrible foe – is archaic, even in the tenth century, deliberately looking back to a 'Golden Age' of heroic culture, mobilising nostalgia for a time which may never, really, have existed.

Most startling, perhaps, is that *The Battle of Maldon* invents its ideals of Englishness even as it evokes a context of loss and decline. Already, by the tenth century, nostalgia is a powerful tool for shaping ideas of English identity and nation.

3.

Conquest and Resistance

'The Death of King William' from the Peterborough Chronicle (around 1087)

1066: a date so familiar that it's become almost a byword for history itself. In the early years after the Battle of Hastings, the Norman Conquest and the deeds of King William I of England – the Conqueror – were chronicled in Latin and, later, Anglo-Norman French, by Norman historians, celebrating his achievements and shaping an authorised version of events. That's history written by the victors – though even among the Norman chroniclers there are touches of ambivalence and doubt about William's leadership. But what about those who were conquered? Where are their stories?

The impact of the Norman Conquest on England – and especially on the English land-holding and ruling classes – was cataclysmic. Norman rule brought not only economic displacement and dispossession, but cultural and even linguistic losses, too, as imported traditions and the practices of a new social elite took hold. It's partly because of this displacement and erasure that few traces of the English experience in the immediate wake of the Conquest survive. The English sources are scarred with silence: we glimpse the impact beyond the battlefield only in fragments, such as the image of a woman and child fleeing a burning building, stitched (perhaps by English wives and widows) into the Bayeux Tapestry.

This poem is a rare response to the Norman Conquest in an English voice, from an English perspective. Written in a version of the Anglo-Saxon Chronicle kept by monks at Peterborough Abbey in modern-day Cambridgeshire, it records the death of King William in 1087. In English words, it speaks defiantly back to the Conqueror and his project of occupation and colonisation. This is writing as resistance, partisan literature – guerrilla poetry.

Castelas he let wyrcean 7 earme
   men swiðe swencean.
Se cyng wæs swa swiðe stearc 7
   benam of his underþeoddan man
manig marc goldes 7 ma hundred
   punda seolfres.
Ðet he nam be wihte 7 mid
   mycelan unrihte
of his landleode for littelre neode.
He wæs on gitsunge befeallan, 7
   grædinæsse he lufode mid ealle.
He sætte mycle deorfrið, 7 he
   lægde laga þærwið
þet swa hwa swa sloge heort oððe
   hinde, þet hine man sceolde
   blendian.
He forbead þa heortas swycle eac
   þa baras;
swa swiðe he lufode þa headeor
   swilce he wære heora fæder.
Eac he sætte be þam haran þet hi
   mosten freo faran.
His rice men hit mændon, 7 þa
   earme men hit beceorodan.
Ac he wæs swa stið þet he ne rohte
   heora eallra nið,
ac hi moston mid ealle þes cynges
   wille folgian
gif hi woldon libban oððe land
   habban,
land oððe eahta oððe wel his
   sehta.

He had castles built and wretched
   men sorely oppressed.
The king was so very harsh and
   seized from his subject men
many a mark of gold, and
   more hundreds of pounds
   of silver.
He took that by weight, and with
   great injustice
From the people of his country, for
   little need.
He was fallen into avarice, and he
   loved greediness above all.
He set up great game-preserves,
   and he laid down laws for them,
that whosoever killed hart or hind,
   he must be blinded.
He forbade hunting the harts,
   likewise also the boars;
He loved the stags so very much, as
   if he were their father.
Also he decreed for the hares that
   they might go free.
His powerful men lamented it, and
   the poor men complained of it.
But he was so hard that he did
   not care about the misery of
   all of them,
but they had to follow the king's
   will in everything
if they wanted to live or have land –
   land or property or his good favour.

Walawa þet ænig man sceolde modigan swa,	Woe, alas, that any man should be so proud,
hine sylf upp ahebban 7 ofer ealle men tellan.	raise himself up and reckon himself over all men.
Se ælmihtiga God cyþæ his saule mildheortnisse	May the Almighty God show mercy to his soul
7 do him his synna forgifenesse!	and grant him forgiveness of his sins!

Unsurprisingly, the Peterborough Chronicle poem depicts William as an oppressive, brutal ruler. He was 'so very harsh' ('swa swiðe stearc'), it tells us, and 'oppressed' the 'wretched' people of England ('earme men swiðe swencean'). The lines of the Chronicle just before this poem have acknowledged the hardship suffered during William's reign, when 'men had great toil and very many insults' ('hæfdon men mycel geswinc 7 swiðe manige teonan'). That word *teon* ('insult', 'abuse' or 'damage') hints at some of the humiliations and degradations suffered by a conquered people, at the hands of an occupying power.

The poem also dwells on William's greed and avarice. He 'seized from his subject men / many a mark of gold, and more hundreds of pounds of silver' ('benam of his underþeoddan man / manig marc goldes 7 ma hundred punda seolfres'). The poem claims that he took this wealth 'by weight' – that is, at a vast scale – and 'with great injustice' and 'little need'. 'He was fallen into avarice', the poem declares, and 'he loved greediness above all'.

Later in the Chronicle poem, it notes that William's subjects had to 'follow the king's will in everything / if they wanted to live or have land – / land or property or his good favour'. There's a sense of the capriciousness of an autocratic ruler, and his power to dole out – or withhold – wealth and land on a whim, or on the basis of personal favour. English land, of course, was meted out in reward to William's Norman barons – but wrested from its pre-Conquest owners.

At William's death, his vast project to assess the wealth of England – the 'Great Survey', recorded in the Domesday Book, completed in

1086 – would have been recent and raw. The Domesday survey – and the subsequent taxation based on it – was part of a much larger programme of appropriation of English property, and especially land. By 1086, only 8 per cent of the total landed wealth of England was still held by English people, with the other 92 per cent under Norman control. In Kent, to take one striking example, the Domesday Book lists most of the English landholders on the eve of the Conquest, but, by 1086, not a single English name remains.

In fact, the Peterborough Chronicle records the death of King William in the annal for 1086, instead of the correct year of 1087, placing the poem alongside its comments on the Domesday survey. 'By his astuteness,' the Chronicle remarks, 'it was so surveyed that there was not one hide of land in England that he did not know who had it or what it was worth, and afterwards set down in his record'. Perhaps the Chronicle's conflation of the 1086 and 1087 annals is merely an accidental slip. But it hints that the monks saw some connection between William's ruthless Domesday accounting, and their poem's purpose in summing up his life.

The poem also surveys the major changes wrought on the landscape of England by the Conquest. The very first word, 'Castelas', focuses on the new geography of power inscribed across England – and beyond, across Britain and Ireland – in the castles built by the Normans. A new technology of war, castles of earth and timber, and later stone, transformed England into a militarised landscape, a map of colonisation and control.

But the Chronicle poem pays much more attention to another of William's impacts on the English landscape, and – besides warfare and conquest – another of his preoccupations. 'He set up great game-preserves' ('He sætte mycle deorfrið'), the poem tells us, with strict laws that any unauthorised person who killed a deer should be blinded. This is more, evidently, than a zero-tolerance policy towards poaching. In the poem's account, it becomes a symbolic gesture, excluding the English – dispossessed and desperate – from the rich natural resources of their own land.

As the poem lingers over its depiction of William's new royal forests – land protected by law for royal uses such as hunting – it becomes clear that it's saying something more. William forbids hunting harts and wild boar and, the poem notes, 'he loved the stags so very much, as if he were their father' ('swa swiðe he lufode þa headeor swilce he wære heora fæder'). And then there's the language of kingly authority and mercy: 'also he decreed for the hares that they might go free' ('eac he sætte be þam haran þet hi mosten freo faran'). Brutal and cruel to his conquered people, William lavishes love and kindness on his forest animals. To the deer and boar he's paternal and protective, while the English suffer and starve. The words practically spit irony. It's a grotesque distortion, the poem implies, of the proper care and responsibility of a good king.

Sellar and Yeatman famously garble this passage, to comic effect, in their humorous rendition of English history, *1066 and All That* (1930). William the Conqueror, they tell us, 'is memorable for having loved an old stag as if it was his father, and was in general very fond of animals'. But forests and hunting, it turned out, were not a good thing for William's dynasty. William's second son, Richard, was killed while hunting in the New Forest in 1070, when he was still in his teens, reportedly in a collision with an overhanging hazel branch. William's third son and successor as King of England, William Rufus, was killed by an arrow in a probable hunting accident in the New Forest in 1100 – though theories of a possible assassination refuse to die. William may have loved his forests, but it seems they didn't love him back.

Writing this verse obituary for William the Conqueror in the English language is a political statement – an act of resistance in itself. We can't be sure that the poem itself dates from 1087 precisely, due to the complexities of the Peterborough Chronicle's textual history. The monks at Peterborough were continuing a chronicle kept, at various locations across England, since the time of King Alfred: a record of the nation's history in its own words. But, in August 1116, disaster struck the monastery at Peterborough. A fire destroyed the library, including the Chronicle manuscript. By 1121, Peterborough's monks had taken up the Chronicle endeavour again: one single scribe made a fresh copy, starting from the very beginning and running up to 1131, using a range of sources, as well as adding in some material not found in other versions. A few decades into the twelfth century, most of the other chronicles across England were no longer being updated. But, at Peterborough Abbey on the edge of the fenland, the monks still added annals, year by year: a defiant continuation of English history, in English, in which Norman voices didn't dictate the terms.

Over the centuries after 1066, the Norman Conquest would enrich the English language, drawing in more words of Latin and continental European origin, and broadening vocabulary. But, in the late eleventh century, English was the language of the dispossessed, the powerless, the subjugated. We can still trace some of the social and economic impact of the Norman Conquest through its enduring impact on the English language. Our names for animals – and the meats which derive from them – is an often-cited example. A pig becomes pork (French *porc*) when it's butchered and cooked; cow becomes beef (*boeuf*); sheep becomes mutton (*mouton*). The Old English or Saxon name in the mud of the farmyard – where the conquered English laboured – and the Norman French name on the table – where the new wealthy elite dined. Quietly, though, Old English is still in use after the Conquest, even in written documents. Religious texts like homilies or guides to pastoral care, especially, suggest that English was still the language for grassroots guidance and learning and, perhaps, a powerful marker of continued tradition. 1066 isn't the absolute watershed we might imagine.

Even so, it's a bold and purposeful choice to write poetry in English after the Norman Conquest: a deliberately partisan act. And it's rare and striking to have this account from the English perspective at all. When we look to the English vernacular sources – those texts which continue to be written in English after 1066 – we're met with gaps and silences. For the English, the Conquest, it seems, was unwriteable: traumatic recent history beyond the reach of words.

When we use the term 'trauma', we're using a metaphor. Derived from the Ancient Greek word for 'wound' (τραῦμα), our notion of psychological damage or pain is made speakable by a word for physical injury. Writing much later, at the end of the twelfth century, the historian William of Newburgh – an Augustinian canon of English descent – gives an account of the Battle of Hastings in his Latin *History of English Affairs* (*Historia Rerum Anglicarum*). William of Newburgh uses that same metaphor of the wound to concretise the trauma of violence and conquest, surfaced in the earth itself at Battle Abbey. He writes:

> [I]n that same monastery, the place at which the greatest destruction was done to the English fighting for the fatherland, whenever it is wet with a little rain, real and seemingly fresh blood oozes out, as if it were being openly proclaimed on the very evidence of this event that the voice of all that Christian blood is still crying out to God from the earth, which opened its mouth and received that blood spilled by the hands of brothers, that is, fellow Christians.

William of Newburgh's powerful image of the battlefield as an unhealed, reopening wound suggests something of the ongoing pain and trauma of conquest. History is not safely in the past, but still bleeds into his own present. But it's significant, too, that his account of the Battle of Hastings is written over a century after the event. The telling of collective trauma, as we know all too well from twentieth-century horrors, tends to skip a generation or generations, to be fully voiced only by those with more distance from the original events. It's impossible to know how many medieval records of the Norman Conquest and its aftermath have been destroyed by the ravages of time or human destruction. But the impact of this momentous event in England's history reverberates, curiously, with silence.

We can see the Peterborough Chronicle poem straining to find the right words for its account of the death – and life – of William the Conqueror. The poem is written into a historical text, but marked with highly emotional language – the cry of 'Walawa', roughly translated as 'Woe, alas' – and the performative exclamation at the end – 'May the Almighty God show mercy to his soul /

and grant him forgiveness of his sins!', which sounds more like the rhetoric of the pulpit than a chronicle account.

The poem is also shaped by a specific literary tradition: the forms and conventions of the epitaph, or poem 'on' (literally or metaphorically) the grave. As with many other medieval epitaphs – whether incised on a tomb or written into a manuscript – the poem on William the Conqueror surveys the subject's life, memorialises his deeds, and then asks for God's mercy. Medieval epitaphs are often quite transactional in language and tone: tallying up a lifetime's achievements, undertaking a reckoning of the soul (and anticipating the heavenly reckoning ahead), and asking (either explicitly or implicitly) for the prayers of the reader in return for the edifying example given to them.

But here, there's a sense of the reckoning being skewed. The calculations are off, the scale is wrong: William has already counted himself far above all other men. 'Woe, alas', the poem laments, 'that any man should be so proud, / raise himself up and reckon himself over all men'. The Old English word for 'reckon' is *tellan* – the direct linguistic ancestor of our modern word 'tally'. This poetic epitaph attempts to reckon up the Conqueror's life – but William has got there first. He's all about counting, William: in the Great Survey and the Domesday Book with its cramped, abbreviated lists of properties and values and taxes. Now, the Chronicle poem imagines William turning that same bureaucratic attention to himself – and cooking the books. The Chronicle epitaph – and even God's final judgement of William's soul – are pre-empted by the king's own grotesquely distorted reckoning, which inflates his value above all other people. The poem goes through the motions of the genre but, really, it's more an anti-epitaph. The final invocation of God's mercy sounds more like an exclamation of despair or contempt than a genuine prayer.

There's an implicit sense throughout the poem of a sardonic, defiant response to the Domesday project – underlined by the placing of the poem in the annal for 1086, alongside the reference to the Great Survey, rather than in the correct year of William's death: 1087. The poem isn't just an account of William's life – it's an accounting of it; an audit which scrutinises the Conqueror's own ledgers. It shows up his deficits as a king and a man, and his failures, on his own terms, as an accountant: one who tallies himself up wrong and forgets to count what's right.

And there's another nice resonance between the Chronicle poem and the Great Survey. Could it be that the monks of Peterborough were reflecting simultaneously on the book which came to be known in English as Domesday (meaning, in Old English, 'Judgement Day') and the ultimate Day of Judgement they believed would be waiting for William after his death? The Chronicle is scrupulously even-handed as it weighs William in the balance, acknowledging, just before this poem, the 'good order' he maintained in England, and finally opening out the question of judgement to its readers. 'We have written these things about him,' the Chronicle adds, after the poem, 'both the good and the evil, that good men may take after the goodness and wholly flee the evil, and go on the path that leads us to the kingdom of heaven'.

Stories of resistance to Norman rule in the first years after the Conquest soon enter medieval English myth and folklore. They include that of Hereward the Wake: the English nobleman who led rebellions against the Normans in East Anglia, from his base in the fens at Ely. Among other sources, his story is recorded in the Peterborough Chronicle.

Not all resistance is violent or bloody. We can place this quiet, defiant poem alongside other kinds of rebellion in England immediately after 1066: a guerrilla text, written in English, which lifts the language out of the mud and takes its cool, steady appraisal to William's life, holding the Conqueror to account.

Anarchy: The Land Torn Apart

'Who Will Give Me a Fountain of Tears' by Henry of Huntingdon (around 1146)

Some time in the middle of the twelfth century, near the village of Woolpit in Suffolk, locals are busy in the fields gathering the harvest, when two children – a boy and a girl – emerge out of the ground. They wear clothes of strange colour and material, speak their own language – and their bodies are entirely green all over. Much later, when the girl has learned to make herself understood, she explains that they had come from a place called 'St Martin's Land', where there are churches, just as in England, but where it is always twilight, and a shining country is visible far across a wide river.

The story of the Green Children, who climbed out of a ditch in the ground near Woolpit, is recorded by a contemporary historian, the Augustinian canon William of Newburgh (and, slightly later, by the Cistercian monk Ralph of Coggeshall). It's a strange aside in William's serious, sober account of the reign of King Stephen (1135–54) and the events of England's first, bloody, civil war. Long before Roundheads and Cavaliers, or even the Wars of the Roses, the brutal and chaotic years in the middle of the twelfth century were a social collapse and crisis so extreme they were named the 'Anarchy' by nineteenth-century historians. King Henry I had died without a direct male heir, after his son William Adelin was drowned in the *White Ship* disaster. He had named his daughter, Matilda, as successor, but instead, on Henry's death, his nephew Stephen of Blois seized the throne, supported by his brother Henry of Blois, the powerful Bishop of Winchester. Later, from 1148, the so-called 'Empress Matilda' retreated to Normandy and her campaign was pursued by her son, Henry FitzEmpress – eventually to become King Henry II. The civil war reached across three decades, from 1138 to 1153, blighting a century.

So, what's the story of those strange Green Children doing in a sober historical account of England's catastrophic medieval civil war? A poem by another twelfth-century chronicler, Henry of Huntingdon, in his *History of the English (Historia Anglorum)*, can help us understand what it felt like to live through these brutal decades, and how the horrors of civil war might surface – in strange and uncanny ways – in the contemporary imagination.

It's a difficult poem, written in the medieval language of learning – Latin – by a churchman seeking to show his skill and erudition. But a close look reveals a horrific picture of civil conflict, appalling violence and the collapse of social order. Henry of Huntingdon's poem

Quis michi det fontem – quid enim potius – lacrimarum?	Who will give me a fountain of tears (what better?)
Vt lacrimer patrie gesta nefanda mee?	So that I may weep for the wicked deeds of my country?
Aduenit caligo Stigis dimissa profundo,	Stygian darkness has come, sent forth from the underworld,
Que regni faciem conglomerata tegit.	And thickly covers the face of the realm.
Ecce furor, fremitus, incendia, furta, rapine,	Behold rage, uproar, arson, robbery, pillage,
Cedes, nulla fides, consociata ruunt.	Murder, lack of faith, rush together to ruin.
Iam furantur opes et opum dominos et in ipsis	Already they are stealing riches, and (oh, new robberies!)
Sopitos castris – o noua furta! – premunt.	They bear down upon wealthy lords, even as they sleep in their castles.
Periurare, fidem mentiri, nobile factum;	To perjure, to make false promises, is a noble deed;
Prodere uel dominos actio digna uiris.	To betray even lords is the worthy way for men to act.

Contio predonum cimiteria, templa refringit,	A band of robbers breaks into graves and temples,
Iamque sacerdotes – res miseranda! – rapit.	And now (a pitiful thing!) drags priests away.
Detorquent unctos Domini, simul et mulieres,	They torture the anointed ones of the Lord, and at the same time
Proh pudor! ut redimant excruciare student.	They are zealous to torture women too (for shame!) to gain ransom.
Affluit ergo fames, consumpta carne gementes;	Their flesh consumed, hunger fills the wailing people;
Exalant animas ossa cutisque uagas.	Skin and bones breathe out their wandering souls.
Quis tantos sepelire queat cetus morientum?	Who will bury these great crowds of the dying?
Ecce Stigis facies consimilisque lues.	Behold! here is the face of the Styx and a kindred pestilence.

shows us what it feels like when hell breaks loose: when your land is torn apart and the very ground beneath your feet gives way.

The poem presents a torrent of violence and a terrifying impression of social breakdown and disorder: from 'rage, uproar, arson, robbery, pillage' to 'murder' and 'lack of faith' – in Henry's eyes, loss of the moral compass or God-fearing righteousness which should guide proper social relationships and community. While some present-day historians have questioned the Victorian notion of the 'Anarchy' – that total disintegration of law and social order – contemporary medieval sources certainly depict it that way. Just before this poem, Henry observes that 'there was no peace in the realm, but through murder, burning, and pillage, everything was being destroyed, everywhere the sound of war, with lamentation and terror'. The *Deeds of Stephen* (*Gesta Stephani*), another contemporary account, focuses on the acute, intimate horror of civil war, as friends turn against each other and families are torn apart. The author laments how 'the sacred bonds of hallowed friendship were rapidly broken among the people; the closest links of relationship were undone'. The Peterborough

Chronicle, written in English by the monks of Peterborough Abbey, Cambridgeshire, includes an unusual first-person comment on the horrors of the conflict:

> I am neither able, nor wish to, tell all the horrors nor all the tortures that they did to the wretched men in this land; and that lasted nineteen winters while Stephen was king, and it always became worse and worse.

Some things, the chronicler admits, are beyond the reach of history-writing: too terrible and traumatic for a direct account.

The poem's reference to castles captures a particularly distinctive feature of the twelfth-century civil conflict, effectively a protracted war of attrition. Henry's poem pictures warmongers who 'bear down upon wealthy lords, even as they sleep in their castles': an image of the siege warfare which characterised so much of this period. While Empress Matilda eventually came to control mostly the south-west of England and much of the Thames Valley, and Stephen the south-east, the lines of control were constantly being redrawn. And in large swathes of the country, barons refused to support either side and instead took the opportunity to exert their own power locally. William of Newburgh – the historian whose account of the civil war includes the story of the Green Children – depicts England fractured into countless fiefdoms, each with its own castle and belligerent 'king'. These local tyrants plunder and burn their neighbours, amid spiralling feuds and rivalries. In an England once 'most fertile', William of Newburgh explains, even bread became vanishingly scarce.

Some of the most famous stories of the conflict are those of sieges and counter-sieges. Stephen's attempted siege of Wallingford Castle in 1139, for example, and the notorious dungeon of its lord, Brien FitzCount, who sought to use the war to extract wealth from the region and crush his rivals. Or the besiegement of Empress Matilda and her forces at Oxford Castle in 1142 – from which Matilda sensationally escaped in the snows of midwinter, cloaked in white, across the frozen Thames.

Several contemporary chroniclers write with horror of how churches and monasteries were also turned into 'castles' by opposing factions: taken and held as defensive positions, their wealth and resources exploited. Henry of Huntingdon may have been a churchman – Archdeacon of the Diocese of Lincoln – but he wasn't cloistered away from the violence of war. He tells of how, in 1144, the rebel baron Geoffrey de Mandeville took the abbey church of Ramsey and turned it into his own stronghold. 'While that church was being held as a castle', Henry recounts, 'blood bubbled out of the walls'. Henry maintains that he saw this directly himself – his is an eyewitness account. Some say that God slept during those turbulent years, Henry reflects, but no: those bleeding walls were a sure sign that he was watching, and judging.

Attrition warfare drives the collapse of supplies, resources, food. In England's 'Anarchy' it led to widespread hunger and starvation, as Henry's poem depicts. The final lines paint an image as graphic and terrifying as any post-apocalyptic horror. 'Skin and bones breathe out their wandering souls': a scene of skeletal bodies and the spirits of the dead which can find no resting place.

Henry of Huntingdon's *History of the English*, from which the poem is taken, surveys English history from its very beginnings – drawing on Bede – to 'The Present Time' covered in Book 10, which deals with events of Henry's own lifetime. Like Bede's *History*, and the authoritative classical and medieval histories Henry's trying to emulate, the *History of the English* is written in Latin: the language of ecclesiastical language and authority. Much of England's literature in these early centuries is written in Latin, rather than the English vernacular: the association between English language and literary tradition only comes much later. Latin is also the language of classical tradition: the literatures and cultural worlds of ancient Rome and, through it, ancient Greece. Henry deliberately composes his poem in a classical form: elegiac couplets. And the choice of language steers the verse towards classical allusions. The River Styx (with its 'Stygian darkness') is the mythological river of the classical Underworld, the land of the dead, where the boatman

Charon ferries souls across into Hades. The poem laments how robbers break into graveyards and 'temples' – 'templa' in the Latin, but clearly a choice of elevating, classicising language to describe the Christian churches of Henry's England, just as the Underworld might suggest a Christian vision of hell. The whole poem has a highly rhetorical, performative quality, with its exclamations and asides: the language of the pulpit, or of classical oratory.

Most of Henry's *History of the English* is in prose. Just occasionally it moves into poetry, at moments of high intensity: praise, lament, crisis or jeopardy. And, most of all, the poetry comes in Book 10, in the midst of its account of England's terrible civil war. There's another hint here of what the Peterborough chronicler was trying to express: that some history is beyond the reach of conventional historical prose. Perhaps only poetry can begin to capture these moments of extreme experience.

Henry's poem plays with the idea of a world turned upside down. The darkness and torment of the Underworld is thrown up and exposed to sight, instead of being contained and hidden below ground. Hell, literally, has broken loose. And Henry adopts a sarcastic, scathing tone to depict what he regards as a new, topsy-turvy morality of these brutal years. Perjury is now a 'noble deed'; betrayal is a 'worthy way for men to act'. Codes of honour are seemingly inverted, turned on their head. Henry tells of the desecration of graves and churches, and how wicked people torture priests and are 'zealous' or eager to torture women, too. Here, again, another horrible inversion: a zeal for righteousness and honour twisted into an insatiable desire for violence and cruelty.

Although most of the *History of the English* is in prose, Henry did write verse elsewhere. Books 11 and 12 of the *History* are in fact collections of epigrams: short poems on a range of themes, showing different styles and forms of composition. One of these, in Book 11, is a verse 'On England's Troubles', reflecting again on the years of the twelfth-century civil war. Again, this poem deals in imagery of inversion, distortion, corruption. England is imagined as a 'pure fountain' now polluted and obstructed. Its fertile crops are ruined, its beautiful flowers crushed. Formerly a land of 'sweet honey', it is now a country filled with 'poisons'. This epigram is a searing indictment of England's moral and social collapse during the civil war. But it's striking that the imagery Henry deals in is the very same pastoral which shapes mythologies of England and its 'green and pleasant land'. Here, the political unmaking of England goes hand in hand with its literary and imaginative making: an imaginary of the nation forged in collapse and crisis.

Henry's poem in Book 10 on the civil war centres on one appalling, horrifying image. The earth itself is seemingly split apart, ruptured. The deadly gloom and darkness of the Underworld spill out into the realm of the living. The final line of the poem is an exhortation to look, to witness 'the face of the Styx', as if through a great fissure in the ground. Is this how it felt, for Henry and his contemporaries living through England's 'Anarchy'? The land fractured, riven beneath them? The earth split apart, ruptured under their feet? Henry's poem has an uncanny affinity with the story of the Green Children, who climb out of the ground and unsettle and perplex the villagers of Woolpit – as well as with a collection of other strange stories William of Newburgh tells alongside, folded into his careful, sombre account of the civil war.

A solid rock is discovered in a quarry which, when split open, reveals two dogs rather like greyhounds, but smelly and hairless. One dies almost immediately, but the other is kept for some time as a pet by Henry of Blois, Bishop of Winchester – King Stephen's brother. In another quarry, workers find a beautiful double-stone (two parts joined with a seam). When it's broken apart, a small toad is found inside, wearing a golden chain around its neck. Witnesses are astonished, but the bishop orders the stone to be sealed up again and buried back in the depths of the quarry for ever. And in the north of England, near a place where wondrous springs have been known to burst forth out of the ground, William recounts the story of a man who, returning home at night, hears voices singing. In the side of a hill he finds an open door and steps into a large, well-lit, underground chamber, where men and women are feasting. He steals a cup and the subterranean revellers give chase – but he escapes on his horse. The curious cup eventually finds its way into the posses-sion of King Henry I, and then at last to Henry II.

These are stories of the strangeness and precarity of the solid ground beneath our feet, of the unsteady English soil which might once have been thought firm and stable. At King Henry I's death in 1135, the Anglo-Norman kingdom was still young: less than seventy years since the Battle of Hastings and William the Conqueror's tri-umph. Do these stories reflect a kind of anxiety about the fragility of post-Conquest rule – about the limits of governance and authority in these islands? The Green Children, like the strange revellers under the hill, might suggest the haunting presence of other peoples, other traditions and cultures, beyond the knowledge of kings and chron-iclers, which linger around the edges and margins of Norman power. After all, Wales and Scotland still lay beyond Norman control. The nascent Anglo-Norman nation had too easily disintegrated into fac-tions and gangs. Who knew what other realms and agencies – past and present – were folded into the fabric of the land?

Most of all, these stories evoke a sense of English ground – the land itself – as a deep and capacious archive: of buried stories, won-ders, forgotten lore and peoples. They point to the fundamental association between the idea of 'land' – nation – and the land itself: ground, earth and rock; all the layers of time and territory, power and trauma. This land might be a kingdom – even if contested and fought over, as in the twelfth-century civil war – but it is also unknowable, strange, potentially treacherous, alien. It is a repository of miracles and monsters, which cannot always be buried and con-tained. Just as Henry of Huntingdon shudders at the sight of the Styx – the Underworld – as his country is torn apart, these other stories present glimpses into the strange underworlds of England and its history.

In 1153, Henry FitzEmpress returned to England to begin another phase in his campaign against King Stephen. After another cycle of siege, counter-siege, stand-offs and skirmishes, the war reached a turning point. Stephen's son and heir Eustace fell ill and died.

Fighting continued. But, that summer, Stephen and Henry met at Winchester and Stephen agreed to name Henry FitzEmpress as his successor. They sealed their agreement with a kiss of peace. 'Thus', writes Henry of Huntingdon, 'the mercy of God brought a dawn of peace to the broken realm of England, after a night of misery'. This wasn't a 'conquest' of England, Henry adds in his *History*, but rather a 'resuscitation'. One of Henry's first acts, as the newly named heir to the throne, is to press for all those castles 'built for wicked uses', which had become such symbols of division and conflict across England, to be pulled down.

Henry of Huntingdon ends Book 10 of his *History of the English* with a poem in lavish praise of Henry II. Stephen has died, on 25 October 1154, and England awaits the arrival of its new king. The verses capture Henry of Huntingdon's hopes for the new era of peace and order in England: among the qualities and virtues he attributes to the new king are 'proper punishment, sweet correction' – the return of law and order after years of crisis and social breakdown. He depicts Henry II as a hero saving the frail and grieving kingdom: he revives the country from its near-fatal sickness and warms it into new life. The final words of Book 10 of the *History of the English* point to new beginnings: 'And now a new book must be given to a new king'. But the historical narrative ends there. It seems that Henry of Huntingdon died before he could write the history of England's recovery and revival under its new monarch.

Perhaps it is only during civil war that anxieties about the *terra firma* of the nation can emerge so acutely; only when the earth feels torn asunder and ripped from beneath your feet that you look into its depths. Many accounts of the 'Anarchy' tell us about the horrific warfare of those turbulent years. But Henry of Huntingdon's poem shows us how it feels to live through a time when the land is broken apart, when the earth gives up its secrets, and the strange, unsettling underworlds of the nation can be glimpsed.

Mice, Monks and 'Merry England'

'Sumer Is Icumen In' (around 1260)

Children of 1970s Britain – and their parents, and perhaps their off-spring, too – will remember Bagpuss, the pink-and-white-striped 'saggy old cloth cat' who belonged to a little girl named Emily. In the much-loved television programme, Bagpuss – together with his companions Professor Yaffle the mechanical woodpecker, Madeleine the rag doll and Gabriel the toad – would help to mend lost and broken old toys found by Emily and brought back to her magical shop. While Bagpuss presided, the real workforce were the mice who lived in the 'mouse organ': an adorable miniature army of stop-motion labourers, stitched in grey felt, who would bustle eagerly about their business singing their 'We will fix it!' song. That catchy ear-worm wasn't a new tune. It was based on a medieval English part song, 'Sumer Is Icumen In', from a manuscript put together for one of the monks at Reading Abbey around the middle of the thirteenth century. The choice of music came from eminent folk musicians Sandra Kerr and John Faulkner – the voices of Madeleine and Gabriel, respectively.

The original medieval song is a celebration of the arrival of spring, with frolicking – and farting – animals and a noisy cuckoo. With its cast of barnyard animals and their sounds, it might seem that we're in the territory of a children's rhyme like 'Old MacDonald'. But 'Sumer Is Icumen In' is written in a prestige manuscript for the use of monks at Reading Abbey. And alongside the English lyrics – as well as the musical notation – are alternative words in Latin on the crucifixion of Christ.

What's a poem about farting farmyard antics doing in this religious environment? And what on earth can it tell us about religious and secular cultures in medieval England? 'Sumer Is Icumen In' casts light on a period often characterised lazily as the 'Age of Faith'. It gives us a glimpse into the cultural magnificence of medieval monastic life – as well as its downfall at the Dissolution and Reformation. And it prompts us to reflect on some of our assumptions about the Middle Ages as a more innocent, childlike time: an imagined 'Merry England' at the childhood of the nation.

Sumer is icumen in,	Summer has come in!
Lhude sing cuccu!	Loudly sing, cuckoo!
Groweþ sed	The seed grows
and bloweþ med	and the meadow blossoms
and springþ þe wde nu	and the wood springs (into leaf) now.
Sing cuccu!	Sing, cuckoo!
Awe bleteþ after lomb,	Ewe bleats after lamb,
lhouþ after calue cu.	Cow lows after calf.
Bulluc sterteþ,	Bullock leaps,
bucke uerteþ,	Stag farts,
murie sing cuccu!	Sing merrily, cuckoo!
Cuccu, cuccu	Cuckoo, cuckoo,
Wel singes þu cuccu	You sing well, cuckoo,
ne swik þu nauer nu.	Don't ever stop now!
Sing cuccu nu; sing cuccu.	Sing cuckoo now; sing cuckoo.
Sing cuccu; sing cuccu nu.	Sing cuckoo; sing cuckoo now.

The first line of the Middle English is a bit of a false friend: 'sumer' doesn't equate directly to 'summer' in modern English, but suggests a longer warm season lasting up to six months and starting with what we'd call spring. And though 'is icumen in' sounds like 'is coming in', the song's joyful announcement is that it has already arrived – it 'is come in'. The picture is unmistakably one of springtime renewal and flourishing: seeds growing, the landscape blooming and trees bursting into leaf. The animals have been busy, too: the ewe and cow calling after their newborn young in a flurry of onomatopoeic animal noises. The short lines and jaunty rhythm capture spring's exuberant energy, as do sing-song internal rhymes in the Middle English like 'Groweþ sed / and bloweþ med' or 'ster-teþ' and 'uerteþ'.

The cuckoo is there too: that archetypal herald of spring, the cherished two-note music of the new season. In Old English poetry – mostly written before the Norman Conquest – the call of the cuckoo is traditionally described as a mournful sound, evoking feelings of melancholy and regret in the listener. But here, it's that welcome, joyful harbinger of spring, recognisable and familiar in continuing traditions today. The cuckoo and its distinctive call are woven right through this springtime song – not only in the words, but in the music, too. The song is a round, described in the Latin instructions which accompany it as a *rota*, meaning 'wheel'. While the top four parts circle around the main melody, a two-part repeated *pes* underpins the harmony (these are shown here as the last two lines of the poem). 'Sing cuccu' in the sixth line of the song moves between two notes, like a cuckoo, repeating and piercing through the round just as a cuckoo's call rises up through the chorus of spring birdsong in a wood.

This is a complex piece of polyphony, or multi-layered music, with parts moving independently along their own melodic lines, when this style of music – even in as many as four parts – was still rare in Europe. In the thirteenth-century manuscript, the song comes with (Latin) instructions on how to sing it. The singers are described not as monks or religious brothers, but as 'sociis' – companions. Anyone who's ever sung a round – 'London's Burning' or 'Kookaburra Sits in the Old Gum Tree' or 'Three Blind Mice' – will know that it's sociable, fun: elaborate harmonies conjured out of a single tune, and always that possibility that the music might run away from you and fall apart into laughter.

For those of us sniggering at the back, let's talk about farting.

The bad news: some scholars have suggested there's no farting at all in the song and, instead, we have a goat 'cavorting'. But *uerten* – to fart – spelt with an initial 'u' is a common variant in Middle English, found in a wide range of sources. There was also, believe it or not, a strong association in the Middle Ages between farting and sex. A vigorous fart was evidence of virility and a promise of energetic coitus. So, the farting stag is a sign that he's in fine form and ready to strut his stuff: the alpha male of the woodland. More widely in medieval poetry – not just in England, but across European traditions – springtime is associated with sex and romance. A time for new dalliances, affairs and getting busy among the greenery. It's not just the farmyard animals up to monkey business.

All these details make it, perhaps, all the more perplexing that this poem is written in a manuscript for medieval monks, living lives supposedly devoted to celibacy and religious contemplation. And not only that, but written as lyrics to a song alongside a Latin alternative which meditates on the crucifixion of Christ – perhaps the holiest and most solemn subject in Christian devotion. The Latin words to the 'Sumer Is Icumen In' round are quite different.

Perspice Christicola	Observe, Christian,
que dignacio	such honour!
Celicus agricola	The heavenly farmer,
pro vitis vicio	because of a flaw in the vine,
Filio non parcens	not sparing the Son,
exposuit mortis exicio	exposed him to the destruction of
Qui captivos semiuiuos a supplicio	death.
vite donat et secum coronat	He gives life to the captives half-
in celi solio	dead from torment,
	and crowns them with himself
	on the throne of heaven.

How do we make sense of the relationship between the two sets of lyrics: the sacred text and the apparently secular, barn-storming English version? One connection is pretty clear – and it's the seasonal link.

The *Perspice Christicola* text fits with the church's liturgical season of Easter, or the period of Holy Week and Passiontide leading up to it. While the date shifts each year, it always falls at some point in the spring. But, at a first look, there's seemingly a total contrast between the two sets of words. One is serious, religious, focused on the death and resurrection of Christ, while the other larks around in the mud of the farmyard: playful, even bawdy and secular.

It's a big contrast. But one familiar from surprising juxtapositions across medieval ecclesiastical art and culture, from the buildings of churches and great cathedrals to the decoration and illumination of manuscripts. The medieval period is often labelled as the 'Age of Faith': dour, ignorant, relentlessly pious. But medieval ecclesiastical artefacts themselves tell a different story.

The Rutland Psalter, roughly contemporary to 'Sumer Is Icumen In', and made in London, displays the biblical Psalms in exquisite gothic script with lavish illustrations. On one page, the words of the psalm cry out to God for mercy 'in the day of my tribulation' and distress. Below, in the margin, a strange white man, with a fish tail instead of legs, bares his buttocks while another, red-faced grotesque shoots an arrow into his arse. In another serious, penitential psalm ('O Lord hear my prayer, and let my cry come onto thee'), a naked man, wielding a club, shimmies along the body of a serpent-like creature at the bottom of the page. Rabbits, goats and strange hybrid creatures play musical instruments. Mice gather around a cat they've hanged on a gallows. And, on folio sixteen, the elegant red and blue decorative band running down the left-hand margin of the page abruptly disappears into the spread buttocks of an upside-down naked man. The Rutland Psalter isn't unique: similarly playful marginal images – bared bums, phallic motifs, grotesque comic creatures, nonsense pictures and, strangely often, knights battling snails – appear across medieval illuminated manuscripts from England and beyond.

In churches and cathedrals, too, we find these jaw-dropping juxtapositions. Misericords – the 'mercy seats' designed to discreetly support the buttocks of tired monks and clerics during lengthy periods of standing for prayer – hide multitudes of weird and wonderful creatures. When the main wooden seat is down, the carved misericord ledge is out of sight. When raised, the carved misericord design is visible – but only briefly, before it's hidden again under the cheeks of a prayerful churchman. Grotesque and hybrid creatures jostle with scenes from saints' lives. Mermaids, dragons and monsters alongside farmyard animals. Wives beating husbands with their distaffs. Bare bums and breasts. In Tewkesbury Abbey, a misericord carving of a flatulent man reminds us that farting was just as funny in the Middle Ages as today. As Piers Plowman laments, in the great fourteenth-century English allegorical poem, he has none of the gifts for being entertaining in company: 'I can neither drum nor trumpet, nor tell stories; neither fart nor fiddle at parties, nor play the harp'.

From farting around with misericords we can move on to look at church buildings themselves. Grotesques, gargoyles, monstrous faces and impish corbels. One carving, high in the rafters of All Saints Church, Hereford, has become something of a local celebrity. Carved in wood in the fourteenth century, a man, naked from the waist down, holds his legs up over his head, baring his buttocks – and cock and balls – in an eye-popping display. This cheeky medieval figure was tucked away in the church roof for hundreds of years – until a new mezzanine café in the 1990s suddenly brought him face to face (and a lot more) with amused visitors. He's not the only bit of medieval Herefordshire which might require a Parental Advisory. Just down the road, in the Herefordshire village of Kilpeck, the famous Sheela Na Gig, carved into one of the twelfth-century corbels of the church, grins broadly at the viewer while pulling open her enormous vulva.

Alongside the soaring fan vaulting, gothic arches and transfiguring stained glass of medieval churches and cathedrals, we find these lewd images and bawdy jokes. In the pages of the holiest books: profanity and comedy. They raise – more vigorously – a similar question to that posed by 'Sumer Is Icumen In'. What are these naughty images doing at the edges of the most sacred spaces and texts?

We might assume they're subversive, undermining the central

focus of the church: the service going on in the cathedral, or the solemn text set out in the middle of the page. But they're now more often understood as a way of allowing the expression of more unruly, playful, crude human instincts in safely limited spaces around the edges of religious practice. Those marginal manuscript decorations, misericord carvings and figures tucked away in church buildings acknowledge and play out human desires, impulses, bodily functions and the more animal and comic parts of life, around the edges of higher and holier aspirations. Those bawdy, comic images might seem childish, but they're part of a sophisticated and highly developed trad-ition; a careful balance between the church's authority and control, and the need for ordinary human nature to find its outlets.

'Sumer Is Icumen In' is different, though. The fun English words, with their farting animals and perhaps bawdy hints at sex and pro-creation, aren't confined to the edge, but are right at the centre of the page. Which came first: Latin or English? Musical clues – how the words fit the notation – hint that the Latin might have been the original (though this is still disputed). The five notes of the under-pinning *'pes'* are also the same as the first five notes of an Easter antiphon (a choral work), *Regina Caeli*, which includes words about the resurrection. So, the balance probably tips towards the piece having emerged, initially, out of religious traditions and sources. The English words are given first in the manuscript, directly under the music, suggesting their priority. But the Latin text is written in red – a marker of importance and status in medieval manuscript conventions. (Important dates, for example, were 'rubricated' or inked in red, giving us the phrase 'red letter day'.) Did the monks at Reading actually sing the English words aloud? Or did they sing the solemn Latin, all the while looking at those alternative lyrics about animal noises and flatulence?

The English and Latin texts might seem completely at odds with each other. But a closer look finds some surprising thematic links. The Latin verse imagines God as 'the heavenly farmer'. He's depicted as cultivating a vine – a conventional biblical image for his creation, and especially humankind. Somehow, a sacred poem on the crucifixion and resurrection is nudging us back to the farmyard. There might, also, be another more implicit hint of connection here. The cross on which Christ was crucified can also be known as the 'Tree of Life', and is often depicted in medieval art literally springing into leaf. Perhaps that's another subtle resonance with the English song's springtime wood bursting into new life.

It's hard to be certain: are the English words a joke, subverting the seriousness of the Latin text, and applying a ridiculous literalness to the idea of God as a farmer, Old MacDonalding on a noisy springtime farm? Or should we understand the English and Latin lyrics more in terms of dialogue: sparring, playful, but ultimately mutually enriching?

Who were the 'sociis' or 'companions' singing this song, and how did it fit into the cultural life of Reading Abbey in the thirteenth century? Reading Abbey was founded by King Henry I in 1121, on a site between the rivers Kennet and Thames, ensuring excellent connections for trade, pilgrimage and royal visits. Henry's daughter, Matilda, gifted the monastery a holy relic – the hand of St James the Apostle – making the abbey an important destination for pilgrims. When Henry I died in 1135, the abbey was still unfinished, but the king was buried close to the high altar. The first monks introduced into the abbey were Cluniacs, but by the thirteenth century they followed the Benedictine rule. A typical day for the monks would have been structured by regular prayer: Matins and Lauds (in the middle of the night), Prime (at sunrise) continuing on until Vespers at sunset and Compline before bed. Reading, learning and contemplation were an important part of Benedictine life, whether private reading in monks' cells, as part of the liturgy in the abbey church, or listening to religious texts during meals in the refectory.

The manuscript which contains 'Sumer Is Icumen In' (modern catalogue name: Harley 978) was just one of many books held in the library of Reading Abbey in the Middle Ages. Folio 11 verso – the page bearing the song words and music – is the only surviving medieval copy, which explains the conspicuous grime along its margin, where generations of singers and scholars have pored over the text. Today, the manuscript is in the collection of the British Library. What else was in the book, alongside this famous English song? The contents are diverse: Latin works on moral and biblical topics, but also satirical poems in Latin and French, medical texts and pieces showing an interest in recent political and religious history. The manuscript also includes the only complete version of the *Lais* – courtly tales of love and adventure – by Marie de France, as well as a treatise on the aristocratic occupation of hawking. And, of course, plenty of music and songs, mostly in Latin, but with some English.

The physical make-up of the book suggests that it was put together at Reading Abbey (though some scholars have suggested it was made in Oxford). It's a compendium, an anthology, a treasure trove of textual delights which the monks wanted to keep. The contents range across what we might think of as 'sacred' and 'secular' materials. Perhaps it's a surprise to find monks immersed in Marie de France's stories of forbidden, adulterous love, or reading up on the latest hawking techniques. The book is also strikingly multilingual, reflecting medieval textual cultures and traditions which spanned Europe. Marie de France herself is a good example of how culture transcended the boundaries of kingdoms and emerging nations. Possibly born in France – as her name suggests – Marie lived in England in the late twelfth century, but wrote in a form of French, while also being proficient in English, Latin and possibly Breton. We might expect a medieval monastery to be closed and inward-looking, but books like the 'Sumer Is Icumen In' manuscript were a window to the world.

We don't know the first owner of the manuscript, but many scholars have been keen to connect it with a name noted in the book. A list of polyphonic music at the end is headed 'Ordo libri W. de Wint'. William of Winton (that is, Wintonia, or Winchester) was a monk of Reading Abbey who later went on to be sub-prior of Leominster, its daughter house. He was ordered to appear before the Bishop of Hereford, charged with fornication with Agnes de Avebury – an Augustinian nun – and with 'certain other women'. There's an appeal in tying up the manuscript with this scandalous history. But, in the absence of further evidence, it's perhaps just a reminder that not all monks lived exemplary lives.

By the time of the Dissolution of the Monasteries, Reading was valued as the second wealthiest rural abbey (after Glastonbury) and fifth wealthiest in the entire country. The last Abbot of Reading, Hugh Faringdon, was an ally of Henry VIII, who exchanged gifts and hunted with the king, and had been involved in the requiem mass and burial services for Jane Seymour in 1537. A few years earlier, Hugh had even made the library of Reading Abbey available for Henry as he sought to put together the case for the annulment of his marriage to Katharine of Aragon. But Hugh's religious convictions remained conservative, and he was open that he continued to pray for the Pope.

In 1538, Hugh gave up the abbey's holy relics, including the Hand of St James. But he refused to surrender the abbey to the king. The full reasons remain unclear even today, but Hugh was charged with treason, found guilty, and hanged, drawn and quartered in the streets of Reading. Two of Thomas Cromwell's agents had already ransacked the abbey, listing in their report the 'Plate, vestements, copys and hangyngs' which they were conveying back to London. Cromwell's visitors had previously compiled a meticulous inventory of the abbey's holy relics: a strangely evocative glimpse of a vanishing medieval world.

Back to our barnyard animals and the origins of the Bagpuss song. It's all too easy to look at the frolics and farting of 'Sumer Is Icumen In' – or the comic and bawdy drolleries of medieval art – and imagine a more childlike age of guileless japes and jests, and innocent belief. In the early twentieth century, the great historian Johan Huizinga characterised the European Middle Ages as a time when the world was 'half a thousand years younger' and 'all experience had yet to the minds of men the directness and absoluteness of the pleasure and pain of child-life'. Such a narrative casts the medieval period as the infancy of present-day culture and society; the childhood of our history.

But close analysis of 'Sumer Is Icumen In' gives us a window into a far more complex and sophisticated world. Close reading reveals a poem far more subtle than a nursery-rhyme round-up of animal noises. It holds its own in dialogue with a Latin religious text. It represents a world in which sacred and secular are in finely poised balance; the high spiritual ideals and lofty authorities of religion always in counterpoint with the impulses and functions of human bodies. Perhaps the astonishing music of the 'Sumer Is Icumen In' round gives us the best metaphor of all: the religious and secular, sacred and profane entangled and interwoven in a rich polyphony. Multiple voices sustaining different melodies. The farting stag on the same page as the heavenly farmer. And wood – trees in the farm down the road, just as much as the holy cross of Christ – springing into vibrant new life.

6.

What Women Want

Extract from 'The Wife of Bath's Tale'
by Geoffrey Chaucer (probably 1390s)

Gap-toothed, a bit deaf, garrulous and quick to laugh, with a fond-
ness for travelling, flamboyant personal style, and four husbands
she's outlived (so far . . .) We meet the Wife of Bath on the road
to Canterbury, on pilgrimage to the shrine of St Thomas Becket,
having set off from the Tabard Inn, Southwark. With the Wife
of Bath – Alison – we reach the first poem in this book voiced,
it seems, by a woman. Her words beckon us towards a different
perspective on medieval society and culture; her story opens out
questions about women's desires, agency and opportunities in
fourteenth-century England. Alison's larger-than-life character
spills over the edges of the page: more than just a historical figure,
she's a personality, almost a celebrity. In 2023, she even got her
own biography. But, of course, the Wife of Bath is the creation of
a male author: Geoffrey Chaucer, in his most famous work, *The
Canterbury Tales*. Our first explicitly female voice is ventriloquised
by a man.

But the Wife of Bath and Chaucer together – through their stor-
ies and experiences, both imagined and real – give us a way into
women's lives in medieval England. From the Wife's experiences
of domestic abuse, to her defiant, outspoken independence; from
Chaucer's poetic depictions of women, love and marriage, to his
own entanglement with the law over the case of Cecily Chaum-
paigne, a London servant: Alison and Geoffrey pose questions about
women's place and power.

This extract comes from the very end of the tale the Wife of Bath
tells her fellow pilgrims in their sociable exchange of stories. It's often

overshadowed by her much longer Prologue: the preamble in which she shares her own life experiences and holds forth on her opinions. The knight of Alison's tale has been sent on a quest by Queen Guinevere for a year and a day, to discover what women most want ('What thing it is that women moost desiren'). After a magical encounter with some ladies – who vanish into thin air – the knight meets an old woman. She's loathly, hideous – no one could be 'fouler'. But she promises to grant him the answer to his question. Together, they return to Arthur's court, and the knight gives his response. What women most desire is mastery ('maisterie') over their husbands. The loathly lady asks Guinevere for a reward: she should be granted whatever she asks of the knight. To the knight's horror, the old crone asks to be his wife. Miserably, he marries her. But then she offers him a choice.

'Chese now,' quod she, 'oon of thise things tweye:	'Choose now,' she said, 'one of these two things:
To han me foul and old til that I deye,	To have me foul and old until I die,
And be to yow a trewe, humble wyf,	And to you to be a true, humble wife.
And nevere yow displese in al my lyf;	And never to displease you in all my life;
Or ells ye wol han me yong and fair,	Or else you can have me young and fair,
And take youre aventure of the repair	And take your chances regarding the crowd (of suitors)
That shall be to youre hous by cause of me,	Who'll come to your house because of me,
Or in soom other place, may wel be.	Or in some other place, as it may well be.
Now chese yourselven, wheither that yow liketh.'	Now, choose for yourself, whichever you like.'
This knight aviseth him and sore siketh,	This knight deliberates and sighs painfully,
But atte laste he seyde in this manere:	But at last he said in this manner:

'My lady and my love, and wyf
  so deere,
I put me in youre wise
  governance;
Cheseth yourself which may be
  moost pleasance,
And moost honour to yow and me
  also.
I do no fors the wheither of the two;
For as yow liketh, it
  suffiseth me.'
  'Thanne have I gete of yow
  maistrie,' quod she,
'Sin I may chese and governe as
  me lest?'
  'Ye, certes, wyf,' quod he, 'I
  holde it best.'
  'Kis me,' quod she, 'we be no
  lenger wrothe;
For, by my trouthe, I wol be to
  yow bothe,
This is to seyn, ye, bothe fair
  and good.
I prey to God that I moote
  sterven wood,
But I to yow be also good and trewe
As evere was wyf, sin that the
  world was newe.
And but I be to-morn as fair
  to seene
As any lady, emperice, or queene,
That is bitwixe the est and eke
  the west,
Dooth with my lyf and deth right
  as yow lest.

'My lady and my love, and wife
  so dear,
I put myself in your wise
  governance.
Choose yourself which may be
  the most pleasure
And most honour to you and to
  me also.
It's no matter whichever of the two;
For as it pleases you, it is enough
  for me.'
  'Then have I got mastery from
  you,' she said,
'Since I may choose and govern as
  it pleases me?'
  'Yes, certainly, wife,' he said, 'I
  consider it best.'
  'Kiss me,' she said, 'we're no
  longer angry;
For, by my word, I will be to you
  both –
That is to say, yes, both fair
  and good.
I pray to God that I may
  die mad,
Unless I am to you as good and true
As ever was a wife, since the world
  was new.
And unless I am tomorrow as fair
  to behold
As any lady, empress, or queen,
That is between the east and also
  the west,
Do with my life and death just as
  you wish.

Cast up the curtin, looke how that
  it is.'
  And whan the knight saugh
  verraily al this,
That she so fair was, and so yong
  therto,
For joye he hente hire in his
  armes two,
His herte bathed in a bath of blisse.
A thousand time a-rewe he gan
  hire kisse,
And she obeyed him in every thing
That mighte doon him plesance or
  liking.
  And thus they live unto hir
  lives ende
In parfit joye; and Jhesu Crist
  us sende
Housbondes meeke, yonge, and
  fresh abedde,
And grace t'overbide hem that we
  wedde;
And eek I praye Jhesu shorte
  hir lives
That wol nat be governed by hir
  wives;
And olde and angry nigardes of
  dispence,
God sende hem soone verray
  pestilence!

Lift up the curtain, look how
  it is.'
  And when the knight saw truly
  all this:
That she was so fair and so young
  as well,
For joy he embraced her in his
  two arms,
His heart bathed in a bath of bliss.
A thousand times in a row he
  kissed her,
And she obeyed him in every thing
That might give him pleasure or
  enjoyment.
  And thus they live unto their
  lives' end
In perfect joy; and may Jesus Christ
  us send
Husbands meek, young, and good
  in bed,
And grace to outlive those whom
  we wed;
And also I pray Jesus shorten
  their lives
Who will not be governed by their
  wives;
And old and angry niggardly
  misers,
God send them soon the very
  pestilence!

The Wife of Bath's story begins in a time before England, in
'th'olde days of King Arthour', of whom the ancient Britons told
with such 'great honour' ('greet honour'). It's a distant time when
this familiar ground was 'fulfild of faerie': fairies, elves and magic

still abounded in the land. Why have the elves disappeared, the Wife wonders? All those prayers and blessings cast around by men of the church, she supposes. She imagines them accumulated thick in the air, like motes of dust in a beam of sunlight ('As thikke as motes in the sonne-beem').

Times have changed since back then, the Wife says. Now women can travel freely in safety, without fear of the 'incubus' – a demon in folklore which might rape and impregnate a sleeping woman. But the Wife of Bath's story begins with a rape. And not from a supernatural creature or monster, but from a 'lusty bacheler' – a fine young 'knight' riding out in the countryside. He sees a maiden walking ahead of him and, despite her resistance, 'by utter force, he stole her virginity' ('By verray force, he rafte hire maidenhed'). There's an outcry, and a formal legal petition ('pursute') brought to King Arthur. The knight is sentenced to death, but Guinevere and her ladies intervene. He can keep his head, they decree, if he can return in the alotted 'twelf-month and a day' to tell them what women most desire. It's a strange story of mercy, reprieve, education and reward, which begins with an act of brutal violence.

The Wife of Bath knows plenty about violence against women, both in deeds and words. She explains that her fifth and current husband, Jankyn the clerk, is the reason she's deaf in one ear. Jankyn's favourite pastime, Alison tells us, was reading from his book of 'wikked wives': a collection of anti-feminist writings from church authorities, decrying the flaws and failings of women from Eve onwards. One night, she's had enough, and while Jankyn's sitting by the fire, reading his misogynist anthology, she snatches it and rips out three pages. She smacks him on the cheek and Jankyn topples backwards into the fire. He leaps up, like a 'furious lion' ('wood leoun'), and strikes her so hard on the head 'That in the floor I lay as I were deed (dead)'. 'I was beaten for a book, by God!', Alison exclaims to her fellow pilgrims ('I was beten for a book, pardee!').

Alison's rage at clerical anti-feminist teaching shows its power to hurt and diminish women. While Jankyn's book is fictional, the texts anthologised in it are very real: Valerius and Theophrastus and a roll-call of authoritative writers who heap opprobrium on women. Jankyn's reading is high-brow and learned, but medieval misogyny tipped into more popular and light-hearted contexts, too. A late fifteenth-century manuscript, now in the Bodleian Library, includes a rhyming poem, apparently on the virtues of women. The first verse, for example, opens with a declaration that

> In every place ye may well see
> That women be trewe as tirtil on tree . . .

> In every place you may well see
> That women are as faithful as the turtle-dove in the tree . . .

But there's a trick. The two-line refrain running through the whole poem is in both English and Latin:

> Of all creatures women be best:
> *Cuius contrarium verum est.* [*The opposite of this is true.*]

All of the poem's statements about the virtue and excellence of women are to be turned on their head. It's no accident that the joke is available only to those who are trained in clerical or scholarly Latin – in other words: (mostly) men.

You could turn the Wife of Bath upside down and find her to be made of these anti-feminist clichés and stereotypes. She's gossipy, sexually voracious, unruly and always looking to get the upper hand over her husbands. But she's more than simply a character made out of a collection of quotes and commonplaces. Much more than that, Alison is quick-witted and wry: she knows herself and her own weaknesses, and knows what she wants. She even gets to the heart of the matter when she asks, reflecting on Jankyn's book, 'Who painted the lion?' ('Who peyntede the leon, tel me who?'). These wicked women are all written by men, she points out. 'By God', she wonders, 'if wommen hadde writen stories . . .' How different the world would look if women were the ones making history, she muses: all those tales might be turned on their head. Perhaps we might catch an echo here with another strong woman in fiction, three centuries later, when Jane Austen's Anne Elliot in *Persuasion* debates with Captain Harville the relative faithfulness of men and women. He claims that all books speak of woman's 'inconstancy' and 'fickleness' – but then concedes that these 'were all written by men'. Yes, Anne agrees, 'men have had every advantage of us in telling their own story'.

To be a woman in medieval England is to contend with misogyny and systemic violence. But, of course, there's more than one way to be a woman: context, age, position and social status all make a difference. And the many women in Chaucer's life, and writings, reflect a range of roles and possibilities. Chaucer's wife, Philippa, came from a high-status family, sister to Katherine Swynford (third wife of John of Gaunt) and, before their marriage, was a *domicella* or lady-in-waiting in noble and royal households. One of Chaucer's early poems, *The Book of the Duchess*, was probably written under patronage to commemorate the death of the noblewoman Blanche of Lancaster, first wife of John of Gaunt.

Chaucer's poetry reflects a serious interest in women, their stories and voices. His long poem *The Legend of Good Women* answers back to so much classical and medieval misogyny by retelling the stories of famous women – even notorious characters like Cleopatra, Medea, Lucretia – possibly in response to a request by Anne of Bohemia, first wife of King Richard II. In other texts, he reimagines well-known myths from the woman's perspective: Dido's own version of her affair with Aeneas, for example (in *The House of Fame* and elsewhere), or the full ethical and emotional complexity of Criseyde's infidelity in his great poem set during the Trojan War, *Troilus and Criseyde*. The Scots poet Gavin Douglas, in the early sixteenth century, described Chaucer as 'evir . . . all womanis frend' ('ever . . . a friend to all women'). But his poetry has been associated with rape culture by modern readers, too. Stories of sexual violence, coercion, trafficking and objectification abound in his work. Chaucer's verse points us to complicated, knotty issues around women, power and agency – and especially around their bodies, emotions and sex.

So, it was, and remains, confronting and uncomfortable for scholars of English history and literature when, in 1873, Chaucer's name was discovered in a fourteenth-century legal document. The case related to Chaucer and a London servant, Cecily Chaumpaigne. What light could this shed on his dealings with women in the real world? And what can it add to our understanding of women's lives in medieval England?

In 1873, Frederick J. Furnivall, founder of the Chaucer Society, discovered a quitclaim from Cecily Chaumpaigne, daughter of a London baker, in the Close Rolls of the English Chancery – a collection of legal records. Dated to 4 May, 1380, it released Chaucer from 'all manner of actions relating to my *raptus*'. *Raptus* is a slippery word in medieval legal contexts: its meaning can range from 'abduction' to 'rape', with plenty of grey areas in between.

The discomfort and embarrassment to Furnivall, and other early Chaucer scholars, was extreme. Chaucer's reputation and status were bound up with England and Englishness. John Dryden had revered him as the 'father of English poetry', whose genius was to capture distinctively 'English' traits in character and human nature, which endured over time. In *The Canterbury Tales*, Dryden argues, Chaucer had captured 'the various Manners and Humours (as we now call them) of the whole English Nation, in his Age', still recognisable centuries later. The beginning of the General Prologue to *The Canterbury Tales* is often used as a literary touchstone for pastoral Englishness – our 'green and pleasant land' in the making. The opening lines, depicting spring bursting out across England, are endlessly anthologised:

> Whan that Aprille with his shoures soote
> The droghte of March hath perced to the roote . . .

> When April with his sweet showers
> Has pierced the drought of March to the root . . .

Then, Chaucer tells us, 'longen folk to goon on pilgrimages' ('folk long to go on pilgrimages'). He imagines them coming 'from every shires end' as they travel to Canterbury. His fictional band of diverse pilgrims – from different places, social estates and walks of life – offer a kind of microcosm of English community.

A charge of *raptus* against the father of English poetry was a serious problem. Over the decades, some scholars sought to defend Chaucer's reputation. How could a poet who paid such sensitive attention to women's stories and perspectives be a rapist? How could the Chaucer depicted in *The Canterbury Tales* – a self-deprecating portrait by Chaucer himself – be violent or vicious? In the *Tales*, Chaucer is famously described by the character Harry Bailey, the company's host, as a little 'poppet' ('doll'); plump, small and always looking down at the ground. Feminist readers of Chaucer, though, have found much to think with in the suggestion that Chaucer's relationship with women may have been more complicated and ambivalent than early champions allowed.

In 2022, scholars in the UK and Canada discovered game-changing new evidence for our understanding of Chaucer's *raptus* case: a writ from 1379 and a 1380 warrant. The writ, dated 16 October 1379, was from a Thomas Staundon, who alleged that Geoffrey Chaucer had 'admitted and retained Cecily Champayn, formerly the servant of the aforesaid Thomas', without permission or licence. Then, in a warrant of 9 April 1380, Cecily Chaumpaigne appoints two attorneys to act on her behalf. But they weren't appointed against Chaucer: instead, they were to act against Staundon, with Cecily as defendant, rather than plaintiff.

These new discoveries radically change our understanding of Chaucer's *raptus* case, setting it in the context of new regulations put in place in the restricted labour market following the Black Death, when workers were in short supply. These statutes were intended to control wages and to prevent the poaching of servants by employers with deeper pockets. Cecily Chaumpaigne, it seems, had moved from Thomas Staundon's employment into service with Geoffrey Chaucer, without Staundon's permission. Chaucer and

Chaumpaigne, together, defended themselves against the charge of *raptus*, and the original quitclaim, found by Furnivall, was Cecily's declaration that she had left Staundon's service of her own free will, without the involvement of Chaucer or others.

We know a great deal about Geoffrey Chaucer, but who was Cecily Chaumpaigne? Describing her as the daughter of a London baker doesn't tell the whole story. Her father, William Chaumpaigne, also did business as a corn merchant and held property in the city. On his death, Cecily's mother, Agnes, married William Pickerel, a well-to-do London saddler, who'd been Master and Warden of the Saddlers' Company in the 1320s and later King's Saddler to Edward III. An astute businesswoman herself, Agnes brought her own prosecution under labour regulations in 1368 against a Matthew Winfield of Doncaster, for leaving her service before the end of the agreed term.

In 1380, Cecily was in her early thirties and unmarried. She had come from an affluent, upwardly mobile family, where she would have enjoyed status, luxury goods and fine possessions. Since her mother's death, life had been more complicated and uncertain, under the protection of her brother Robert, who seems to have had various financial difficulties and run-ins with the law. But, through her brother, Cecily retained connections with the royal household. She wouldn't have been employed by Chaucer in a menial role, but likely as a senior servant or housekeeper. What did Cecily Chaumpaigne want? As a single woman entering service in the household of Chaucer – merchant, senior civil servant, diplomat, rising courtly poet – was she seeking security? Financial or social advancement? Marriage opportunities? What were her ambitions and desires?

Of course, Cecily Chaumpaigne's move into Chaucer's employment may still have involved coercion, pressure or abuse – even physical or sexual violence – but this doesn't find a place in the medieval written record. Medieval documents reflect uncertainty – or silence – around women and consent. The experiences of Cecily Chaumpaigne, her mother and wider family, suggest a world in which women navigated power through careful relationships with men:

marriage, employment, service – though, in the streets and houses of medieval London and other towns and cities, they were also running businesses and households, working as skilled artisans and managing trade. The Wife of Bath's confident assertion, at the beginning of her tale, that 'Wommen may go now saufly (safely) up and down', belies the resourcefulness, ingenuity and wariness with which women negotiated what was still, predominantly, a man's world.

Cecily Chaumpaigne is a real medieval woman, but her voice is (any future discoveries aside) absent from the archive. Her silence is in contrast with the Wife of Bath's loud and expansive voice, unapologetically taking up space in *The Canterbury Tales*. But, of course, we're listening to Geoffrey cosplaying Alison all along. While women's words appear in a wide range of medieval sources – from legal documents to business records and domestic accounts, even religious writing – locating real women's voices in premodern poetry is challenging. Often women are ghostwritten, or their words retold by unreliable narrators, or they simply disappear off the edge of the page. Women – especially royal and noble women – undoubtedly played crucial roles as patrons, but any creative contribution they made to the poetry itself isn't clear. Even a key figure like Marie de France, whose 'Lais' are collected alongside 'Sumer Is Icumen In' in the Reading Abbey manuscript, is hard to pin down as a real historical figure. Women poets in this period are elusive, fugitive. If Chaucer is the 'father of English poetry', it's much harder to find its mothers.

Let's get back to 'The Wife of Bath's Tale' and the quest to discover what women want. The knight finds little agreement: a flurry of diverging opinions from both men and women. Alison herself interjects to say that what women like best is flattery: with compliments and attentive behaviour, she observes, women are 'ylimed' – that is, caught like birds in glue pasted on a tree branch. The loathly lady gives the knight the correct answer, which he offers to Guinevere:

> 'Wommen desiren to have sovereintee
> As wel over hir housbond as hir love
> And for to been in maistrie him above.'

'Women desire to have sovereignty
As well over their husband as their love
And to be in mastery above him.'

But then the ending of Alison's tale has dismayed and angered some readers. Everything seems to go the knight's way. The loathly lady transforms into a beautiful young woman – who will also be 'good and trewe' and obedient to him forever. The tale begins with the knight's violent rape of a maiden; it ends with him 'bathed in a bath of blisse', with his beautiful new wife ready to do 'every thing' which might bring him pleasure or delight. It's an uncomfortable kind of 'happy ever after'. What's the moral of the story?

The Wife of Bath takes it into her own hands – and her concluding lines don't quite match up with the tale we've just heard. She bids Jesus Christ send us 'Housboundes meeke, younge, and freshe abedde', and to grant wives the 'grace' to outlive their husbands. She wishes 'pestilence' – plague – on those men who won't be governed by their wives. The Wife of Bath's story is part of a wider conversation among the pilgrims in *The Canterbury Tales* about mastery, sovereignty and the power dynamics between the sexes and in marriage. She wrests the ending of her tale back to her own agenda and purpose. Hers is a powerful, strident voice – but also likable, human, self-aware, pragmatic, funny, relatable. It connects with us across time.

At the end of her tale, the Wife of Bath shoulders back in to take control – to give her own spin on the story and her own irreverent, outspoken message. But gaining 'maistrie' over a story isn't so easy. The narrative machine the Wife has put in motion risks a very different set of conclusions: the rapist rewarded, masculine desire fulfilled, the loathly lady transformed into a by-the-numbers male fantasy of youth, beauty and sexual obedience. The unnamed maiden at the start of the tale, raped by the 'lusty bacheler', now seems forgotten – more a plot device than a character, jettisoned by the story. 'Maistrie' over women's stories, as we've seen, is especially tricky when they're ventriloquised by men.

The Wife of Bath rips pages from Jankyn's book of 'wikked wives' in her own, infuriated, bid for mastery. But what about the real historical figure of Cecily Chaumpaigne, in fourteenth-century London? How far did she have 'sovereintee' over her choices and destiny? We will almost certainly never know whether she was pressured into making her quitclaim, or the desires and aspirations she carried as she began her service with Chaucer's household. What do women want? 'The Wife of Bath's Tale' claims to give us the answer, but medieval sources all too often leave us with silences and questions. Nevertheless, we glimpse women negotiating their world with resilience and ingenuity, seeking 'maistrie' over books, stories and their own lives.

7.

Love and Loss in a Time of Plague

Extract from Pearl *(around 1390)*

What was it like to live through a medieval pandemic? The plague which swept through Western Eurasia and North Africa from 1346 onwards had a truly vast reach and devastating impact. From the origins of the *Yersinia pestis* pathogen, now traced back to the Tibetan-Qinghai Plateau, it moved across Central Asia, the Middle East, North Africa and Europe, killing probably 40 to 60 per cent of the human population as it went.

The Black Death – known at the time as the Great Pestilence or Great Mortality – landed in England in summer 1348, at the Dorset port of Melcombe (modern-day Weymouth). From one sick sailor, landing from Gascony, the disease spread rapidly, and by summer 1349 the entire country was stricken. But that was just the first wave. Peaks of infection and mortality continued through the following decades and beyond. Sources from medieval England record contemporary perceptions of the horror. The *Polychronicon* – a history book – by the Chester monk Ranulph Higden declares that 'scarcely a tenth of mankind was left alive'. The Chronicle of the Cistercian Abbey of Louth Park, Lincolnshire, remarks in 1349 that 'it is thought that so great a multitude of people were not killed in Noah's Flood'.

But how do we make sense of those huge numbers and sweeping, horrifying statements? How did it actually feel to survive the Black Death? Those of us who've lived through the Covid-19 pandemic know all too well that figures and statistics don't tell the full story or count the true human cost. Poetry offers us an alternative way into the familiar history: an intimate, personal encounter with the emotion and anguish of lived experience.

A father, wracked by grief, mourns for his young daughter, in an idyllic garden haunted by reminders of plague and disease. A jeweller grieves for the beautiful pearl which slipped through his fingers – the most perfect treasure he ever held, now lost and buried. The 1212-line poem *Pearl*, written around 1390, takes the metaphor of an exquisite pearl for a young girl who has died in early childhood. Her father – symbolically the jeweller, who has lost his dearest and most precious gem – falls asleep and meets with a strange dream: the Pearl-Maiden now grown up, in a strange and beautiful Otherworld, speaking to him about a marvellous kingdom beyond death.

Pearl has left us with a raft of unanswered questions. Who wrote the poem? Who was it for? Was there a real-life Pearl-Maiden – a young girl who had died – and who was it who mourned her? And, given its late fourteenth-century context, did the Pearl-Maiden die of the plague? We can't know for certain, but the poem returns – compulsively, repeatedly – to images which suggest the horror of the Black Death. It communicates the terrible human cost of medieval disease, the tangible pain of loss and grief, the fear and doubt stirred by this time of crisis, and the visceral anguish behind the stark statistics for historical child mortality.

At the beginning of the poem, the Dreamer speaks to us in the first person as he wanders in a beautiful garden. At first, it seems he's a jeweller, remembering his most excellent, perfect pearl. But it quickly becomes apparent that this pearl is more than just a jewel, and the Dreamer's loss is far more agonising. The language is intricate and highly wrought – like the filigree setting of a gemstone itself. It's complicated, ornate, elaborate: one thing can be many, and sometimes metaphors turn out to be real. If the poem seems disorienting and strange, remember that we're stepping inside someone else's dream, where things are not always what they seem.

Perle pleasaunte, to prynces paye	Lovely pearl, which would please a prince
To clanly clos in golde so clere:	To cleanly enclose in gold so clear,
Oute of oryent, I hardyly saye,	Out of all the Orient, I firmly declare,

Ne proued I neuer her precios pere.

So rounde, so reken in vche araye,

So smal, so smoþe her sydeȝ were,

Quere-so-euer I jugged gemmeȝ
   gaye,

I sette hyr sengeley in synglere.

Allas! I leste hyr in on erbere;

Þurȝ gresse to grounde hit fro
   me yot.

I dewyne, fordolked of luf-daungere

Of þat pryuy perle wythouten spot.

Syþen in þat spote hit fro me
   sprange,

Ofte haf I wayted, wyschande
   þat wele,

Þat wont watȝ whyle deuoyde my
   wrange

And heuen my happe and al
   my hele.

Þat dotȝ bot þrych my hert
   þrange,

My breste in bale bot bolne and
   bele;

Ȝet þoȝt me neuer so swete a
   sange

As stylle stounde let to
   me stele.

For soþe þer fleten to
   me fele,

To þenke hir color so clad
   in clot.

O moul, þou marreȝ a myry
   iuele,

My priuy perle wythouten spotte.

I never proved her precious peer.

So round, so noble in every setting,

So slender, so smooth her sides were.

Of all the bright gems I judged
   anywhere,

I set her apart in uniqueness.

Alas! I lost her in a garden,

Through grass to the ground it fell
   from me.

I languish, pierced with love-longing

For that dearest pearl without a spot.

Since it sprang from me in
   that spot,

Often have I waited, wishing for
   that treasure,

Which drove away my want
   and grief

And lifted my spirits and all my
   health.

That loss crushes my heart with
   agony.

My breast burns and swells with
   sorrow.

Yet no song ever seemed to me
   so sweet

As the silent moments when her
   memory stole to me.

In truth, many of those moments
   came to me.

To think of her colour, so clothed
   in clod!

Oh earth, you mar a merry
   jewel,

My dearest pearl without a spot.

Þat spot of spyseȝ mot nedeȝ
   sprede,
Þer such rycheȝ to rot is runne;
Blomeȝ blayke and blwe and rede
Þer schyneȝ ful schyr agayn þe sunne.
Flor and fryte may not be fede
Þer hit doun drof in moldeȝ
   dunne;
For vch gresse mot grow of
   grayneȝ dede;
No whete were elleȝ to woneȝ
   wonne.
Of goud vche goude is ay bygonne;
So semly a sede moȝt fayly not,
Þat spryngande spyceȝ vp ne sponne
Of þat precios perle wythouten
   spotte.

To þat spot þat I in speche expoun
I entred in þat erber grene,
In Auguste in a hyȝ seysoun,
Quen corne is coruen wyth crokeȝ
   kene.
On huyle þer perle hit trendeled
   doun
Schadowed þis worteȝ ful schyre
   and schene,
Gilofre, gyngure and gromylyoun,
And pyonys powdered ay bytwene.
Ȝif hit watȝ semly on to sene,
A fayrre flayr ȝet fro
   hit flot.
Þer wonys þat worþyly, I wot
   and wene,
My precious perle wythouten spot.

Spices had to spread out from
   that spot,
Where such riches were run to rot.
Flowers white and blue and red
Shine so brightly there in the sun.
Flower and fruit can never fade
Where that pearl fell down into
   dark earth,
For each grass must grow out of
   dead grains,
Or no wheat would ever be
   harvested home.
Every good thing comes out of good;
So lovely a seed could not fail to root
Nor flourishing spices spring up
From that precious pearl without
   a spot.

In that spot which I have described
I entered into that green garden,
In August, on a holy day,
When corn is cut down with the
   sharp scythe.
The mound the pearl had rolled
   away down
Was shaded with plants bright and
   beautiful.
Gilly-flower, ginger and gromwell,
And peonies sprinkled in between.
If it was lovely to look at,
Fairer still was the fragrance that
   floated there.
I believe and know where that
   lovely one lives,
My precious pearl without a spot.

Bifore þat spot my honde I spenned	I clasped my hands before that spot
For care ful colde þat to me caȝt;	For the cold grief that gripped me there.
A deuely dele in my hert denned,	A desolating pain ached in my heart,
Þaȝ resoun sette myseluen saȝt.	Though reason should have reconciled me.
I playned my perle þat þer watȝ penned	I mourned for my pearl that was prisoned there,
Wyth fyrce skylleȝ þat faste faȝt;	My feelings fought against my faith and reason;
Þaȝ kynde of Kryst me comfort kenned,	Though the mercy of Christ gave me comfort,
My wreched wylle in wo ay wraȝte.	My wretched spirit was tormented with sorrow.
I felle vpon þat floury flaȝt,	I fell down upon that flowery grass,
Suche odour to my herneȝ schot;	Such an odour rushed into my head;
I slode vpon a slepyng-slaȝte	I slipped into a deathly sleep, to dream
On þat precios perle wythouten spot.	Of that precious pearl without a spot.

The opening lines of the poem dazzle with a description of the pearl's exquisite beauty. The narrator's voice speaks with the authority of an experienced jeweller: this pearl is unparalleled, finer than any others, even those from the 'Orient', which were especially highly prized in the Middle Ages. The jeweller tells us that he's never found an equal to it, out of all the many gems he's known. This pearl is fit for the pleasure of a prince, we're told, 'to cleanly enclose in gold so clear' ('To clanly clos in golde so clere'). (If anyone ever sneers at a split infinitive, point them to the beginning of this magnificent poem, and suggest they think again.)

While the poem imagines the beautiful pearl in its setting or 'araye', the verse itself is like a finely wrought ornament – the work of a master craftsman. The form is so intricate that it presents difficulty for modern translators: the use of alliteration on stressed syllables within each line (a feature of a movement in fourteenth-century English poetry, looking back to Old English forms, called the 'Alliterative

Revival'), as well as end-rhymes. On top of that, in each section of the poem, the verses each begin and end with a line repeating a key word or phrase – here, the word 'spot'. My translation aims to give the meaning of each line, not contorting itself into strange language or word-order to preserve rhymes, but keeping the sense of alliterative rhythm where possible.

There's another reason why the language of *Pearl* is tricky. The poetry of Chaucer, roughly contemporary, is written in the London dialect of Middle English which, through an array of economic and political chances and accidents, became the forerunner of our modern-day Standard English. But *Pearl* uses the regional language of the north-west Midlands – somewhere around Cheshire, north-west Staffordshire, or north-east Shropshire. The poem is sprinkled with local words and its spelling suggests a north-west Midlands accent – just like the other works likely by this same poet, including the Arthurian romance *Sir Gawain and the Green Knight*. Alongside more recognisable words for 'man' in *Pearl*, for instance, we find 'gome', 'hathel' and 'lede' – all with their origins in Old English and part of the poet's rich local vocabulary.

Already in the first lines of the poem, our precious pearl is slippery. Notice the pronouns: first the pearl is referred to as 'her', four times, and then as 'it'. Is this pearl a jewel or a person? The more detailed description only adds further ambiguity. The pearl is 'so noble in every setting' ('so reken in vche araye'). Do we take that literally – a description of a gem set in fine jewellery? Or is this a metaphor? Perhaps, rather than a precious stone, we should imagine a young girl, nobly dressed in rich garments, and beautifully behaved in every situation. The pearl's sides are described as 'So slender, so smooth' ('So smal, so smoþe') – the glossy sleekness of a pearl, but also the ideal of feminine beauty at this time. Chaucer's poem *Troilus and Criseyde* depicts Criseyde's 'slim arms, her straight and soft back, / Her slender sides, soft, smooth and white' ('Hir armes smale, hir streyghte bak and softe, / Hir sydes longe, fleshly, smothe, and whyte'). Indeed, it doesn't take much to move us from a gemstone to a girl. The Latin for 'pearl', *margarita*, was a common name in medieval England: Margaret, Margery, Maggie.

If this pearl is a girl, then who is she? The poem itself is cagey. We're never told explicitly that the Pearl-Maiden is the Dreamer's daughter. Instead, later on in the text, the Dreamer mentions that 'She was nearer to me than aunt or niece' ('Ho watz me nerre þen aunte or nece'), implying this close relationship. The age of the girl when she died is also vague: later in the poem, the Dreamer remarks that she 'lived not two years in our world' ('lyfed not two ȝer in our þede'). Here, the Dreamer's anguish is palpable as he is torn from memories of the girl's beauty to the thought of her cherished body buried in the earth: 'To think of her colour, so clothed in clod!' ('To þenke hir color so clad in clot!').

These opening verses set the scene for the coming dream, describing the remarkable 'spot' where the vision will take place. It's a beautiful garden – but not just any garden. It's a green 'erber': a place associated with courtliness, love and even romance, where the Dreamer will see his beloved again. It's a stylised, formulaic description, steeped in literary conventions, from the gentle shade of plants down to the carpet of many-coloured flowers. But perhaps this beautiful garden suggests something else, too? Its splendour hints at more than an earthly garden – perhaps a glimpse or foreshadowing of Paradise itself. The reference to the Orient in the poem's opening lines might have already planted this idea for a fourteenth-century audience: medieval *mappae mundi* (world maps) depicted the Garden of Eden at the far eastern edge of the world, an earthly mirror of the eternal heavenly Paradise.

The medieval manuscript which contains *Pearl* is highly unusual for a book of poetry in the English language at this time: it includes coloured illustrations. Rather rough and ready, they nevertheless depict the beauty of the garden with exuberant colour: leafy green trees, red and white flowers, the Dreamer lying on the ground in his scarlet tunic and bright blue cloak. Later, when he sees the Pearl-Maiden across a flowing river, we can make out the pen-outline shapes of fish swimming amid the azure ripples.

But is there something slightly off in this beautiful garden? The Dreamer has come here on a holy day in August 'When corn is cut down with the sharp scythe' ('Quen corne is coruen with croke3 kene'). It may be the feast day of Lammas, the time associated with gathering in the harvest. But the poem's imagery might take us somewhere else instead: the personified figure of Death – the Grim Reaper – hewing down lives with his fearsome scythe. Even here, the Dreamer can't escape pictures of death and mortality.

Perhaps the Dreamer has even sought out this beautiful garden to avoid contagion or disease. The poet John Lydgate's *A Doctrine for Pestilence* – a 'How To' poem on warding off the plague, written soon after *Pearl* – advises readers to 'Walk in gardens sweet of fragrance' to avert the foul vapours and airs of disease. The flowers the Dreamer describes in the garden – gilly-flower, ginger, gromwell, peonies – were all used for their medicinal properties against the Black Death. But Lydgate also warns sternly against the risks of 'meridian sleep' or napping during the day. And that's just what the Dreamer does, in the last lines here. More than that, he falls into a 'slepying-sla3te' – literally, a 'sleeping-slaughter' – a sleep so deep and heavy it's like the blow of death itself. What lulls him into this risky slumber? An intense odour, which rushes ('schot') into his head. Is this the purifying, cleansing scent of the garden, as prescribed by John Lydgate? Or something more sinister: the miasma and evil air of the Black Death itself? Even in this idyllic garden, the poem unsettles us, keeps us watchful and alert, and hints at the present dangers of contagion and death when the plague is nearby.

Insidiously, the taint of plague and disease infects the language of all five opening verses. The hook word here, after all, repeated insistently in the first and last lines of each stanza, is 'spot'. It's the term the poem chooses for the place of the garden, where the Dreamer lost his pearl. And it's the feature the Dreamer returns to, again and again, when remembering the perfection of his lost jewel / daughter: his precious pearl 'without a spot'. The effect is creeping, cumulative. Are we to imagine that the Dreamer's insistence on his daughter's spotless perfection betrays a darker reality: that she died marked with the spots or buboes of the plague? Throughout the poem, spots and blemishes (literal and metaphorical) are a constant preoccupation. The Pearl-Maiden describes herself as 'maskelles' ('spotless'): transfigured after death into a perfect, unblemished, flawless creature. In the heavenly kingdom where she lives, the Lamb of Christ is a symbol of perfect purity, without 'black spots' ('spottez blake').

For a poem about grief and consolation, *Pearl* doesn't shy away from the grim, vivid realities of death and decay. In the third verse, the Dreamer describes the beautiful garden as the place where 'such riches were run to rot' ('such ryche3 to rot is runne'). He runs through, in his mind, how the fertility and beauty of the garden are grown out of death and decay beneath the ground. 'For each grass must grow out of dead grains', he notes ('For vch gresse mot grow of grayne3 dede'). It's an astonishing image of death and decomposition as part of the life cycle: his buried pearl seeding new growth. But it's uncompromising, stark – the poem doesn't avert its eyes from the rot and ruin of the Pearl-Maiden's body, deep down in the earth.

With this strangely decorative, moralising picture of rot and decay, we're not so far from the imagery of medieval cadaver tombs, suddenly popular a generation after the Black Death's first wave and on across the following centuries. Also known as 'transi' tombs, these depicted the transition from life to death, with the full body horror of physical decomposition. Alongside (or sometimes instead of) the carved stone effigy lying in dignified repose, cadaver tombs displayed the rotting corpse, as a reminder of the vanity and transience of earthly pride and glory. The earliest surviving example in England is the memorial to Bishop Richard Fleming, who died in 1431, in Lincoln Cathedral. Below his robed body, hand lifted in blessing, the carved corpse slips out of its stone shroud, revealing shrunken flesh, protruding bones and bulging eyes. Cadaver tombs from continental Europe add worms, flies and toads feeding on the decaying flesh, but in England and Wales the emphasis is purely on the horror and pathos of the human body rotting and returning to dust.

What did it feel like to feel grief in fourteenth-century England? Or to feel love, or loss? Are emotions the same across history, or do they change over time? In *Pearl*, the Dreamer's pain is raw, immediate, recognisable to us today. He speaks of the agony and joy bound together as he remembers his daughter, confides in us the heartbreaking truth that 'no song ever seemed to me so sweet / As the silent moments when her memory stole up to me'.

But some of the language of the poem is stranger, hinting at less familiar emotional worlds and touchstones. The Dreamer tells us that 'My breast burns and swells with sorrow' ('My breste in bale bot bolne and bele'). The notion of his heart burning and swelling recalls earlier English ideas about the mind and how it functioned within the body. In pre-Conquest England, texts suggest that the mind was understood as a physical container, located in the chest, which could be affected by heat, cold and pressure. Evidence suggests that this 'hydraulic model' of the mind was more than just a metaphor, but how people actually experienced and understood their embodied emotions. The Dreamer also speaks of the pain of 'love-longing' – literally 'luf-daungere' or 'love-danger'. A term borrowed from the courtly romance tradition of forbidden passion, knightly devotion and courtship, it suggests the agony of a love which cannot be requited – but also, for us as modern readers, makes strange use of an erotic concept to articulate a parent's grief.

Before the Dreamer slips into his sleep, we witness the turmoil as his inconsolable grief collides with his dutiful Christian faith and attempts at reason. He clasps his hands together as he mourns in the garden ('my honde I spenned'). Is he praying, or simply wringing his hands in despair? When he sees the Pearl-Maiden in his vision, his bewildered, desperate joy is perhaps even more devastating than his grief. At first, he doesn't realise that this beautiful, queenly maiden, clothed in white, is his lost daughter. That's hardly surprising: in this heavenly country she has been transformed from the little toddler he once knew. But, gradually, as he looks at her face, he tells us 'I knew her more and more' ('I knew hyr more and more').

But this reunion with his daughter is strange: their relationship has changed, and now the Pearl-Maiden speaks with command and authority about the kingdom of heaven and the theology of salvation. It's hardly surprising that the Dreamer barely knows how to address her: he slips into awkward small talk, trying to adjust to this astonishing new reality. 'We meet so seldom, by tree or stone' he tells her ('We meten so selden by stok oþer ston'). It's a banal little phrase – like saying 'How've you been? I hardly ever see you around these days'. And the Pearl-Maiden expects him to take in a lot. As well as a meditation on grief, *Pearl* is a sophisticated debate poem, packed with learned allusions, scholastic argument and detailed biblical analysis. The Dreamer seems very much an ordinary fellow, dropped into this wondrous world. He constantly gets the wrong end of the stick, and misunderstands what the Pearl-Maiden tells him, despite his eagerness to please her.

There are hints throughout the poem of the radical new religious ideas and heated theological arguments emerging in the later fourteenth century, in the wake of the Black Death. The horrors of the plague contributed to frustration with the Church, and helped foster new movements. Lollardism, the Wycliffites: innovative approaches to Christianity which centred the English vernacular and were sceptical of the Roman Catholic Church's lucrative monopoly on salvation. Later in the poem, the Dreamer asks his daughter, puzzled, how she could have earned a place in heaven when she lived only two years on earth. It's a truly heart-wrenching question, and the Pearl-Maiden's reply is perhaps the most moving moment of consolation in the whole poem. She refers to the biblical Parable of the Vineyard, in which the labourers are all paid the same, regardless of how long they worked for. It doesn't matter, she tells the Dreamer: she is saved by grace, not by any tally of her own good works. Her life isn't valued by a balance sheet of minutes and hours. We might read this as a pushback against Catholic doctrine – or, equally, as an anti-Wycliffite defence of infant baptism. Importantly, while this is a personal consolation, it's also on the front line of religious debate, politically charged and live.

So, was there a real-life Pearl-Maiden? Who was the poem written for? *Pearl* is deliberately allusive and enigmatic, perhaps partly to ensure that its power is universal, perhaps as a mark of discretion in a work written for a noble or courtly patron. Modern scholars have suggested a range of possibilities for the poem's patronage and subject – all necessarily speculative and unproven. Perhaps it was written on the death of Margaret, daughter of John Hastings, Earl of Pembroke. Or for Margaret, granddaughter of King Edward III. (Edward's own young daughter, Joan, died of the plague in summer 1348, while travelling through France.) The poem has been linked with a Cheshire circle at the court of Richard II, and the death of Richard's wife Anne of Bohemia in 1394, of plague, has been suggested as one possible occasion for its composition. But Anne, while lavishly mourned by Richard, was a woman of twenty-eight, not a young child. We will probably never solve the mystery of the poem's author and subject – but the unending scholarly guesswork reflects the sophisticated, allusive and cryptic nature of the poem itself.

At the end of *Pearl*, after a dazzling vision of the heavenly Jerusalem, built radiantly from gemstones, the Dreamer can't contain his delight and his desire to be reunited with his beloved daughter. He flings himself into the river which separates him from the Pearl-Maiden (the symbolic division between earthly life and the afterlife, which he's been warned not to cross), only to wake up, cast out of the wonderful dream. He's back in the beautiful garden, but now with a message of consolation: our Lord in heaven is waiting for us, and we must all endeavour to be 'precious pearls, to our Prince's pleasure' ('precious perlez vnto His pay'). The poem is as perfect and circular as a pearl itself, ending exactly where it began.

Grief and consolation aren't a neat, linear process, and even after his miraculous vision of heaven, the Dreamer can't let go of his pain. The lovely garden – and indeed, the whole world – is now merely a 'prison of sorrow' ('doel-doungoun') where he will mark time until he can, at last, enter that heavenly city and be with his daughter once more. *Pearl* is a poem with a lofty religious message, but also tender compassion for the lived reality of loss and bereavement.

Just occasionally, you might hear someone suggest that, in times of high infant mortality, people loved their children less. That's a catastrophic failure of empathy and imagination, with profound implications for the present day, as well as the past. *Pearl* lets us listen in on an old, faraway grief, as raw and affecting now as ever. It transforms unfathomable statistics of medieval disease and death into just one, devastating loss, and shares with us the human story. It calls for our compassion and sympathy, even across the centuries.

8.

Once More unto the Breach: Neighbours and Adversaries

'Agincourt Carol' (1415)

St Crispin's Day, 1415. King Henry V and his men gather after battle to receive word from the French herald. The day is England's: victory against all the odds and triumph over the flower of French nobility. The red-cross flag of St George unfurls and ripples in the breeze, against blue sky, billowing clouds and, in the distance, a castle known as Agincourt. The green fields of battle roll away, still scattered with bodies in their colourful liveries, while a few stray horses gallop into the woods. As Henry accepts victory, voices break into song. 'Our king went forth to Normandy, / With grace and might of chivalry' – the opening lines of the 'Agincourt Carol', celebrating the triumph of England and the king. But this king is Laurence Olivier, and the battlefield panorama is in brilliant Technicolor. The words of the 'Agincourt Carol' are sung to a setting by composer William Walton. This is the 1944 film adaptation of Shakespeare's *Henry V*, made to boost British morale during the Second World War, just as another invasion of France was looming, and released in the autumn following D-Day.

England the underdogs: honour, courage and victory against the odds. Agincourt: a byword for patriotic pride and valour. The 'Agincourt Carol', composed shortly after the battle, glories in victory for England – 'Anglia' – and its brave king, at this pivotal moment in what proved to be the Hundred Years War. But Englishmen weren't the only ones pitted against the French on the battlefield.

The story of Agincourt we're familiar with – via Olivier and Shakespeare before him – is a carefully crafted one of unity and co-operation. Shakespeare's play features a cast of diverse characters: Gower the Englishman, Captain Jamy the Scot, Macmorris the Irishman and Fluellen (Llewellyn) the Welshman – bickering and japing, but nevertheless coming together to fight. Longbowmen, including those from Wales, were Henry's secret weapon and a decisive factor in victory. Yet, in 1415, relations between neighbours in Britain were far from comfortable. Back across the Channel, the rebellion of Owain Glyndŵr had threatened English control for over ten years. Political tensions and resistance to the English crown rumbled on.

The 'Agincourt Carol' trumpets English triumph, but there's another, unspoken, story here about those others on the battlefield and troubles back home. What happens if we read around the edges of this exuberantly patriotic, jingoistic verse? The poem points us to something not just about England's belligerent history with France, but also its fractious, predacious relationships with its neighbours within Britain, too.

Deo gracias anglia	England give thanks to God for
redde pro victoria.	the victory!
Our kyng went forth to normandy	Our king went forth to Normandy,
Wyth grace and myth of chyvalry	With grace and might of chivalry,
Þer god for hym wrouth	There God for him wrought
mervelowsly	marvellously.
Qwerfore ynglond may cal and cry	So England may call and cry:
deo gracias.	Thanks be to God!
Deo gracias anglia	England give thanks to God for
redde pro victoria.	the victory!
He set a sege for sothe to say	He set a siege, truth to say,
To harflu toune wyth	On Harfleur town, with the
ryal aray	royal army.

Þat toune he wan and mad
 a fray
Þat fraunse xal rewe tyl
 domysday
deo gracias.

That town he won, and made
 affray,
That France will rue till
 Judgement Day.
Thanks be to God!

Deo gracias anglia
redde pro victoria.

England give thanks to God for the
 victory!

Than went hym forth owr kyng
 comely
In achyncourt feld he fauth
 manly
Thorw grace of god most
 mervelowsly
He had both feld and vyctory
deo gracias.

Then he went forth, our
 comely king,
In the field of Agincourt he fought
 manfully.
Through the grace of God, most
 marvellously,
He had both the field and victory.
Thanks be to God!

Deo gracias anglia
redde pro victoria.

England give thanks to God for the
 victory!

Ther lordys eerlys and baroune
Were slayn and takyn and þat
 ful soun
And summe were browth in to
 londoune
Wyth ioye and blysse and greth
 renoune
deo gracias.

There lords, earls, and barons
Were slain and taken prisoner, and
 that very swiftly,
And some were brought to
 London.
With joy and bliss and great
 renown.
Thanks be to God!

Deo gracias anglia
redde pro victoria.

England give thanks to God for the
 victory!

Almythy god he kepe
 our kyng

May Almighty God keep
 our king,

Hys pepyl and al hys weel-welyng	His people and all those who wish him well.
And ȝeve hem grace withoutyn endyng.	And give them grace without ending.
Þan may we calle and savely syng deo gracias.	Then we may call and safely sing: Thanks be to God!
Deo gracias anglia redde pro victoria.	England give thanks to God for the victory!

Written soon after the battle, the 'Agincourt Carol' survives in two medieval manuscripts. The earliest, from which this version is taken, is an early fifteenth-century manuscript roll now held at Trinity College, Cambridge. Manuscript rolls like this were a format often intended for use in performance: they could be transported relatively easily and used by singers without awkward page turns. Today, carols are indelibly associated with Christmas, but in the Middle Ages they had a much wider range of topics and uses. Still, they were typically linked to religious festivals and themes, and a secular subject like this is unusual. In reality, it's unlikely the 'Carol' was first improvised on the field at Agincourt (properly Azincourt) in the immediate wake of battle. It's a complex piece of polyphonic music, written for three voice parts, with words which alternate between English and Latin. Appealing as the scene in Olivier's film might be, it's hardly plausible that a band of exhausted soldiers would spontaneously break into sophisticated words and music like this.

The 'Carol' focuses wholly on the triumph and glory of England. The Latin refrain (*'Deo gracias Anglia / redde pro victoria'*) is typical of the 'macaronic' style of many medieval carols, which switch between languages. It's a reminder that medieval England was a multilingual environment, with English, ecclesiastical Latin, French and many other languages a familiar part of the soundscape. With 'England give thanks to God for victory!' the 'Carol' repeatedly returns to the idea that God is responsible for the English triumph – just as in the words Shakespeare puts into Henry's mouth: 'God fought for us'.

History presents the English at Agincourt as the underdogs, engaging at huge disadvantage, against all the odds. And that's broadly in line with the evidence. Henry's men were significantly out-numbered by the French forces – though medieval English sources exaggerate the difference and present-day scholars don't agree on exact figures. The Welsh lawyer and chronicler Adam Usk's account of the battle, compiled from reports and news circulating back in England, claims that Henry set out on his campaign 'bravely, like a lion', with 'barely ten thousand soldiers', while the French had 'sixty thousand' in their force. Historians today tend to put the two armies closer in number: perhaps 9,000 English to 12,000 French. But num-bers weren't the only disadvantage facing Henry's men.

The English army had come to Agincourt from the lengthy siege of Harfleur, followed by a gruelling two-and-a-half week march. The 'Carol' presents Henry's victory at Harfleur in heroic terms: the 'ryal aray' or direct royal arrangements for the cam-paign, and the 'afray' or fighting with which he won ('wan') the town. But the protracted siege had depleted Henry's army: a large garrison was left in the town, while sick and injured men were returned home to England. After Harfleur, Henry attempted to lead his army to the safety of Calais, the remaining English stronghold in northern France, but was forced inland, finally crossing the River Somme further south. After all this, English victory on the battlefield at Agincourt might well have seemed something like a miracle.

More likely, terrain and the different tactics of English and French armies proved decisive. Henry's longbowmen flanked the battle-field, driving in stakes to protect them and to force the French into a narrower arena of combat. The initial French cavalry charge aimed to knock the archers out of the battle – but too few French cavalry had volunteered and this opening attack did not succeed. Henry's bowmen tactically targeted horses; wounded animals caused havoc as they panicked and ran through the French foot soldiers. The field had recently been ploughed, and the last few days had seen heavy rainfall. The French infantry were well equipped in heavy armour, but their advance towards Henry's forces was under relentless volleys of arrows, slowing them down so that they crowded in on each other. Struggling through the boggy ground, they were easy targets for Henry's archers – who climbed onto heaps of French bodies – and were hacked down by English foot soldiers where they floundered. French reinforcements pushed into their comrades ahead of them, crushing them and driving them onto the English lances and swords. The French force was funnelled towards annihilation.

Longbowmen were Henry's weapon of mass destruction. And, in a total of perhaps 7,000 archers in the army, around 400 at the battle were Welsh. In a time of uneasy, volatile relations between England and Wales, their road to the battlefield had been winding and complex. The Welsh uprising led by Owain Glyndŵr had only recently been brought under control. By autumn 1415 Glyndŵr himself had disappeared – thought dead, but perhaps still a once and future leader in the hearts of many fellow Welshmen. Tensions continued. Penal laws were already in place to discourage further unrest, but Henry V – who had cut his military teeth leading campaigns in Wales to suppress the rebellion – was reasserting English power and control.

The recruitment of archers from across the lands of Wales in 1415 was an integral part of the English management of the aftermath of the Glyndŵr rebellion. Five-hundred-and-twenty-three men (including mounted archers and foot archers, plus a small number of other men-at-arms) were raised from south and mid Wales: from across the counties of Carmarthen and Cardiganshire, and the lordship of Brecon. No company of archers was recruited from North Wales. This region – the stronghold of Glyndŵr – was still one of suspect loyalties and fermenting resistance. Concerns lingered over risks of the enemy within. Yet the presence of many of the Welsh longbowmen at Agincourt had everything to do with the Glyndŵr uprising and the roiling tensions between England and Wales.

Many of the Welshmen serving at Agincourt were granted pardons for their involvement in the Glyndŵr revolt. Others may have been deliberately seeking to renegotiate loyalties and allegiances and to rebuild favour with the English regime. There's evidence that a number of named Welsh archers recruited in 1415 had taken active part in Glyndŵr's uprising. Like Laurence Dyer, who served with Rustin de Villeneuve in the garrison of Cardigan in 1404 and then fought as an archer from the commote of Caerwedros (Carmarthenshire) in Henry's French campaign. The boundaries between reconciliation, rehabilitation and coercion aren't always clear from the surviving documents: some of the Welshmen in Henry's force may have had little choice but to serve out the consequences of their former rebellion. Not all of the 523 men recruited in 1415 ever left Wales; others were sent home sick from Harfleur. Perhaps 400 Welsh archers served on the battlefield at Agincourt. But Henry's Welsh bowmen weren't just a useful force against the French. They had an important symbolic purpose in domestic politics and governance, demonstrating back home in England and Wales – especially in areas of fragile submission and loyalty – the reach and strength of Henry's power as king.

The 'Carol' offers a compelling portrait of King Henry himself, igniting his cult as a great military leader. The French campaign is cast in the terms of heroic romance and adventure: Henry sets forth to Normandy 'with grace and might of chivalry'. While 'chivalry' here could just mean the military classes, it also conjures the image of a noble, questing knight, straight out of the tomes of Arthurian myth and legend. He's a 'comely' – handsome – young warrior, who fights manfully ('manly'). He's every bit the legend, the pin-up, the charismatic hero, the strong ruler England needs to take back control of its unruly home territories and reclaim the French crown.

Beyond the panegyric of the 'Agincourt Carol', the character of Henry V is a tangle of contradictions: pious, cultured, warlike. It's tricky, today, to square Henry's apparent piety with his steel as a military leader – and, especially, with some of his actions at Agincourt. Most of all, Henry's order for the execution of French prisoners seems repugnant to moral codes of honour, fair play and the rules of war. Perhaps he feared that the large numbers of prisoners might use their combined force against their captors, and sought to protect his own men. Perhaps also, as apologists including Shakespeare have hinted, this ruthless measure might have been a reaction to the French attack on the English baggage train, led by local noble Ysembart d'Azincourt. Shakespeare has the character Fluellen, in his distinctive Welsh accent, lament this cowardly attack against the rules of combat.

> FLUELLEN: Kill the poys [boys] and the luggage! 'Tis expressly
> against the law of arms. 'Tis as arrant a piece of
> knavery, mark you now, as can be offert, in your
> conscience now, is it not?

> GOWER: 'Tis certain there's not a boy left alive.

Generations of insult, rivalry and tit-for-tat atrocity are the hinterland to the 'Agincourt Carol'. Perhaps it's unsurprising that the poem takes delight in the destruction of the French nobility: 'There lords, earls, and barons / Were slain and taken prisoner, and that very swiftly' ('Ther lordys eerlys and baroune / Were slayn and takyn and þat ful soun'). And the 'Carol' crows that this defeat is one 'France shall rue till Judgement Day' ('fraunse xal rewe tyl domysday'). This is a triumphalist celebration, without much room for grace or compassion in victory.

If the 'Agincourt Carol' wasn't originally sung on the battlefield, in the immediate aftermath of combat, when was it first performed? There are clues as to the possible early performance of the 'Carol' – and the Welshman Adam Usk gives us a particularly rich account. Henry returned to England on 16 November, and a spectacular pageant was staged in London on 23 November to celebrate his victory. London had granted a huge loan to Henry to fund the French campaign, and now was the time to celebrate. There are reports in a number of contemporary sources, all giving slightly different perspectives.

Adam Usk tells of a vast procession, which meets Henry at Blackheath and moves into London, following the long tradition of ceremonial royal entries into the city. At London Bridge, huge armed figures tower over the crowds, one carrying a lance and one an axe. Enormous models of a lion and an antelope (the king's badge) guard the middle of the bridge. In Cheapside, a three-storey tower has been specially constructed, decorated with coats of arms and painted to look like marble and porphyry. Six citizens approach the king, carrying two golden basins filled with gold as offerings. Maidens come dancing, with drums, viols and choirs singing. Is this the moment when the 'Agincourt Carol' was first sung, as part of this sumptuous pageant? We can't know for sure. And we can't know whether Adam was there himself as an eyewitness, though the detail of his account makes it a possibility. If he was indeed there, on that remarkable day in London, how did it feel, as a Welshman, to watch the triumphalist return of the all-conquering English ruler?

Adam lends his voice to the general celebration of the king and England's glory. His *Chronicle* includes a poem, in Latin, celebrating the victory at Agincourt, as well as a little mnemonic couplet – just two lines – commemorating the battle.

> Harflu fert Mauric,
> Agincowrt prelia Crispin.

> Maurice has brought down Harfleur,
> Crispin has won Agincourt.

Harfleur surrendered to Henry on the feast day of St Maurice, 22 September, with the Battle of Agincourt won on the feast of St Crispin. It's the now-familiar association between Agincourt and St Crispin's Day, used to such powerful effect by Shakespeare in Henry V's exhortation to his troops on the morning of battle – but here in one of its earliest occurrences.

Adam Usk is unequivocal in his celebration of the king and of England. But his own fortunes show the impact of divisions and internal conflict within Britain in the early fifteenth century. As an Usk boy, from the Welsh borders, making his way in the world of

English church, law and politics in the late fourteenth and early fifteenth century, his prospects had been marred by his Welsh heritage. Adam was abroad during the height of the Glyndŵr rebellion, but was warned that his own loyalty to the English Crown was under suspicion, and that he risked his life if he returned to England. He lost church livings, possessions, wealth and royal favour. His *Chronicle*, at moments, reflects his resentment and anger. Indeed, he's sometimes vague about his allegiances and motivations – and it's hard to blame him, in an England where the very act of being Welsh is precarious, risky, suspect.

For Adam Usk, as well as for those companies of Welsh archers recruited to Agincourt, it's clear that identity and loyalty are far more complex than a simple Welsh/English divide. Local lordships and geographies within Wales make a difference, as do political alliances and patronage bonds which reach across borders. Adam Usk knew when to back a winner. After his hostility to Richard II and disappointment with Henry IV, the young Henry V seemed to be a strong ruler he could rally behind (even if he does mutter about the extortionate cost of foreign campaigns). 'What more can I say?' he shrugs, turning to us in an aside as he wraps up his report of the great London pageant. 'Happiness filled the people – and rightly so.'

The last verse of the 'Agincourt Carol' calls on God to protect ('kepe') King Henry, his people ('pepyl'), and all those who support him (literally, his 'weel-welyng' or 'well-wishers'). In the supremely confident – even obstinate – portrayal of total English victory in the 'Carol', do we detect here just the tiniest chink in the armour? A hint that there may be some within Henry's realms who *don't* necessarily wish him quite so well? Let's not forget that, even as Henry was preparing to embark on his French campaign in 1415, the Southampton Plot was revealed: a scheme to depose him and to install his cousin Edmund Mortimer, the Earl of March, as king. It was Mortimer himself who told Henry, claiming to have only just discovered the plan. On 5 August, the Earl of Cambridge, Henry, Lord Scrope and Sir Thomas Grey were executed for their parts in the affair (the king's friend Scrope, in fact, merely for having had knowledge of the plot which he had not shared). Mortimer was pardoned. It remains uncertain whether the Southampton Plot was a genuine plan of high treason, or a vague rumour seized upon by Henry, or even a purge of potential rivals ruthlessly engineered by the king himself.

A masterstroke of the 'Carol', in its final lines, is its use of the first-person plural – 'we' – to proclaim Henry's triumph. It's typical of the medieval carol form: a voice of collective festivity. Even the typical *carole* dance traditionally associated with this kind of singing was a visual performance of unity: a communal, social dance in which carollers held hands and joined in a circle.

But who are 'we'? The 'Carol' draws everyone into its expression of unity and consensus: a capacious and inclusive version of English nationhood, but also one in which difference and detractors are utterly erased. Threats to English ambitions within the island of Britain came not only from noble plotters or Welsh resistance fighters: the independent kingdom of Scotland was allied with France and, in the years following the crushing defeat of the French royal army at Agincourt, sent thousands of troops in response to requests for aid. No evidence has been found that Scots fought alongside the French at Agincourt. But incursions across the Scottish border in 1415, including the Battle of Yeavering – while Henry was preoccupied with planning his French campaign – tested the edges of English authority.

And what of those Welsh longbowmen and other men-at-arms, returning home with their pardons and uneasy rehabilitations as loyal subjects of the Crown? Contemporary Welsh records themselves remain mute on Henry's triumph of 1415; Agincourt is perhaps the only major battle of the Hundred Years War not recorded in Welsh-language poetry. Henry's triumph of 1415, it seems, is too closely entangled with the disappointment and humiliation of the failed Glyndŵr rebellion to be honoured in verse. But, gradually, over the centuries, the mythology of the Welsh longbowmen at Agincourt, in their knitted Monmouth caps, has grown in popularity and potency, deployed in patriotic narratives both Welsh and English.

Shakespeare's Agincourt constructs a sense of unity through its cast of characters, each emblematic of a different nation, but serving together. Olivier's 1944 film version seeks to muster the whole of the United Kingdom behind the banner of Agincourt as an emblem of honour and courage, against all the odds. But the 'Agincourt Carol' forges unity through a stubborn focus on England only, celebrating the triumphant nation with the valiant Henry – and God – as its champions. The poem transforms a boggy battlefield in France into a glorious feat of noble conquest – but belies an England still fighting, against its nearest neighbours, for supremacy within the island of Britain itself.

9.

Anne Boleyn and All That

'Whoso List to Hunt' by Thomas Wyatt (around 1520s)

May 1536. Thomas Wyatt – diplomat, official, courtier, poet – is imprisoned in the Tower of London. It's a spectacular fall from grace: just over a year before, probably on Easter Day 1535, he had been knighted by King Henry VIII. In 1532, he had been chosen to accompany Henry and his mistress Anne Boleyn on a visit to France, and in 1533 had played a ceremonial role at her coronation. But now, he is locked up as a traitor.

What did Thomas do, during those dark days in the Tower? He probably reflected on the reversal in his fortunes and the precarity of courtly favour. He probably wrote letters and may well have scribbled lines of verse. And, perhaps, from his prison window, he witnessed the execution of five men imprisoned just before him: Mark Smeaton, Sir Henry Norris, William Brereton, Sir Francis Weston and George Boleyn, Viscount Rochford – all accused of adultery (and her brother, additionally, of incest) with Anne Boleyn, now the queen. Perhaps, even, on 19 May, he glimpsed Anne Boleyn herself as she walked to the scaffold and knelt for the swordsman's blow. Why was Wyatt in the Tower? Contemporary records are vague or untrustworthy, with their own political agendas or prurient interests. Scholars have speculated for generations.

'Whoso List to Hunt' is about unrequited or forbidden love, aching with erotic desire and frustrated passion. It's written in coded language and imagery: a puzzle or riddle to be deciphered. The poem is often scoured for evidence of Wyatt's possible relationship with Anne Boleyn – and it seems to offer various hints and clues. But the poem's origins and intent are much more complicated than that. Did Thomas Wyatt have an affair with Anne Boleyn? And is that even the most interesting question to ask? 'Whoso List to Hunt' opens a window into Tudor passions, intrigues and rivalries. But it also offers insights into the risky business of making verse in the royal court. What happens when poetry goes under cover in the court of Henry VIII?

> Whoso list to hunt, I know where is an hind,
> But as for me, hélas, I may no more.
> The vain travail° hath wearied me so sore,
> I am of them that farthest cometh behind.
> Yet may I by no means my wearied mind
> Draw from the deer, but as she fleeth afore
> Fainting I follow. I leave off therefore,
> Sithens° in a net I seek to hold the wind.
> Who list her hunt, I put him out of doubt,
> As well as I may spend his time in vain.
> And graven with diamonds in letters plain
> There is written, her fair neck round about:
> *Noli me tangere*, for Caesar's I am,
> And wild for to hold, though I seem tame.

On the surface, it's a poem about hunting. But you hardly have to dig deep for the hidden message. Key is the pun on 'deer' and 'dear' – the quarry of the hunt and the beloved or lover who is the poem's subject. It's a poem about the thrill of the chase – and the misery when desire can never be fulfilled. The speaker, in fact, is declaring his intention to give up: he's exhausted by the endless pursuit, the 'vain travail' or futile effort and labour, with no hope of success. But it's not that easy. Try as he might, 'Yet may I by no means my wearied mind / Draw from the deer, but as she fleeth afore / Fainting I follow'. He just keeps coming back for more. She's impossible to catch, this 'hind' or lady who's the object of the speaker's desire. It's like trying to catch

° labour   ° Since

the wind, he tells us: 'in a net I seek to hold the wind'. So, who was the woman who inspired this aching, irresistible desire, yet who remained always beyond reach? Was Thomas Wyatt another of Anne Boleyn's lovers? And could his poetry be the smoking gun?

Contemporary sources paint a picture of Anne as the perfect female courtier: elegant, accomplished, beautiful. Portraits show her with chestnut-brown hair, a high forehead and arched brows. She spoke French fluently, after her years serving Queen Claude of France as a maid of honour. She was a fine dancer, lutenist and singer. By New Year 1522 she had gained a position in the English court as a lady-in-waiting to Queen Catherine. This wasn't the Boleyn family's first intimate association with the court of Henry VIII: Anne's older sister Mary had been the king's mistress and possibly bore him one or more children, though they were never formally acknowledged.

Before becoming an established figure in Henry's court, Anne herself had been linked to other men. Rumour had it that she'd been the mistress of the king of France himself, but her supposed nicknames 'the English mare' and 'the royal mule' are probably defamatory later inventions. She had been recalled from France to England in 1521 to marry her Irish cousin, James Butler, 9th Earl of Ormond. But the marriage plans were broken off. In 1523, she was secretly betrothed to Henry Percy, son of the 5th Earl of Northumberland. But again the marriage was called off, when Percy's father refused to support the match. Anne was an alluring presence at court – Wyatt wasn't the only nobleman trying to catch her. In 1525, Wyatt charges his wife, Elizabeth Cobham, with adultery, and leaves her. It seems to be around this time that he becomes more closely involved with Anne. But she has also caught the king's eye. Henry's interest in Anne intensifies from around 1526 onwards.

Wyatt's poem hints at the lady's romantic entanglements in a startlingly brazen way. The speaker doesn't just reflect on his own desire and pursuit of the 'deer' / 'dear', but implies that a few others are up to the same game. It's a surprisingly laddish opening line. 'Whoso list to hunt, I know where is an hind.' It's a call to the chase, and a kind of rowdy invitation – a shout-out to anyone else who's up for it. It presents the poem's lady – Anne? – as fair game. The speaker complains that 'I am of them that farthest comest behind'. He's just one of many, and grumbling that he's last in the race. Are others succeeding, and winning their prize? The poem's not just a private reflection on the speaker's own predicament, but advice to others, too. 'Whoso list her hunt, I put him out of doubt, / As well as I may spend his time in vain.' It's not worth it: a waste of time. But that repeated word 'whoso' – 'whoever' – is astonishingly capacious, addressing itself to all-comers as they try their shot with this lady. The final line of the poem is perhaps most audacious of all. This beautiful quarry is 'wild for to hold', even if she seems 'tame'. Of course, this fits with the extended metaphor of the deer for the lady which is the poem's central conceit. But the sexual connotations of 'wild' are unmistakable. 'Whoso List to Hunt' doesn't evoke a distantly unattainable, virtuous, chaste lady, but a character far more erotic, wanton and dangerous.

So, did Thomas Wyatt and Anne Boleyn have an affair? The surviving documentary evidence is biased and unreliable, riddled with rumour, hearsay and salacious speculation. Nicholas Harpsfield, a sixteenth-century Roman Catholic propagandist, claims that Wyatt told the king Anne had been his mistress, and warned him against marriage. Harpsfield gives as his source one Antonio Bonvisi, a merchant of Lucca with various courtly connections. But there's no hard proof. A version of the story by the French ambassador Eustace Chapuys, in a letter to Charles V, remarks that Anne had been 'trouvee au delit avec un gentilhomme de court' ('caught in the act with a nobleman of the court'). The snitch is the Duke of Suffolk – the man whom, later in life, Wyatt blames for his imprisonment in the Tower in that spring of 1536. The most detailed account appears in a letter supposedly written from Wyatt to King Henry from prison, after the execution of Anne's other lovers. It gives an extraordinarily graphic account of a visit Wyatt paid to Anne's bedroom. But the text comes from the notoriously unreliable Spanish *Crónica del Roy Henrico*: another piece of Roman Catholic hand-wringing at the depravities of the English court on the cusp of the Reformation.

The date of 'Whoso List to Hunt' is unclear. It was perhaps written in the period in the 1520s when Wyatt was increasingly involved with Anne, but before Henry had made clear his intention to marry her. The poem is written in a shrinking window of opportunity: there's still room for ambiguity, hope and self-delusion. But the final lines make clear that the object of desire is out of reach, possessed by someone far more powerful. The lady wears a jewelled necklace and 'There is written her fair neck round about: / *Noli me tangere*, for Caesar's I am'.

'Noli me tangere': it's a quote from the Vulgate Latin text of the Bible – the version familiar to most educated early modern European readers. The phrase comes from John's Gospel, when Mary Magdalene recognises the risen Christ in the garden by the empty tomb. Christ tells her 'Noli me tangere': 'Do not touch me'. He's preparing her for a transformation in their relationship once he ascends into heaven: they will be parted physically, and instead of embodied human contact, they must be together in spiritual communion. But it's a charged and multi-layered text. By the end of the Middle Ages, a tradition was firmly established which depicted Mary Magdalene as a fallen woman or prostitute. And some heretical teachings even held her to be the wife of Christ. The scene of Christ telling Mary not to touch him has gathered illicit and dangerous erotic associations.

'For Caesar's I am' also conjures a particular cultural allusion. The Roman author Solinus, writing in the early third century, had told of white stags found in the Roman Empire 300 years after Caesar's death, which still wore collars bearing the inscription 'Noli me tangere, Caesaris sum' ('Do not touch me; I am Caesar's'). So great was Caesar's power that the marvellous white stags still belonged to him, even generations later. The meaning in Wyatt's poem is clear: hands off. The object of the speaker's desire is out of bounds. She's owned by 'Caesar': that is, the most powerful of all men – perhaps even a king. The risk and danger of holding on to her is simply too great. The detail of the jewelled inscription leaves us with a lingering image of the lady's 'fair neck': sensual, erotic; soft skin touched by lovers' hands and kisses. Reading the poem after the events of

1536, we might think, all too easily, of its fragility and vulnerability: the scaffold, the block, the executioner's blade.

What happens next in the story needs little recapitulation. In his pursuit of Anne, Henry seeks annulment of his marriage to Catherine of Aragon, which Pope Clement VII refuses. The failure is Cardinal Wolsey's ruin, and the whole matter precipitates the English break from Rome and the Reformation. Anne and Henry marry in January 1533, with Anne crowned queen consort on 1 June. Their daughter Elizabeth is born that September. But it doesn't take long for the marriage to unravel. Another Wyatt poem, about a 'Brunet', refers to 'Her that did set our country in a roar', later carefully amended, in Wyatt's own hand, to 'set my wealth in such a roar'. Was this another lyric about Anne? She had certainly caused commotion and calamity which could hardly have been foreseen. Written words could be risky. If Wyatt was writing about Anne, then he needed to take care.

But the biography of 'Whoso List to Hunt' is far more complex. It didn't start life with Wyatt's pen, in sixteenth-century England. In fact, it's a translation, of a sonnet by the fourteenth-century Italian poet Petrarch – now often known as the 'Father of Humanism'. What does that mean for interpreting the poem's authenticity and motivation? And how does it affect our understanding of how poetry operates in the Tudor court?

Wyatt made an important contribution to the development of English literature by importing and adapting verse forms and styles from continental Europe. In an anthology of English poetry printed by Richard Tottel in 1557, only about fifteen years after Wyatt's death, 'depewitted sir Thomas Wyat' is credited with the transformation of English poetry. The 'workes of divers Latines, Italians, and other' are known to be excellent and praiseworthy, Tottel writes. But the verse of Wyatt, and a handful of his peers, shows that 'our tongue is able in that kynde to do as praiseworthely as the rest'. The Elizabethan writer George Puttenham remarks that Wyatt, having travelled in Italy, 'there tasted the sweet and stately measures and stile of the Italian Poesie' and then 'greatly polished our rude and homely maner' of English verse. Wyatt shows that the English language is more than equal to making its own poetic tradition. In 'Whoso List to Hunt' we see the fourteen-line form borrowed from the Italian sonnet, as well as other artful European touches such as the exclamation, in French, of 'hélas' ('alas') in line two. Wyatt brings together courtly continental styles with English words and innovations.

Translation at this time is understood as a freer process – more like adaptation, rather than strict and exact reproduction of meaning. We can look for what's different in Wyatt's poem compared to the Petrarch original: the choices and alterations he makes. Petrarch's earlier poem certainly lacks the rather laddish depiction of multiple suitors chasing the lady. Instead, it presents an intense and almost mystical private encounter between the speaker and his beloved, appearing as a white doe. She's not 'wild', but instead 'sweet and proud'. She also wears the inscription around her neck which warns that she belongs to Caesar. But hers is adorned with diamonds and topazes – the topaz symbolic of chastity. Is it significant that Wyatt removes those topazes and leaves only the sparkling diamonds?

Writing a translation gives Wyatt room for manoeuvre. It offers licence to speak on a dangerous topic. The safety of translation allows secret truth-telling about the Tudor court and its most powerful figures. Typically, for a high-status writer at this time, Wyatt's poetry isn't public. It's not designed to be printed or published, but to be circulated in manuscript among friends and fellow nobles – those who can decipher its clues and catch its coded, unspoken messages.

Poetry in the Tudor court is about going under cover, using verse to say things which can't be voiced openly. This is a historical moment in which words are uniquely dangerous. The Treason Act of 1534 made it high treason to 'maliciously wish, will or desire by words or writing, or by craft imagine, invent, practise, or attempt any bodily harm to be done or committed' to the king, queen and their heirs. Suddenly, treason was a crime not just of physical violence but of words, thought and imagination. Now, also, high treason could exist in the eye of the beholder: a matter of opinion.

Wyatt himself fell foul of what he called this 'law of words', when he was accused of speaking treasonously against the king. These later accusations were first made in 1538, but blew up again in 1540 after the downfall of Wyatt's patron and protector, Thomas Cromwell. In his defence, Wyatt recalled that he had indeed once said that 'he feared that the king should be cast out of a cart's arse' (that is, be thrown off the back end of a cart). But, he explained, this was spoken without malicious intent – just a careless figure of speech. These words sent Wyatt back to the Tower (in January 1541) and almost cost him his life. He protested that they showed 'whereby a malicious enemy might take advantage by evil interpretation'. Words needed careful guarding.

The influential Elizabethan guidebook on poetry and rhetoric, *The Arte of English Poesie*, probably by George Puttenham, is preoccupied throughout with questions of literary disguise and dissembling. Puttenham reflects on the poetic use of *Allegoria* – allegory, or what he translates as 'the Figure of false semblant'. Poetry with a hidden meaning allows the writer to 'dissemble', he explains: 'I meane speake otherwise than we thinke, in earnest as well as in sport'. Such 'disguisings' are the everyday business of those in the court: the 'profession of a very Courtier, which is in plaine termes, cunningly to be able to dissemble'. Puttenham covers his back by claiming that, while foreign courtiers might be slippery and deceitful, the 'English maker' or courtly poet is fundamentally honest. He's only really a dissembler in terms of the effort and labour of his art, Puttenham suggests: disguising the artifice of his style to give the impression that his verse is natural and spontaneous. But Puttenham keeps coming back to that fraught and tricksy relationship between poetry, truth and disguise. Amid the intense pressures of the Tudor court, shifting politics and the fickleness of royal favour, the art of poetry – giving praise, advice, critique or complaint – all too often needs its disguising 'cloak'.

Wyatt's many other poetic translations include a version of the biblical Penitential Psalms, attributed in the Old Testament to the authorship of David. The seven psalms known as 'penitential' are laments about sin and guilt, as well as personal misfortune, hardship and the trials of God's people. Wyatt's translation is beyond reproach: a devout and pious rendering of a biblical source. Yet, while taking inspiration from the Old Testament text, they give him space to complain about 'myne enemyes' and the 'troubles that compass me'. They make room for expressions of discontent and venting of a sense of injustice: a safe guise for dangerous thoughts and words.

Another of Wyatt's poems is sometimes linked to the collapse of his possible relationship with Anne Boleyn and the sudden unravelling of his fortunes in the mid-1530s. 'They Flee from Me' looks back with regret at past intimacies, now withdrawn: 'They flee from me that sometime did me seek'. The subject of loss and regret shifts between 'they' and a singular 'she'. The speaker recalls secret visitors 'With naked foot, stalking in my chamber', who once 'put themself in danger / To take bread at my hand'. One moment is remembered vividly:

> When her loose gown from her shoulders did fall,
> And she me caught in her arms long and small;
> Therewithall sweetly did me kiss
> And softly said, 'Dear heart, how like you this?'

The speaker is left bereft, forsaken, in thrall to a memory of passion and shunned by his former friends. Yet there's no evidence that this poem is about Anne Boleyn: it could be about any, or indeed many, of Wyatt's illicit dalliances and sexual relationships in the Tudor court. Wyatt can write all these things, within the conventions of literary genre and with intense feeling, without them being true in the world outside the poem. Indeed, perhaps the whole pleasure of the poem – then and now – lies in the variable relationship between poetry and reality, and the way Wyatt skirts the borders.

And it's possible the poem is about something quite different. Verse about a thwarted love affair is expected fare from a courtly poet. But when Wyatt writes about being spurned and rejected, is he actually talking about something else? Perhaps, under the guise of love poetry, he's really voicing his sense of injustice and anguish at his treatment by King Henry himself. Is Henry the real preoccupation of these poems? Perhaps this is love poetry as the ultimate misdirection.

After his imprisonment in the Tower in May 1536, Wyatt was released by mid-June. He soon returned to royal favour, granted many of the estates of the recently dissolved Boxley Abbey. But, in 1540, that old treason charge resurfaced, and in January 1541 Wyatt was back in the Tower. Past grievances and accusations were dredged up again. This time, Wyatt's release was in part due to the intervention of Catherine Howard. He was granted a full pardon and regained his role as ambassador. But he became ill and died in October 1542, aged less than forty.

So, why was Wyatt in the Tower in May 1536? In reality, there is no smoking gun. Contemporary evidence for his relationship with Anne Boleyn is inconclusive – despite the wishful thinking of countless scriptwriters and historical novelists. 'Whoso List to Hunt' isn't hard proof: it may be about someone else, or it might depict desire and fantasy rather than any consummated sexual relationship. The lady of the poem is less a living, breathing person than an object: the quarry of the hunters and the possession of 'Caesar'. His warning words hang around her neck in jewels, while her own voice is absent.

And perhaps, rather than Anne or any other lady, Wyatt's real obsession in the poem – and in so much of his other verse – is actually other men: rivalry with those courtiers who defeat him in the 'hunt', jealousy of Henry's power and sexual prerogative, and resentment at the nobles who turn against him when he's vulnerable. Yet the route Wyatt navigates along the marches of artistic play and the realities of power is one he is able to take because he knows other men will understand it. Wyatt's poetry has cultural traction because the culture of the court is one of generalised anxiety, precarity and risky words. Sex might be the dangerous truth of this poem – or just another one of its cloaks and guises. Almost 500 years later, Wyatt remains deep under cover.

10.

Words for Burning

'The Ballad Which Anne Askew Made and Sang When She Was in Newgate' by Anne Askew (1546)

Smithfield, London, 16 July 1546. A large crowd gathers below the imposing stone tower of St Bartholomew the Great. People jostle, gossip and brawl, dogs bark over scraps, riders on skittish horses draw near to view. Boys scramble onto carts and wagons to see over the tops of heads. Today, four people are to be burned as heretics: John Lascelles, Nicholas Belenian (also known as John Hemsley), John Adams and a woman, Anne Askew.

Anne has to be carried to the stake on a chair and chained up to prevent her falling. Torture on the rack, in the Tower of London, has already left her body broken. Attendants bustle with bundles of wood and kindling. On a large stage, raised high above the crowds, sit the lord chamberlain and other counsellors of King Henry VIII, the lord mayor, and City of London aldermen. From here they can both see and be seen: a public show of their power and authority. Nicholas Shaxton, latterly Bishop of Salisbury – himself a former religious reformist who has now recanted – climbs a pulpit to preach. At least some of those at the stake that day, it's reported, have had gunpowder tied to their bodies, to hasten death as the flames rise.

The scene comes from a wood-cut illustration in John Foxe's *Acts and Monuments* (also known as *Foxe's Book of Martyrs*), published in 1563. It commemorates Anne Askew as a Protestant martyr, and presents her account of her two 'Examinations' or interrogations as a supposed heretic: the first under the questioning of Edmund Bonner, Bishop of London, as well as the lord mayor and others, and continuing in the second, led by the Lord Chancellor, Sir Thomas

Wriothesley, Stephen Gardiner, Bishop of Winchester, Sir Richard Rich and more. Before Foxe's publication, Askew's 'Examinations' had already been printed by the Protestant writer John Bale in 1546, with his own substantial accompanying commentary. Askew's own account of her trials, 'by her own hande wrytinge' was smuggled abroad, Bale explains in his introduction, and was rushed to print in the greater safety of Germany. But the 'Examinations' aren't the only surviving texts attributed to Anne Askew. She also leaves two poems, including this ballad, composed in Newgate Prison, London, while she awaited her execution.

A woman from a respectable Lincolnshire gentry family, Anne Askew ended her life at the centre of the fevered power struggles and ideological upheaval following Henry VIII's break from Rome. Her story gives an insight into the violence and fervour of religious reform and resistance, as well as its dark political motives. But she is no weak or passive victim: in the writings attributed to her, her voice is confident, bold – even sardonic – and resilient.

Poems take us to all kinds of strange and surprising intimacies in the past; they invite us into unexpected empathy with individuals and moments far away. But perhaps this poem is the strangest and most difficult for present-day readers in our largely secular world – and leaves us with challenging questions about the ethics of reading. It's a slight poem, but bursting with defiant power. What does Anne Askew want her words to do? And what do we do with them?

> Like as the armed knight
> Appointed to the field,
> With this world will I fight
> And Faith shall be my shield.
>
> Faith is that weapon strong
> Which will not fail at need.
> My foes, therefore, among
> Therewith will I proceed.

10: Words for Burning

As it is had in strength
And force of Christes way
It will prevail at length
Though all the devils say nay.

Faith in the fathers old
Obtained rightwisness°
Which make me very bold
To fear no world's distress.

I now rejoice in heart
And Hope bid me do so
For Christ will take my part
And ease me of my woe.

Thou saist, lord, who so knock,
To them wilt thou attend.
Undo, therefore, the lock
And thy strong power send.

More enmyes now I have
Than hairs upon my head.
Let them not me deprave
But fight thou in my stead.

On thee my care I cast.
For all their cruel spight
I set not by their haste
For thou art my delight.

I am not she that list
My anchor to let fall
For every drizzling mist
My ship substancial.

° righteousness

125

Not oft use I to wright
In prose nor yet in rime,
Yet will I shew one sight
That I saw in my time.

I saw a rial° throne
Where Justice should have sit
But in her stead was one
Of moody cruel wit.

Absorpt was rightwisness°
As of the raging flood
Sathan in his excess
Suct up the guiltless blood.

Then thought I, Jesus lord,
When thou shalt judge us all
Hard is it to record
On these men what will fall.

Yet lord, I thee desire
For that they do to me
Let them not taste the hire°
Of their iniquity.

   The word 'faith' appears three times in the first four verses of the poem. Straight away, we meet Anne Askew's resolute, forthright, defiant voice. So, what exactly was the faith she was willing to die for, as a Christian woman condemned and burned by fellow Christian countrymen? At the heart of Askew's 'heretical' thinking was her belief that the bread and wine of the sacrament were a token or sign only: they symbolised the body and blood of Christ, but didn't actually transform into the physical substance of his flesh and blood

---

° royal   ° righteousness   ° wage / cost

when consecrated. In her own words, under interrogation, Askew explains that 'the bread is but a remembraunce of hys [Christ's] death, or a sacrament of thankes gevynge for it, whereby we are knytt unto hym by a communion of Christen love' ('the bread is but a remembrance of his death, or a sacrament of thanksgiving for it, whereby we are knit unto him by a communion of Christian love'). But Askew's belief was against the Catholic teaching of the transubstantiation – the notion that the bread and wine physically changed into the body and blood of Christ – which was still official doctrine in England at this time.

Henry VIII had broken away from Rome, partly through his pursuit of annulment of his marriage to Catherine of Aragon, compounded with a desire for greater autonomy over religious and secular affairs in England, and with an acquisitive eye on the vast wealth of monasteries and other religious houses. The First Act of Supremacy, in 1534, made Henry Supreme Head of the Church of England, followed by the Treasons Act (1534), making it punishable by death to deny royal supremacy, and finally, in 1536, the Act against the authority of the Pope, removing any further papal jurisdiction in disputes around religion or scripture.

That, of course, wasn't the end of the matter: Reformation was a protracted, tumultuous and non-linear process which stretched on over generations. But, unsurprisingly, there was popular anxiety and resistance to change – and Henry himself remained conservative in matters of theology. In 1539, Parliament passed the Act Abolishing Diversity in Opinions, setting out the 'Six Articles' which maintained Catholic doctrine as the basis for belief and practice in the new English Church, and underlined existing heresy laws. Intended to affirm continuity and familiarity, and to reassure the public, the Six Articles include a definitive statement on the sacrament. In the sacrament of the Eucharist, the bread or wafer and wine become:

the naturall bodye and bloode of our Saviour Jesu Criste, conceyved of the Virgin Marie, and that after the consecracon there remayneth noe substance of bread or wyne, nor any other substance but the substance of Criste, God and man.

the natural body and blood of our Saviour Jesus Christ, conceived of the Virgin Mary, and that after the consecration there remaineth no substance of bread or wine, nor any other substance but the substance of Christ, God and man.

During her interrogations, under relentless questioning and pressure to recant, Anne Askew remains firm in her beliefs on the sacrament. As well as drawing on scripture, she works calmly and logically through a series of arguments. How can the sacrament really be the body and blood of Christ, she contends, when the Creed (the authorised statement of faith) says that he sits at the right hand of God in heaven? Some of her analogies border on the provocative, even contemptuous. 'As for that ye call your God, is but a pece of breade', she says: 'As for what you call your God: it's just a piece of bread'.

For a more profe therof (marke it whan ye lyst) lete it lye in the box but iii. months, and it wyll be moulde, and so turne to nothynge that is good. Wherupon I am persuaded, that it can not be God.

For further proof thereof (observe it whenever you like), let it lie in the box just three months, and it will be mouldy, and so turn to nothing that is good. Whereupon I am persuaded that it cannot be God.

What about Christ's words at the Last Supper – 'This is my body' – her interrogators demand? She remains unshaken, pointing to Christ's use of metaphorical language on multiple occasions recorded in the Gospels: I am the vine, I am the door, I will raise up this temple in three days . . . The substance and detail of her answers suggests the influence of the Protestant writer John Frith, but ultimately she turns to the Bible for instruction. She tells her questioners: 'I believe as the scripture infourmeth me' – itself a heretical statement rejecting the authority of the Church and its ministers.

The energies expended on Anne Askew's questioning and later torture by her interrogators have a clear central purpose: to force her to confess, recant and reject her heretical beliefs. But there are other, obscurer and more shadowy motivations too. The inquisitors ask for names: her heretical associates and allies. Askew refuses to speak, and claims, in her own text, little understanding of what the interrogators want. It's possible they are pushing her to incriminate Catherine Parr, Queen of England as Henry's sixth wife, who was known for Protestant sympathies and composed her own books on religious matters.

The opening image of Anne Askew's 'Ballad' is that of a knight, armed for fighting and '[A]ppointed to the field'. It's a seemingly masculine image, while Anne foregrounds her identity as a woman in her account of the 'Examinations'. Especially in the first 'Examination', she frustrates her interrogators' questions with silence, and reminds them that 'Solomon says, that a woman of few words is a gift of God' ('Salomon sayth, that a woman of fewe words, is a gyfte of God'). When they accuse her of breaking the rules of scholastic debate – as practised in learned Catholic tradition – she answers that, as 'but a woman', she can't know about such things. When the inquisitors ask her to interpret a text of St Paul – perhaps a trap to catch her in the heretical act of preaching as a woman – she replies it's against St Paul's own teaching for her to interpret scripture, especially with 'so manye wyse lerned men' gathered around her.

But Anne Askew did break the rules for women – both social and religious. Born in Lincolnshire in 1521, Anne evidently received an education good enough for her to read and write confidently herself. Her father had arranged for her older sister, Margaret, to marry Thomas Kyme, a wealthy local landowner, but Margaret died before the marriage could take place. The match was transferred to Anne, so that the lucrative alliance would not be lost. The marriage was not successful: Anne later petitioned for divorce, and continued, pointedly, to use her maiden name. By 1545, when she was first examined for heresy, she had been living in London, associating with reformists and disputing with priests, earning her a reputation as an – illicit – woman 'preacher'. Anne Askew's short life saw her dangerously overstepping boundaries of many kinds.

Of course, that apparently masculine image in the first lines of the 'Ballad' isn't what it seems. It comes from the Bible (Ephesians 6): an allegory for the good Christian, whatever their gender, who should 'put on the full armour of God' and fight against evil and the world. The 'Ballad' extends this metaphor throughout the first and second stanzas, adapting the biblical imagery of the shield of faith, and declaring that '[w]ith this world will I fight', armed with faith, once again, as a 'weapon strong'. The poem is steeped in scriptural quotation and allusion – just like Anne's assured answers in her 'Examinations'. Stanza six, for example, reminds us that 'Thou saist, lord, who so knock / To them wilt thou attend' (Matthew 7), while Askew borrows the words of the Psalmist to lament that 'More enmyes now I have / Than hairs upon my head' (Psalm 69). She looks back to the 'fathers old' – the Church fathers and their writings – and takes courage from their example of faithful suffering.

Despite its depth of learning, the poem presents itself simply: a forthright, unadorned and unaffected text. The form is simple: three-beat lines and a basic ABAB rhyme scheme. The choice of ballad form itself aligns with popular and oral traditions, not high culture or sophisticated artistry. In stanza ten, Askew claims that 'Not oft use I to wright / In prose nor yet in rime' ('I didn't often use to write / In prose or yet in rhyme'). It's a profession of humility sometimes used by women writers in this period: Askew tells us she's not a skilled fashioner of words, not crafty with language. But it's astute, too: the straightforward simplicity of the poem, together with Askew's comment, present something which suggests authenticity and honesty – even authority.

The plainness of Askew's poem contrasts with the slippery, treacherous eloquence of the great men who confront her in her interrogations. In her testimony, Askew describes the 'glorious words' ('gloryouse words') of Sir William Paget (the king's principal secretary). She refers to the entreaties of Sir Richard Rich and the Bishop of London as 'flatterynge wordes' and 'glosynge pretenses' – deceitful language with its glossy veneer over the truth. Askew is involved in setting up a contrast here between the language of the court and politics – polished, mannered, untrustworthy – and the simple, straightforward language of her true faith.

There's even more invested in this contrast. Stephen Gardiner, one of Askew's interrogators and the traditionalist, reactionary Bishop of Winchester, is a prominent voice railing against the dangers of 'plain speaking' in this period. Along with others, he viewed plain speaking as dangerous – implicitly associated with wider availability of religious knowledge and threats to the vested interests of the Church and its authority. Gardiner sees plain speaking as a tool of heresy, in which a preacher makes a 'pretence to speak plainly and professes simplicities', all the while leading others into error.

Whatever their clever, smooth words, Anne is more than a match for her interrogators. As well as using the agency of silence and speaking through biblical quotation, she repeats key points insistently, without compromise. Her plain speaking sometimes borders on insolence: a wry, mocking voice which refuses to be cowed by her questioners – some of the most powerful men in the land. She responds to one question merely with a smile. At another point, when asked for her interpretation of scripture, she says that she will not 'throwe pearles amonge swine, for acornes were good enough'. Askew repeatedly outwits her captors. Unbroken, resilient, even obstinate: she persists.

The 'Ballad' points to the enemies Askew feels pressing around her – but carefully and with a deliberate ambiguity. The second verse refers to 'My foes'; stanza seven to 'enmyes'; pronouns through the poem seem to refer to 'these men' (stanza 13) attacking her. But some instances are more ambivalent. Are the 'devils' of stanza three spiritual assailants – Satan's demons come to test her faith – or could this be another reference to her human persecutors and adversaries? There's a safety in ambiguity as well as licence, but the uncertainty here also elevates Askew's situation to allegory or exemplar. Less hinged on specific historical detail, her struggles become a timeless, universal model of the beleaguered, suffering, but faithful Christian soul.

Near the end of the 'Ballad', Askew describes a 'sight' or vision, in which heavenly judgement replaces and supersedes earthly power and authority. After her condemnation as a heretic, Askew did write letters to the king, seeking mercy. Those appeals failed. The image of a 'royal throne' ('rial throne') empty of justice, and instead the seat of 'moody cruel wit' – caprice and vindictiveness – is bold and risky.

But this is not a poem of despair. Instead, it's an assertion of defiance, even triumph. The 'Ballad' is structured around the three theological virtues. We've seen faith already, shaping the first verses of the poem and appearing again in stanza nine in the image of the anchor (an allusion to the biblical passage in Hebrews 9). The second virtue on which the poem hinges is hope, foregrounded in stanza 5. Askew writes that 'I now rejoice in heart / And Hope bid me do so'. It's challenging – to say the least – for us to imagine: as Askew looks ahead to her execution at the stake, she writes of feeling joy and even 'delight'. The final virtue is charity, or love, most evident in the poem's final stanzas. The last verse echoes Christ's own words of compassion on the cross, as he asks forgiveness for his killers (Luke 23:24). These concluding words form a prayer to God, begging mercy for those who have caused Askew's suffering and death. It's an audacious feat of empathy from Anne herself: an act of mercy as grace, resistance, defiance.

If Anne did compose this poem in Newgate, awaiting her execution, then she was already grievously injured. In her own testimony in the 'Examinations', Anne is reticent about her torture on the rack, and gives little detail – though she says enough to shame her tormentors, who acted outside of all normal lawful practice. She writes:

> Then they ded put me on the racke, bycause I confessed no ladyes nor gentyllwomen to be of my opynyon, and theron they kepte me a longe tyme. And bycause I laye styll and ded not crye, my lorde Chancellour and master Ryche, toke peynes to racke me their owne handes, tyll I was nygh dead.

> Then they did put me on the rack, because I confessed no ladies nor gentlewomen to be of my opinion, and thereon they kept me a long time. And because I lay still and did not cry, my lord Chancellor and master Rich took pains to rack me with their own hands, till I was nearly dead.

Thomas Wriothesley, the lord chancellor, and Richard Rich turn the wheels of the rack with their own hands, until Anne's joints are dislocated. Afterwards, she tells us she was 'brought to a house, and laid in a bed, with as weary and painful bones, as ever had patient Job' ('brought to an howse, and layed in a bed, with as werye and payneful bones, as ever had paycent Job'). Once again, this is an instance where Askew withholds and claims the agency of her silence, deflecting our attention away from her suffering body.

But Askew's first editor, John Bale, adds graphic detail, drawing the reader's gaze to Anne's pitiful body and its mutilation by Wriothesley and Rich. He tells us that:

> . . . lyke a lambe she laye styll without noyse of cryenge, and suffered your uttermost vyolence, tyll the synnowes of her armes were broken, and the strynges of her eys perysshed in her heade.

> . . . like a lamb she lay still without noise of crying, and suffered your [the torturers'] utmost violence, till the sinews of her arms were broken, and the strings of her eyes perished in her head.

We're witnessing the violation of Askew's body – described by Bale in his introduction as 'very young, dainty, and tender' ('verye yonge, dayntye, and tender') – and the vivid details of her martydom. Bale wants us to look, but Anne refuses to make herself a spectacle. Does lingering over representations of her torture and execution, then, make us complicit? Are we colluding in the voyeurism of the rabble gathered at Smithfield, doing her further violence, joining those who have used the display of her suffering for their own, various, ideological ends?

Askew's words, in the 'Examinations' and her poems, were used by others for their political and ideological purposes. Bale and Foxe each remake her text, with Bale, in particular, adding extensive commentary and interpretation. Recovering Anne's own authentic voice is tricky: the words she leaves have been shaped and repackaged by others. The big and unavoidable question is whether Anne Askew actually wrote the 'Ballad' herself. The final three verses seem to draw on the verse paraphrase of the biblical *Ecclesiastes* by Henry Howard, Earl of Surrey. Is this Askew's own poetic imitation, or Bale's misattribution of the text? Bale was notorious for making changes and additions to his sources, but this ambiguity points to wider uncertainties surrounding women's authorship of early texts. Reclaiming the words of women from their unreliable editors is a difficult process – and sometimes a leap of faith.

What does Anne Askew want her words to do? What does she want from us, as readers? The purpose of the 'Ballad' is crystal clear: it's devotional poetry, meant to inspire, to kindle true faith and godliness. The poem is positioned emphatically against 'the world'. It points us away from earthly, secular life, from human power, and from history itself. It asks us to follow Askew's example and turn, instead, to heaven. Is to read Anne Askew's *Ballad* as a commentary on history – as a window into a historical moment – to do her a disservice? At the very least such a use of her poem might be missing the point, at worst a fundamental misreading and betrayal of her intention. Here, we are indeed reading the poem for the world, not for God. Poets don't get to determine how we read their poems. But we should pause, here, with this discomfort, this dissonance, in the case of a woman who was burned for her words.

Poems can offer us radical empathy and astonishing intimacy with people in the past. But it's hard to get close to Anne Askew. The boundaries she sets, the distance she maintains, the detail she withholds, her judicious silences: all these hold us apart. There's also, more fundamentally, the position she takes, and how she locates herself: allied with heaven and not with 'the world'. In the 'Ballad', Askew is already withdrawn from the world, already out of reach: beyond the touch of her persecutors, but, in a sense, beyond her readers, too. The 'Ballad' tests the limits of our imagination and empathy as Askew rejoices and delights, even in anticipation of her impending death at the stake, in all its agony.

In the protracted turmoil of the Reformation, England swings, for decades, between reforming Protestant zeal and Roman Catholic reversal. When Askew is burned, Henry VIII is in the last six months of his life. It's just a few years later, in the reign of Edward VI, Henry's son, that belief in the transubstantiation is itself outlawed, and Anne Askew's view – the sacrament as symbol and token – becomes official doctrine. The writings of Askew, Bale, Foxe and others have played their part in this major religious and cultural transformation. But the pendulum doesn't rest there: Mary I pulls the country back to Catholic teaching, and religious disputes and radical movements continue for a century or more. Askew's words, however, are steadfast and immoveable. She writes that 'I would rather die than to break my faith' ('I wolde rather dye, than to breake my faythe'). 'Farewell, dear friend', she bids us in her testimony, 'and pray, pray, pray' ('Fare wel dere frynde, and praye, praye, praye').

Poetry, Prophecy and the Island

'This England' (John of Gaunt's Speech) from Richard II by William Shakespeare (around 1595)

In 1992, conservators at London's National Gallery, working on the fourteenth-century Wilton Diptych, made an astonishing discovery. Made for King Richard II, probably around the time of his second marriage to Isabella of Valois (1396), the Wilton Diptych is formed of two small hinged panels, lavishly gilded and painted. On the exterior, when the diptych is closed, the panels depict a white hart or stag – Richard's emblem – and, on the other side, the heraldic arms of King Edward the Confessor – one of Richard's chosen spiritual patrons – merged with those of Richard himself. When opened, the diptych unfolds into an awe-inspiring blaze of gold and colour. On the left, a young King Richard kneels, as he is presented by three standing saints: the English kings Edward the Martyr and Edward the Confessor, and John the Baptist. Richard faces the right-hand panel, where the Virgin Mary stands cradling the Christ child, who reaches towards the young king in blessing. Around Mary throng angels in robes the exquisite blue of lapis lazuli, each wearing, like Richard himself, the king's emblem of the white hart. One angel raises aloft a staff bearing the red cross banner of St George (also a symbol of Christ's resurrection), unfurling as if caught by a breeze above the rows of feathered wings and floral crowns.

It was the small orb at the top of this staff – plain and dull to the naked eye – that was hiding a remarkable secret. As the diptych was prepared for cleaning, analysis with a powerful microscope revealed a tiny scene painted into the orb itself. A turreted white castle on a jewel-like green island, with trees on the horizon and a blue sky above. In the foreground, a ship in full sail, making its way across a sea of silver leaf, now tarnished to brown. A tiny map, measuring just one centimetre across, which had been there, under the surface, all the time. Commentators immediately reached for Shakespeare's *Richard II* and John of Gaunt's description of England as a 'precious stone set in a silver sea'. Somehow, the script of an Elizabethan play had prefigured a modern-day discovery – and pointed to the detail hidden in a Ricardian royal artwork.

How do we understand a poem in time? The famous 'This England' speech from Shakespeare's *Richard II* was written and first performed in 1595 or 1596, then published in the first quarto edition in 1597 (with further quarto editions following) and later in the First Folio of 1623. Yet these blank verse lines have escaped the original context and confines of the play. Endlessly anthologised as a stand-alone text (but often truncated), recited by generations at school, learned by heart and quoted, they defy chronology. Immediately, the passage triggers a sense of double exposure: a picture of England in the reign of Richard II, 200 years earlier, rather than Shakespeare's own contemporary historical moment. Or is it? What happens to history – and the present – when it's refracted through poetry?

'This England' is a text around which chronologies flow, eddy and snag, showing the power of poetry to disrupt history and send shockwaves through time. Its imagery of England looks back to the earliest myths and legends of the nation. But it is also made to speak forward to later historical crises and triumphs: lines appropriated, mobilised, weaponised across the centuries; words made to praise, rally and agitate. Shakespeare's 'This England' becomes a kind of scripture of English nationhood. And poetry begins to look a lot like prophecy.

> This royal throne of kings, this sceptred isle,
> This earth of majesty, this seat of Mars,
> This other Eden, demi-paradise,
> This fortress built by Nature for herself

Against infection and the hand of war,
This happy breed of men, this little world,
This precious stone set in a silver sea
Which serves it in the office of a wall
Or as a moat defensive to a house,
Against the envy of less happier lands,
This blessèd plot, this earth, this realm, this England,
This nurse, this teeming womb of royal kings,
Feared by their breed and famous for their birth,
Renownèd for their deeds as far from home
For Christian service and true chivalry
As is the sepulchre in stubborn Jewry
Of the world's ransom, blessèd Mary's son.
This land of such dear souls, this dear, dear land,
Dear for her reputation through the world,
Is now leased out – I die pronouncing it –
Like to a tenement or pelting farm.
England, bound in with the triumphant sea,
Whose rocky shore beats back the envious siege
Of watery Neptune, is now bound in with shame,
With inky blots and rotten parchment bonds.
That England that was wont to conquer others
Hath made a shameful conquest of itself.

John of Gaunt's speech, from Act II, Scene 1 of *Richard II*, presents an iconic image of England the nation, the whole 'sceptred isle' imagined as a 'royal throne' or a vessel for royalty; a 'nurse' or 'teeming womb of royal kings'. Most striking throughout these lines is the imagery of England the island, set apart from the rest of the world in destiny, beauty and honour. It's the 'precious stone set in a silver sea', as depicted in the Wilton Diptych. The image of a 'fortress built by Nature for herself', surrounded by the sea 'in the office of a wall / Or as a moat defensive to a house'. The emblems of idealised enclosure keep coming – but right away there's sleight of hand: England has expanded, slyly, to occupy the entire island, stealthily filling that neat insular geography and displacing Scotland and Wales. Seemingly preordained by Providence and Nature, England the island nation is, rather, a feat of politics and rhetoric.

England is even imagined as an 'other Eden', a 'demi-paradise': a counterpart to Adam and Eve's biblical Garden in its beauty and perfect enclosure. Indeed, medieval geography might have suggested this strange and wondrous affinity. Medieval *mappae mundi* – world maps, centred on Jerusalem in the cultural and theological 'middle' of the world – depicted Eden at its very easternmost edge. While inaccessible to humankind, the island of Eden nevertheless retained its location on the map, set apart in the miraculous, fantastical margins, where places were luminous with possibility and marvel. In these medieval maps, Britain was a strange kind of twin to Eden: the island almost at the furthest westernmost point of the world (apart from Ireland), itself located in that strange edgeland where wonders and marvels might be expected. By Shakespeare's time, European geographical imaginaries were changing. The New World now lay to the far west, and England no longer held the same status of a place on the borders of magic and wonder. But the tradition of the island as an 'other Eden' would continue to shape notions of English exceptionalism.

The enclosed beauty of the Garden of Eden is, of course, only one half of the biblical story. It's also a story of deceit, betrayal and downfall. And John of Gaunt's deathbed speech is not one of praise and celebration, but rather lament and warning: a prophecy of the collapse of England under Richard II's rule. Shakespeare's play is looking back to the turbulent later years of Richard's reign: his exercise of royal prerogative, curtailment of the powers of the nobility and reliance on a small group of courtiers. Instead of seeking the support of the baronage, Richard formed his own private military retinue, giving them badges of the white hart like those worn by the king – and the angels – in the Wilton Diptych. Richard was deposed in 1399 by Henry Bolingbroke (the future Henry IV) and died some months later, probably of starvation, in captivity. From Shakespeare's vantage-point, the court of Richard II was a place of extreme decadence and corruption, and Richard's failed rule was the disaster which paved the way for the Wars of the Roses. Shakespeare's John of Gaunt voices that Tudor précis of history, reconfigured as fourteenth-century prophecy.

The paean to England in John of Gaunt's speech begins to turn sour when he praises, over-insistently, his 'dear' land.

> This land of such dear souls, this dear, dear land,
> Dear for her reputation throughout the world . . .

Four uses of 'dear' in two lines – and we can almost hear them spoken on stage with changing inflections: from the 'dear' beloved land, to 'dear' meaning precious or rare, and 'dear' as in too costly. And is it fanciful to detect in 'dear' a surreptitious pun on 'deer', hinting at the white hart badges of Richard's henchmen? John of Gaunt laments how this 'dear' land is 'now leased out', 'like to a tenement or pelting farm'. While a 'pelting farm' might mean something like a 'paltry' or worthless homestead, 'pelting' is also a brutal image for the king's exploitation of the land and enrichment of himself: the nation as bloody and filthy as a fur farm in which the living are skinned for profit.

The speech returns to imagery of enclosure, only to turn it back, vitriolically, on Richard's England. Where England has been 'bound in with the triumphant sea', it is 'now bound in with shame, / With inky blots and rotten parchment bonds'. The warlike people of 'this seat of Mars' are famed as widely as the sepulchre of Christ in Jerusalem, the speech claims (the reference to 'stubborn Jewry' reflecting contemporary antisemitic tropes about the Jews' refusal to accept salvation). But now these brave, chivalrous people have surrendered to the tyranny of paperwork and bureaucracy: the instruments used by Richard to extract the wealth of his subjects. While the island fortress has been bulwarked by Nature against threats and invasions, it '[h]ath made a shameful conquest of itself'.

John of Gaunt's celebration of – and lament for – 'This England' centres on the emblem of the island nation, predestined for greatness but betrayed by an unworthy ruler. Yet, while Shakespeare's lines make the anthologies and the history books, this compelling, seductive image of England goes much further back – even to some of the very earliest medieval writing. Shakespeare weaves together these existing traditions in his iconic depiction of England.

The Venerable Bede, as we've seen earlier, opens his foundational eighth-century *Ecclesiastical History of the English People* with a description of 'Britain, an island of the ocean, formerly called Albion'. Bede's Britain is most certainly a marvellous place, lying in its special location almost at the edge of the world, filled with natural wonders and rich resources. It's a little otherworldly, and certainly quite different from its neighbours across the water: there's jet which can magically drive away serpents, and summer midnights which never get fully dark. And it is an explicitly *English* history Bede is shaping, even though there's that slippage once again between England the emergent nation and the entire bounds of the island. For Bede, England is a Promised Land for the newly arrived peoples from across the North Sea in northern continental Europe: the 'Angles, Saxons and Jutes'. In his formulation of history, the island itself is a kind of self-fulfilling prophecy of English nationhood.

Even Bede wasn't the first to describe Britain in this way. Two centuries earlier (around 550), the British monk Gildas, writing in present-day Wales, imagines the beautiful, fertile island as a gift given to his people by God. With its 'flowers of different hues underfoot', 'clear fountains', and 'brilliant rivers', Gildas compares Britain to 'a chosen bride arrayed in a variety of jewellery'. But Gildas is writing on the cusp of violent change in Britain – the coming of Bede's new peoples, eventually to become the 'English' – and he speaks with the wrath of an Old Testament prophet. He rages against his own people, warning them that they are losing their delightful land through their own internal conflicts and disunity. His image of the island as a beautiful bride suggests its nature as unspoilt, virgin, still perfectly enclosed and intact. But it darkly prefigures the rape, ruin and repossession of the land which he sees in its future.

In the later Middle Ages, a curious myth emerges linking the destiny of the island nation to classical origins. The twelfth-century historian Geoffrey of Monmouth tells the story of Brutus, a descendant of the Trojan hero Aeneas, who is given a prophecy by the goddess Diana. She commands Brutus to travel to the edge of the world, to find 'an island which the western sea surrounds', where 'fate commands to raise a second Troy'. The medieval legend is retrofitted to the name 'Britain' (the Romans' *Britannia*, borrowing from an earlier Brittonic-language form): Brutus gives his name to this new kingdom of Britain, its island enclosure echoing the fortress walls of his ancestral city of Troy. So popular was this story in the Middle Ages, that London itself was sometimes known as 'Troynovaunt' or 'New Troy' (another retrofitting, this time also playing on the name of the Iron Age *Trinovantes* tribe, who lived in the region which became London). But there's another twist. Diana promises that 'time shall never destroy' this great island nation, 'nor bounds confine'. The island prophecy is a clarion call to expansion, conquest and empire.

England's first empire, of course, was within the island of Britain itself. That persistent rhetorical entanglement of England the nation and the entire island is more than just poetics – it becomes an authorising image for internal colonialism, the fantasy of a single national identity created and endorsed by the island's bounds. The emblem of the island nation all too treacherously and aggressively erases other identities and polities from within its bounds. It's an ambition which always belied the realities: local lordships, patchworks of kingdoms, and, later, the fully fledged nations of Wales and Scotland, as well as the messiness of a rocky archipelago with pockets of territory in continental Europe too. And, of course, the deep, rich networks and exchanges – trade, travel, commerce and culture – between Britain the island and its many neighbours across the seas.

In Shakespeare's 'This England' all these images of the island nation – stretching back into the early Middle Ages and on into modernity – gather, swirl and eddy. We see the same emblematic descriptions of the island recur across the centuries in poetry from James Thomson's 'Rule Britannia' to the 'green and pleasant land' of Blake's 'Jerusalem'. Shakespeare's iconography of the island, set apart and blessed with a special destiny, speaks back to the distant past. But it also resonates through later centuries, especially at times of national threat or celebration: made to signify prophetically – and politically – at different historical moments.

'This England' was first anthologised as early as 1600 in a collection titled *England's Parnassus*, in a section 'Of Albion'. Already the verse has broken loose from its moorings in Shakespeare's play: made to speak as a poem in its own right and, in fact, misattributed to the poet Michael Drayton. It appears again in an eighteenth-century poetic miscellany of patriotic extracts compiled during the War of the Second Coalition, when Britain, Austria, Russia, Portugal, Naples and the Ottoman Empire together fought Revolutionary France.

In 1817, the English essayist and literary critic William Hazlitt reflected on 'This England' in his book *Characters of Shakespeare's Plays*. Where other readers had easily coupled the verse to patriotic feeling, he is more sceptical, commenting that he 'should perhaps hardly be disposed to feed the pampered egotism of our countrymen by quoting this description, were it not that the conclusion of it (which looks prophetic) may qualify any improper degree of exultation'. In the context of his own dissatisfaction with English politics, Hazlitt is all too ready to read the darker conclusion of the 'This England' speech as prophecy.

Surfacing repeatedly at times of national turmoil or danger, 'This England' makes a notable appearance in a Blitz-ravaged London of 1941. A special Shakespeare Revue staged at Westminster Theatre by G. Wilson Knight featured the extract alongside scenes from a range of Shakespeare plays. A review in *The Times* noted the play's presentation of 'Shakespeare as the poet and prophet of a free and virile people united under a benevolent monarchy and determined to fight in themselves the evils of greed and corruption and to take up arms against tyranny and the lust for power in others'. In the nation's darkest hour, Shakespeare's iconic verses carried the promise of hope and favoured destiny. The iconography of the island nation persists in Churchill's own calls to popular morale: his vow, after Dunkirk, to 'defend our Island, whatever the cost may be', and, indeed, in the title of the abridged version of his *History of the English-Speaking Peoples*: *Our Island Race*.

Right into the present, the words of John of Gaunt's speech wield power, deployed intentionally – or less so – in vastly varied contexts. Michael Winterbottom and Kieron Quirke's 2022 film about the UK government's handling of the first wave of the Covid-19 pandemic is titled *This England* – having originally had the working title *This Sceptred Isle*. Viewers who'd learned the Shakespeare lines by heart at school might have picked up the ironic allusion to John of Gaunt's fortress nation, defended '[a]gainst infection and the hand of war'. Peter Hitchens' 2015 documentary on the history of the UK's relationship with the EU is *This Sceptic Isle*. While endlessly borrowed for patriotic celebration and flag-waving, Shakespeare's lines still retain their prophetic power to castigate and chastise.

In spring 2023, a British women's clothing brand released a 'British Isles Print Mini Dress', decorated with a repeating map of Britain and Ireland, and lines from Shakespeare's 'This England'. The dress design was named 'Saoirse': the Irish name and word for 'freedom', particularly associated with the struggle for freedom from English rule. Revulsion and mockery on social media led to the dress being rapidly pulled from sale and all traces of the ill-fated product scoured from the internet. Still today, John of Gaunt's words are more than just a neat cultural touchstone or tourist-board cliché; not merely a pretty piece of vintage literary découpage.

Now let's chase our unruly chronology back to Shakespeare's England, and the performance and reception of *Richard II* in Shakespeare's own lifetime. Can we, for a moment, pin the poem in its original historical place? How did Shakespeare's contemporaries understand 'This England'? On Saturday, 7 February 1601, a group of supporters of Robert Devereux, second Earl of Essex, gathered to watch a private performance of a play. It was, as the Earl's steward later told interrogators, 'of King Harry the fourth and of the killing of King Richard the second, played by the Lord Chamberlain's players'. The choice of play was no accident. The Earl of Essex, resentful after military and financial failures and the queen's disapproval, was hatching plans against Elizabeth and her court. Shakespeare's play of Richard II's deposition and death – and John of Gaunt's words decrying the betrayal of England by a corrupt monarch – spoke to the grievances and motives of its audience.

Events moved fast. The Privy Council summoned Essex to appear before them, but he refused. He had now, effectively, declared his position against the queen and lost any advantage of surprise. The following day, four messengers arrived at Essex House from court, led by the Lord Keeper of the Great Seal and the Lord Chief Justice. Essex detained them in the house, under the guard of three musketeers and a caliver. His hand was now forced. Essex and his supporters made their way into the City of London, with the aim of rousing rebellion against the queen. But their efforts stirred no such popular uprising. Essex and his men retreated back to Essex House, and, that evening, surrendered to the queen's men. Less than two weeks later, the Earl of Essex was found guilty of high treason and beheaded at the Tower of London, along with his accomplice Henry Wriothesley, third Earl of Southampton. Five others were also found guilty and executed.

Writing shortly after the trial, Francis Bacon comments on the rebels' choice of *Richard II* for that fateful performance, procured by Sir Gelly Meyrick, Essex's steward. 'So earnest he was to satisfy his eyes with the sight of that Tragedy, which he thought soon after his Lord should bring from the Stage to the State, but that God turned it upon their own heads'. The play, Bacon asserts, was staged as prophecy – but a prophecy which ran awry. Later, in August 1601, according to an apocryphal account, the antiquary William Lambarde visited Queen Elizabeth at East Greenwich with a collection of historical documents. Together, they sit and read through the annals, until Elizabeth reaches the reign of Richard II. She pauses and looks up at Lambarde. 'I am Richard II', she says. 'Know ye not that?'

'This England' spills out of its place in our timeline of English history, sending ripples back and forwards over a thousand years and more. What does it mean for a poem to be prophecy? It's unlikely Shakespeare wrote *Richard II* – or John of Gaunt's iconic speech – as an incitement to rebellion and treason in his own present. Yet its depiction of a proud island nation that 'hath made a shameful conquest of itself' was staged as prophecy by Essex and his followers. The 'precious stone set in a silver sea' on the Wilton Diptych? It's possible that Shakespeare may have seen the diptych himself in the royal collection and consciously copied the motif – but more likely still that both the artwork and blank verse are engaging with the same long-standing tradition of imagining England as the idealised island nation.

All poems speak to multiple historical moments, have multiple lives and afterlives. Readers make them do what they wish, serving different purposes and agendas. 'This England' is a potent text which deals in the magical, the sacral, the foundation myths of English nationhood (however flawed or deceptive). It has scriptural status and power.

Poetry doesn't stay put. The same lines can be a rallying cry, encomium, incitement, condemnation. 'This England' codifies imagery of nationhood developed over a millennium. It draws together traditions and mythologies which continue to shape national discourse. Its readers, then, now and in the future, choose how to make it prophetic.

The Arse-End of England

'Bum-fodder, or, Waste-paper, Proper to Wipe the Nation's RUMP with, or Your Own' attributed to Alexander Brome (1660)

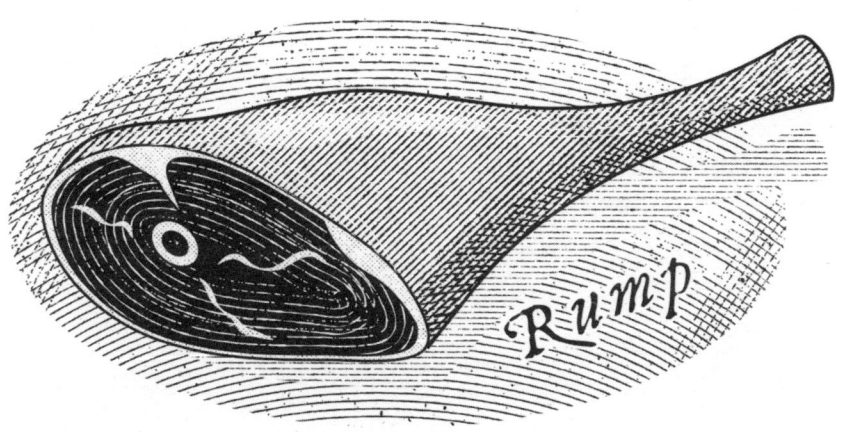

Early 1660, and England's so-called 'Rump Parliament' is almost out on its arse. These have been turbulent years: civil wars, the execution of Charles I, and England's first and only period as a republic – the Commonwealth. Lord General of the army and Commonwealth forces and former Lord Protector Oliver Cromwell is dead. His son, Richard, has proven too weak to hold power. Factions and conflicting ideologies jostle, across political and religious divides: Royalists and republicans, cavaliers and round-heads, conservative Anglicans and hot-headed puritans, civilians and soldiers. Relentless political purges and experiments in different forms of government have repeatedly failed. But word on the street – in pamphlets, broadsides and the other rags – hints that Royalists see an end in sight.

'Bum-fodder' is a satire on the Rump Parliament – the remaining members of the House of Commons left after Colonel Thomas Pride's 1648 purge of all those considered hostile to the New Model Army and opposed to putting the king on trial. After being dissolved by Oliver Cromwell in 1653, the Rump was revived in 1659 – only to be expelled again, in October that year, and called back in December. Now, reviled by Royalists and widely unpopular, the Rump seems on its last legs. The poem doesn't hold back on the scatological humour: all twenty-one stanzas (you can skim them) of bum, fart and poo jokes. It lets us inside seventeenth-century Royalist banter and political gossip. 'Bum-fodder' was first printed as a broadside ballad, part of the street culture of early modern England: cheap, topical, disposable. It sets out to wipe Parliament's arse – leaning in to the double meaning of 'wipe' as beat, strike or hit. But, the title points out, you could also use it to wipe your own. This throwaway rag is pragmatic that its own destiny is also to end up down the privy.

> Free quarter in the North is grown so scarce,
> That Lambert with all his men of Mars
> Have submitted to kiss the Parliaments Arse,
> Which no body can deny.
>
> If this should prove true, (as we do suppose)
> Tis such a wipe as the RUMP and all's Foes
> Could never give to old Olivers nose:
> Which no body can deny.
>
> Theres a Proverb come to my mind not unfit,
> When the head shal see the RUMP all be-shit,
> Sure this must prove a most lucky hit:
> Which no body can deny.
>
> Theres another Proverb which every Noddy
> Wil jeer the RUMP with, and cry Hoddy Doddy,
> Here's a Parliament all Arse and no Body.
> Which no body can deny.
>
> Tis a likely matter the world wil mend
> When so much blood and treasure we spend,
> And yet begin again at the wrong End:
> Which no body can deny.
>
> We have been round and round about twirl'd,
> And through much sad confusions hurl'd,
> And now we are got into the arse of the world:
> Which no body can deny.

But 'tis not all this our courage wil quail,
Or make the brave Seamen to the RUMP strike sail,
If we can have no head, we wil have no Tail:
Which no body can deny.

Then let a Free-Parliament be turnd trump,
And nere think any longer the Nation to mump
With your pocky, perjur'd, damnd, old Rump:
Which no body can deny.

But what doth Rebel Rump make here
When their proper place (as Will. Pryn doth swear)
Is at the Devils arse in Derbyshire:
Which no body can deny.

Then thither let us send them a tilt,
For if they stay longer, they wil us beguilt
With a Government that is loose in the Hilt:
Which no body can deny.

Youl find it set down in Harringtons Moddle,
Whose brains a Commonwealth do so coddle,
That t'as made a Rotation in his noddle:
Which no body can deny.

Tis a pitiful pass you men of the Sword
Have brought yourselves to, that the Rumps your Lord,
And Arsie-Versie, must be the word,
Which no body can deny.

Our powder and shot you did freely spend,
That the Head you might from the Body rend,
And now you are at us with the But-end,
Which no body can deny.

Old Martin and Scot have still such an itch,
That they will with the Rump try to'ther twitch;
And Lenthal can grease a fat Sow in the britch:
Which no body can deny.

Thats a thing that would please the Butchers and Cooks,
To see this stinking Rump quite off the hooks,
And Jack-Daw go to pot with the Rooks.
Which no body can deny.

This forward Sir John (who the Rump did never fail)
Against Charles Stuart, in a Speech did rail;
But men say it was without head or tail,
Which no body can deny.

Just such is the Government wee live under,
Of a Parliament thrice cut in sunder;
And this hath made us the worlds wonder,
Which no body can deny.

Old Noll when we talkt of Magna Charta,
Did prophecy well we should all smart-a,
And now wee have found his RUMPS Magna Fart-a,
Which no body can deny.

But I can't think Monck (though a Souldier and sloven)
To be kin to the Fiend, whose feet are cloven,
Nor will creep i'th Rumps Arse, to bake in their Oven,
Which no body can deny.

Then since he is coming, e'ne let him come
From the North to the South, with Sword and Drum,
To beat up the quarters of this lewd Bum;
Which no body can deny.

12: The Arse-End of England

And now of this Rump I'le say no more,
Nor had I begun, but upon this score,
There was something behind, which was not before;
Which no body can deny.

The ballad begins at the end of a tumultuous year for the Rump Parliament, and for John Lambert – a senior Parliamentary soldier and politician, once widely tipped to be Oliver Cromwell's successor – who is named in the second line. At the start of 1659, tensions between the Third Protectorate Parliament, Richard Cromwell as the new Lord Protector, and the army had grown unmanageable. Parliament and the army were as divided among themselves as against each other. The army forced the removal of Cromwell and dissolution of Parliament. Lambert played a leading role in the subsequent negotiations. Under pressure from his junior officers, Lambert headed a deputation to William Lenthall, Speaker of the House of Commons, listing army demands and calling for the return of the Rump Parliament. The restored Rump gave Lambert prominent roles in government, but he remained ambivalent towards Parliament's authority: 'I know not why they should not be at our mercy as well as we at theirs'. This really was the feeble tail-end of the Parliament formed by Pride's Purge back in 1648, and previously dissolved by Oliver Cromwell in 1653. 'This fagge-end, this Rump of a Parliament with corrupt Maggots in it', as contemporary lawyer and politician Clement Walker described it. Seventy-eight members were now left available to serve, but only sixty-five appeared in May 1659. The weakened Parliament was struggling to agree on a constitution: what sort of republic was this, and how should it be run? It was losing its control over the army and tensions escalated.

In the autumn of 1659, the Rump sent Lambert to suppress army discontent and Royalist risings in the north, but, growing increasingly mistrustful of him and other leading officers, Parliament dismissed (cashiered) them on 12 October. Lambert appealed to troops in London, and marched on Westminster. On 13 October, Lambert's forces surrounded Parliament and expelled the members of the

Rump – again. As they marched out of Westminster Hall, the soldiers gave Lambert a standing ovation: the man who'd given the Rump a good kicking. Lambert now became a member of the Committee of Safety – the interim government which took over in place of the Rump Parliament.

But there was more to come. General George Monck, commander-in-chief of the army in Scotland, had declared in support of Parliament, and now rode to London to its aid. The Committee of Safety sent Lambert north to deal with him. But Lambert's army was disintegrating: years of chaotic government had led to unpaid wages, spiralling deficits and lack of funds, and resentment was fermenting. Lambert's men had had enough of – as the ballad puts it – scrounging for 'Free quarter in the North'. By Christmas Eve, unpaid soldiers across England were clamouring for the return of the Rump, and military Commander-in-Chief Charles Fleetwood formally called for it to be restored. 'Bum-fodder' takes great delight in this about-turn from the strongmen of the English army: the 'men of Mars' who had squared up to the Rump Parliament, now pleading for it to come back. The poem scoffs at these army figures who've 'submitted to kiss the Parliament's Arse': brown-nosing of the most humiliating kind.

It's in late 1659 that the name 'Rump' comes into popular usage: the fag-end Parliament becomes the butt of endless jokes in popular print and Royalist chatter. To select just a few from the ballad's impressive scatological repertoire: it's the 'arse' (stanza 1), the 'butt-end' (stanza 13), the 'lewd bum' (stanza 20), and in so much trouble that, frankly, it's 'all be-shit' (stanza 3).

But the barrage of bum jokes fits into a more extended political metaphor. Running through the ballad is imagery of England turned upside down, a topsy-turvy world gone arse over tit. Stanza 12 settles on the word 'Arsie-Versie' to describe the present state of England, while stanza 6 reels from the giddiness of decades in which the county has 'been round and round about twirl'd'. The idea that civil war – and regicide, or the execution of the monarch – has turned the country upside down is a recurring theme in Royalist ballads, including one titled 'Arsy-Versy', to be sung to the popular tune 'Up tails all'.

And it's more than just an upending of normality. Since the execution of Charles I, the ballad implies, England has been governed by its arse instead of its (severed) head. This isn't just schoolboy humour, but picks up on imagery of the body politic long part of political discourse and symbolism: the nation as a body of parts working harmoniously together, with the monarch as its head. Now, the body of England is unfit and dysfunctional. It's 'all Arse and no Body', as the fourth stanza puts it: there's no united corporate national identity (and, the poem suggests, barely enough bums on seats for the Rump even to count). The ballad revels in the absurdity of a nation led by its arse rather than its head: the very real state of affairs, from a Royalist perspective, after regicide. If they can't have a head – the king – then they don't want a rump, either: 'If we can have no head, we will have no Tail', the seventh stanza declares. These are the chaotic consequences when 'the Head you might from the Body rend' (stanza 13). 'Bum-fodder' caricatures a deformed, monstrous nation. This is a failed, ridiculous parliament – a truncated body, without all its working parts – made laughable and ludicrous.

And if the Rump Parliament has no authority, then all its talk and pronouncements are no more than hot air. Stanza 18 looks back to arguments made against Oliver Cromwell ('Old Noll'), citing Magna Carta ('Magna Charta') and its principles of rights and rule of law. Back then, Cromwell threatened that Royalists would 'smart-a' – feel the pain of his radical political reformation. But now, after all, the Rump is exposed as nothing more than a 'Magna Fart-a': noisy flatulence from the tail-end of a defunct parliament.

When the first Rump Parliament was dismissed by Oliver Cromwell in 1653, he's quoted as saying 'You have sat too long for any good you have been doing lately'. Seventeenth-century medicine attributed the unfortunate ailment of piles (haemorrhoids) to sitting down for too long – another trick the ballad doesn't miss. The 'pocky, perjur'd, damnd old Rump' of stanza 8 hints that members are plagued with lumps and sores for outstaying their welcome on the benches of Parliament. The ballad's mockery of the Rump is relentless, but there's something more than just banter going on here. These are jokes in the face of genuine threat and uncertainty, after the trauma of years of grinding conflict, violence and attrition, and forms of government that were never accepted as legitimate. Comedy, holding back the horror.

On the streets of early modern London, with a penny in your purse, you could buy a loaf of bread or a quart of ale – or, for the same price, a broadside ballad. The news and entertainment of their day, broadsides were ubiquitous, participatory. Broadside ballad sheets circulated in their millions between about 1580 and 1690; hundreds of printers, booksellers and publishers pumped material into the trade. You didn't need to be literate to enjoy a broadside. Ballads were sung to popular tunes. You could listen, join in, memorise the words and pass it on. Images like the 'Rump' rapidly became the viral memes of early modern England.

More popular broadside ballads were printed in 'black-letter' type – a kind of gothic script – often with wood-cut illustrations. They were news, true crime, love and romance, scandal and adventure. Plenty of black-letter ballads dealing with the civil wars survive, from the Royalist 'The Royal Health to the Rising Sun', with its pun on *sun / son* and promise that 'the Sun that sets may after rise again', to the comic 'My Bird Is a Round-head' – a mockery of Puritans. Another kind of ballad was printed in 'white-letter': a Roman font more familiar to us today. These broadsides less commonly included illustrations, and were often associated with more sophisticated political causes and factions. Often given out for free among political cliques and groups, they were also posted up in public spaces, and circulated in well-to-do households. The original broadside printing of 'Bum-fodder' is one of these white-letter ballads, with its learned references and clear political agenda behind the crude humour. It's part of a wider culture of railing rhymes and verse libels in early modern England – poetry as political expression and media. But 'Bum-fodder' is also very much in the popular ballad tradition. It's a song, not just a poem, to be sung to the tune of 'Greensleeves' (fitting the syllables to the notes requires a little ingenuity). We might think of the 'Greensleeves' melody as genteel, courtly, even wistfully romantic. But it's widely used across a range of ballads – not all of them polite – often with the refrain, as here, 'Which nobody can deny'.

Broadside ballads weren't printed to last. Broadsides were ephemera: disposable, throwaway rags, destined to end up as 'waste-paper' – as in the title to our poem. Once they'd had their day, they were put to other uses – including wiping bums. Made out of linen scraps (literally, rags), early modern paper was surprisingly effect-ive for this purpose, probably rivalling today's luxury toilet tissue for comfort. Out of those millions of broadsides printed, only around 10,000 sheets survive. Many of those others were put to good use in the privies of early modern England. 'Bum-fodder' is slang for what you wipe with. We still use the abbreviation for piles of paper we might as well flush: if you've ever complained about a load of 'bumf' (or 'bumph') through the letterbox, you've used this term. The ballad makes a self-deprecating joke about what it might end up wiping.

Of course, there's more than one body part you might wipe. Alongside England's arse, the ballad brings another feature into view: Oliver Cromwell's nose. In the second stanza, the army recalling the Rump is 'such a wipe' (or blow) as successive parliaments and factions 'Could never give to old Oliver's nose'. Today, when we think of Oliver Cromwell, the phrase 'warts and all' might spring to mind: supposedly Cromwell's words to his portrait painter, demanding an unburnished and authentic depiction. The Commonwealth's first Lord Protector was famously warty. But Cromwell's contemporaries – especially his Royalist adversaries – were more interested in his nose. Large and red, it was supposedly a tell-tale sign of private vice and moral hypocrisy: drinking, even sexual promiscuity.

The ballad takes a swipe at other big names of the English repub-lic, too. Stanza 11 mocks 'Harrington's moddle' ('model'), a work of political philosophy by James Harrington titled *The Commonwealth of Oceana*, published in 1656. Dedicated 'To His Highness the Lord Protector of the Commonwealth of England, Scotland and Ireland' (Oliver Cromwell), *Oceana* imagines a utopian republic, grounded in a perfect constitution. The republic of *Oceana* might be fictional, but it's strangely familiar, too: described as 'the most blessed and fortunate of all countries', ever fruitful and fertile, temperate ('not closed with ice, nor dissolved by the raging star'), and clothed in the green of 'continual verdure'. Even night-time doesn't bring the full 'horror of darkness', but 'still some white feather' – a glimmer of light – remains. It's no coincidence, of course, that the opening sketch of Oceana recalls Bede's foundational description of Britain, 'an island of the ocean', written back in the eighth century – the template for so many subsequent celebrations of England's 'green and pleasant land'. Oceana is a metaphor for a more free, just and stable England (and its neighbouring countries within the British Isles), based on meticulous legal principles (around property, power and representation) and planning. But 'Bum-fodder' derides it as total nonsense: the careful system of election and 'rotation' key to Harrington's republican vision becomes nothing more than 'a rotation' in his 'noddle' – the crackpot scheme of someone not right in the head.

Stanza 14 name-checks Henry Martin and Thomas Scot – both former Members of Parliament and regicides who had supported the execution of Charles I. William Lenthall, named in the same verse, was Speaker of the House of Commons for almost twenty years, in a career which took him through a number of pre-civil war and interregnum parliaments, including the first Rump and, later, a period in Oliver Cromwell's answer to the House of Lords, the new 'Other House'. Lenthall was recalled as Speaker of the second Rump – under pressure from the army and despite his own protestations of ill health. In stanza 9, 'William Prynne' is the prominent Puritan lawyer, author and politician, who was removed from the Commons, and imprisoned, during Pride's Purge of 1648. No fan of the Rump Parliament, by May 1659 he had assembled other former members excluded by Pride's Purge and attempted to regain his seat in the House of Commons. The ballad can't resist putting words in his mouth: the (unlikely) taunt that the Rump Parliament belongs at 'the Devils arse' – the famous cave in Derbyshire.

The final stanzas of the ballad bring us right up to the moment in the early days of 1660. George Monck is riding to London – initially called to the defence of the Rump Parliament by William Lenthall.

But things don't seem to be working out that way. Monck arrives in London on 2 February to find riots and disarray. Petitions are raised from across England calling for the removal of the Rump. On 11 February 1660, Monck writes to the Rump, instructing them to issue warrants for free elections, and calls for an immediate General Election. Now, finally, there's a robust move to reinstate the Long Parliament (whose members should put themselves up for election) and bring back stable government. Troops move into the city. On 21 February, soldiers are once again at the gates of Parliament, but this time to enforce the admittance of purged members of Parliament – those men excluded in Pride's Purge, back in 1648. It is, finally, the end of the Rump, and the beginning of steps towards the Restoration.

'Bum-fodder' seems to telescope some of these events. Even though Monck is apparently still on his way to London ('since he is coming, e'ne let him come'), the ballad is boldly confident that he'll 'beat up the quarters of this lewd bum' – give the Rump a good kicking. Other Royalist ballads make much of the notion of 'Saint' George coming to slay the 'dragon' of the Rump Parliament and rescue England. In stanza 19, this staunchly Royalist poem admits a kind of grudging approval of Monck – a Parliamentarian military commander, after all. He might be 'a soldier and sloven', but surely he's not as bad as a devil, 'whose feet are cloven', the ballad reckons, ready to 'creep i'th Rumps Arse, to bake in their oven'. There are long-established associations here between devils, hellfire and rumps – think of the infernal buttocks and demonic farts of the lurid depictions of hell by Hieronymus Bosch. The ballad's confidence that Monck will wipe the Rump's arse is either canny prescience – the writing's on the wall – or an account of those weeks before 2 February 1660, told with the benefit of (pun intended) hindsight.

Of course, 'rump' might conjure another association beyond the virtuoso scatology of the ballad. It is, of course, a cut of meat: a juicy rump steak, a tasty rump of lamb. And 'Bum-fodder' doesn't drop the ball. In stanza 15, the Rump Parliament is a piece of meat which has hung around too long. The 'Butchers and Cooks' would be delighted to 'see this stinking Rump quite off the hooks'. It's another clever double meaning: a rancid steak needs taking down from the butcher's meat hook, but this feeble, enervated Parliament also has to be 'let off the hook' – relieved from its responsibilities and obligations. The stanza goes on to imagine how the 'Jack-Daw' and 'Rooks' will then 'go to pot' – another slang phrase with multiple meanings. Those garrulous, greedy, raucous birds (the Rump MPs) – all noise and bickering over carrion – will be well and truly cooked: finished, done for, let go.

This other association of 'Rump' didn't pass Londoners by, either, when George Monck issued his instructions to Parliament on 11 February, calling for free elections and return of a full House of Commons. Festivities burst out across the city: bells ringing, bonfires blazing, and everywhere Londoners roasting rumps of meat in celebration. Samuel Pepys writes in his diary of seeing bonfires throughout the city, 'and all along burning, and roasting, and drinking for rumps'.

> There being rumps tied upon sticks and carried up and down. The butchers at the May Pole in the Strand rang a peal with their knives when they were going to sacrifice their rump. On Ludgate Hill there was one turning of the spit that had a rump tied upon it, and another basting of it. Indeed it was past imagination, both the greatness and the suddenness of it.

The Royalists are making merry: the Restoration is in sight. By 2 May 1660, Charles II would be recognised by Parliament as king.

'Bum-fodder' is written for a particular moment: it's topical satire, in-jokes, destined to be thrown away or dropped down the privy. But history is full of twists. Already, by late 1659, books are appearing which anthologise some of the many broadside ballads satirising the Rump Parliament. In November, *Rats Rhymed to Death: or, The Rump Parliament Hang'd Up in the Shambles* is published. The Rump lends its title to another large anthology in 1660, including a range of anti-Puritan and anti-Republican verse. Then, in 1662, looking back on the interregnum, comes *Rump: or, An Exact Collection of the Choycest Poems and Songs Relating to the Late Times By the most eminent wits*. It's published by Alexander Brome, bringing together poems by a range of authors, but 'Bum-fodder' is often attributed to him.

The Rump anthology lifts 'Bum-fodder' from the street to the realm of literature. Its frontispiece illustration shows a huge rump of meat being roasted over a fire, next to caricatures of 'The Puritan' and a 'Covenanter', with a seated poet writing at a desk, wearing a crown of laurels in the style of the great classical authors. It's perhaps light-hearted and playful: a scholarly poet scribing humorous and often coarse verse, gathered from rags on the street, into a 'choice' collection. Not all poems in the book are comic – there's a poem on the execution of Archbishop William Laud, for instance, alongside jovial ballads calling for the defence of Christmas. With Charles II now safely on the throne, the Rump Parliament – and all its jokes – have become part of Royalist nostalgia, bonding, sociability and myth-making.

From 'waste-paper' to the bound pages of a prestige book, 'Bum-fodder' makes quite a journey. In his diary for Monday 23 April 1660, Samuel Pepys recalls an evening with friends, one of whom 'fell to singing a song made upon the Rump, with which he played himself well, to the tune of "The Blacksmith" '. 'The Blacksmith' is another name for the 'Greensleeves' melody. There were many satirical broadsides on the Rump, and lots of ballads set to 'Greensleeves'. But, just perhaps, Pepys and his friends were singing along to 'Bum-fodder'.

Not all poems are lofty and high-brow, and not all are pitched at immortality – even if twists of fate might take them there. The broadside culture of early modern England is popular, cheap, ephemeral. Today's news is tomorrow's fish-and-chip paper; seventeenth-century broadsides ended up wrapping parcels, kindling fires, lighting pipes – and, of course, wiping bums. A throwaway poem, 'Bum-fodder' takes us into the thick of the final months of interregnum England, to listen in on its jokes and politics. Now wash your hands.

Out of the Ashes: Making the Metropolis

Extract from Annus Mirabilis by John Dryden (1667)

War, plague, fire: the years 1665 to 1666 brought London to its knees. Yet John Dryden's *Annus Mirabilis* reimagines this period of trials and troubles as a 'Year of Wonders' or 'Year of Miracles'. This long poem – 304 stanzas – looks back at key events of that year, all viewed through Dryden's Royalist perspective, including naval battles against the Dutch and allusions to the devastating Great Plague which swept through the city in the hot summer of 1665. The final part of the poem focuses on the Great Fire of London and its aftermath: a city consumed in flames and reduced to smoking cinders. Alongside other contemporary sources, Dryden's poem helps build a picture of tumultuous events and their impact on individual lives.

The Great Fire reshaped a city already undergoing massive change. In this section, at the very end of Dryden's poem, London rises again, Phoenix-like, once 'Plague and Fire have breathed their last'. Out of the flames and ashes, Dryden forges a new London: the worthy metropolis of a global power, while also strangely magical and other-worldly. This is a pivotal moment in the story of the city we know today: resilient, powerful, wealthy, voracious. Dryden's poem offers an insight into the making and mythologising of London, and its complicated, often coercive, relationships with England, Britain and the world beyond. In 1667, while others are rebuilding with bricks and mortar, Dryden's time-capsule vision of future London writes a new city into existence.

Methinks already from this chemic flame,
 I see a city of more precious mould:
Rich as the town which gives the Indies name,
 With silver paved, and all divine with gold.

Already, labouring with a mighty fate,
 She shakes the rubbish from her mounting brow,
And seems to have renewed her charter's date,
 Which heaven will to the death of time allow.

More great than human now, and more august,
 New deified she from her fires does rise:
Her widening streets on new foundations trust,
 And, opening, into larger parts she flies.

Before, she like some shepherdess did show,
 Who sat to bathe her by a river's side;
Not answering to her fame, but rude and low,
 Nor taught the beauteous arts of modern pride.

Now, like a maiden queen, she will behold,
 From her high turrets, hourly suitors come;
The East with incense, and the West with gold,
 Will stand, like suppliants, to receive her doom.

The silver Thames, her own domestic flood,
 Shall bear her vessels, like a sweeping train;
And often wind (as of his mistress proud)
 With longing eyes to meet her face again.

The wealthy Tagus, and the wealthier Rhine,
 The glory of their towns no more shall boast;
And Seine, that would with Belgian rivers join,
 Shall find her lustre stained and traffic lost.

The venturous merchant, who designed more far,
   And touches on our hospitable shore,
Charm'd with the splendour of this northern star,
   Shall here unlade him and depart no more.

Our powerful navy shall no longer meet,
   The wealth of France or Holland to invade:
The beauty of this town, without a fleet,
   From all the world shall vindicate her trade.

And, while this famed emporium we prepare,
   The British ocean shall such triumphs boast,
That those who now disdain our trade to share
   Shall rob like pirates on our wealthy coast.

Already we have conquered half the war,
   And the less dangerous part is left behind;
Our trouble now is but to make them dare,
   And not so great to vanquish as to find.

Thus to the Eastern wealth through storms we go;
   But now, the Cape once doubled, fear no more:
A constant trade-wind will securely blow,
   And gently lay us on the spicy shore.

Flames and fire are here right away in these lines. But they're not the literal blaze which engulfed the city in 1666. Instead, that great conflagration is transfigured into something more mystical and symbolic. The word 'chemic', at this time, comes from the technical language of alchemy. The new London emerges from the 'chemic flame' like gold magically transformed out of base metals in the alchemist's arcane art. Dryden's vision of a 'city of more precious mould' also recalls the process of forging precious metal in extreme heat: the inferno of 1666 reimagined as a crucible for renewal and remaking. The city's trial by fire has transformed it into something invincible and immortal: 'More great than human now, and more august', she rises from the flames 'New deified'. ('August' – majestic, venerable – also plays on an early name for London: Augusta.) Resurrected from the ashes, the city is transfigured: purified by its fiery martyrdom and elevated beyond the human to become god-like and eternal.

But the flames of September 1666 were very real. As every school pupil knows, the fire broke out shortly after midnight on Sunday 2nd September, starting in a bakery on Pudding Lane and spreading rapidly across the city. By Thursday 6th September, when the fire was finally put out, much of the ancient city within the walls was destroyed: an estimated 13,200 houses burned, perhaps 60,000 people made homeless, many major public and civic buildings lost, as well as 87 parish churches and St Paul's Cathedral.

Eyewitness accounts of the fire bring home the horror. In his diary, Samuel Pepys tells of being woken by his maid in the small hours of the Sunday, viewing the flames from an upper window of his house on Seething Lane (near the eastern edge of the old City), then going down into the street and to a boat on the Thames. He sees:

> Everyone endeavouring to remove their goods, and flinging into the river or bringing them into lighters [small boats] that layoff; poor people staying in their houses as long till the very fire touched them, and then running into boats, or clambering from one pair of stairs by the water-side to another. And among other things, the poor pigeons, I perceive, were loth to leave their houses, but hovered about the windows and balconys till they were, some of them burned, their wings, and fell down [sic].

Later, Pepys and his companions watch the fire from an ale-house on the south bank of the Thames. He writes in his diary how they –

> . . . saw the fire grow; and, as it grew darker, appeared more and more, and in corners and upon steeples, and between churches and

houses, as far as we could see up the hill of the City, in a most horrid malicious bloody flame, not like the fine flame of an ordinary fire.

One of the more fortunate, with wealth and means to fall back on, Pepys makes use of 'a cart to carry away all my money, and plate, and best things'. He returns home briefly to collect other possessions, and buries some of his business papers in a hole in the garden as protection against the flames. Famously, he then digs a second hole, and places in it 'my Paramazan cheese, as well as my wine and some other things'. The fate of Pepys's prized Italian cheese is not recorded: perhaps it remains there to this day. Pepys was one of the lucky ones. Despite the destruction all around, his house, his office – and, of course, his remarkable diary – survived the flames.

Pepys's account of the fire sets up a contrast between the king, Charles II, who listens to advice and intervenes to stop the blaze by ordering buildings in its path to be pulled down, and London's mayor, Sir Thomas Bloodworth, who is slow to recognise the severity of the threat and then feeble in his response. Pepys bumps into him in Canning Street on the first night of the Fire, and paints a pathetic figure.

To the King's message he cried, like a fainting woman, 'Lord! what can I do? I am spent: people will not obey me'.

The account of the Great Fire in Dryden's *Annus Mirabilis*, too, conveys the immediacy and vividness of eyewitness testimony. The poem's imagined narrative of the beginnings of the fire is sinister and unsettling: from the 'fatal birth' of sparks in the 'deep quiet' of a hidden place, to the prowling of a greedy and ferocious predator:

Then, in some close-pent room it crept along,
And, smouldering as it went, in silence fed:
Till the infant monster, with devouring strong,
Walked boldly upright with exalted head.

The fire grows, escaping its confines and rampaging through the city. Dryden describes the scenes in the streets, in the middle of the night, as Londoners rush to tackle the blaze:

> Now streets grow thronged and busy as by day;
> Some run for buckets to the hallowed choir;
> Some cut the pipes, and some the engines play,
> And some more bold mount ladders to the fire.

Here, in just four sparing lines, we have a picture of the full range of defences against the fire, from the fire-fighting pump 'engines' – the most advanced technology of their day – to releasing water from the wooden pipes which served thousands of houses, to desperate individuals up ladders, and the buckets of water traditionally kept on standby in local churches (the 'hallowed choir'). But to no avail: the fire grows relentlessly.

Dryden, a Royalist like Pepys, is also keen to praise the role of Charles II in combatting the fire. He 'Himself directs what first is to be done' and orders buildings in the path of the flames to be torn down or blown up with gunpowder. The king weeps in grief for his beloved city – but leaps into action to its rescue. Dryden's portrayal of Charles's heroics reminds us that this is a partisan poem – just as his attribution of the fire's spread to a 'Belgian wind' reminds us that the politics and hostilities of the Second Anglo-Dutch War hang over the whole of the text. A readiness to blame Catholics, or foreigners, for the fire characterised much of the early popular response in London.

But the eyewitness immediacy of Dryden's poem is a literary trick. He was actually writing *Annus Mirabilis* in Charlton, Wiltshire, at the seat of his father-in-law, Thomas Howard. Dryden had fled London in 1665 – like many of the city's wealthier inhabitants, the nobility, and the king himself – to escape the plague. He was sent news, broadsides, pamphlets and other material, from which he created his picture of the fire. Perhaps this physical distance is why his poem so readily transfigures the realities of the inferno into the symbolic flames of rebirth.

In Dryden's high poetic style, the Great Fire is one of the 'two dire comets which have scourged the town' over the course of the year, visiting their 'utmost malice' on the city. The other, of course, is the Great Plague of 1665. The diary of Samuel Pepys, again, gives us glimpses into that terrible year. Not only the horrific suffering and loss of life – perhaps 15 per cent of Londoners dead – but also the contagion of fear creeping through the city: sightings of dead bodies, reports and rumours of illness, near misses and brushes with infection. As ever, the smallest details are often the most compelling. Pepys writes, in September 1665, of his delight in finally wearing a new wig which he had bought some while ago, but not dared to put on, 'because the plague was in Westminster when I bought it'. He muses: 'it is a wonder what will be the fashion after the plague is done, as to periwiggs, for nobody will dare to buy any haire, for fear of the infection, that it had been cut off of the heads of people dead of the plague'. Pepys's anxieties about the plague are wrapped up with worries about the Anglo-Dutch War: close observation of naval campaigns, hopes for success and concerns about possible Dutch advantages. In 1665, London feels beset and besieged.

In its immediate aftermath, the Great Fire was credited with one enormous service to the city. In the following decades, popular belief was that the fire had cleansed London of plague, purging contamination from its streets and houses. But that was not, in fact, the case. The fire destroyed the area of the ancient city, mostly inside the old city walls, which dated back to the Middle Ages and even to Roman Londinium. The areas worst affected by the Great Plague in 1665 were outside the walls, in the suburbs. After the fire, displaced and homeless people were forced out of the old city, into the suburbs – even if only temporarily – potentially causing even greater overcrowding hazards and conditions susceptible to epidemic disease.

London's expanding suburbs reflect major demographic change in the city in the sixteenth and seventeenth centuries. This was a city in the midst of a population explosion. The population of medieval London had peaked in the early fourteenth century – probably at around 80,000 – but collapsed catastrophically after the Black Death, falling to as low as 35,000. Signs of population recovery by 1500 led to huge sixteenth- and seventeenth-century migration into the city. John Stow's Survey of London (1603) presents a picture of a city changing drastically. Areas outside the walls – once open spaces, green fields or rural parishes – are becoming built up as the city devours more and more land for its booming population. In a personal moment, Stow remembers his boyhood: collecting a 'halfe pennie' of milk from a farm in Goodman's Fields, not far outside the Aldgate, 'always hote from the kine' – still warm from the cow. But now, he observes, those meadows have been leased out for garden plots, and no doubt will soon be houses. It's the seventeenth-century version of 'When I was a boy, all this was fields'. A reminder that London has long had an insatiable appetite for growth and expansion.

Indeed, John Evelyn's pamphlet *Fumifugium*, published before the Great Fire, in 1661, and addressed to Charles II, highlights the negative aspects of London's rapid urban expansion. Evelyn's discourse on the 'inconvenience of the aer and smoak of London' laments the extreme air pollution, caused mainly by burning coal, but also other industrial activities, which hangs over the city, damaging the health of the inhabitants as well as London's buildings. Significantly, this noxious air spills beyond the bounds of the city itself, contaminating counties beyond: 'the weary Traveller, at many Miles distance, sooner smells, then sees the City to which he repairs'. Evelyn's pamphlet has a political purpose: in these years immediately following the Restoration, the dangerously transmissible toxic airs and vapours of the city stand easily for sedition or rebellion which the new monarch must cleanse and quash. But they also show the very real environmental impact of a city growing and industrialising – and the cost for its rural hinterland.

With the Great Fire of 1666, there's an opportunity to reimagine and reshape the most ancient area of the city, within the walls. And the language of Dryden's poem speaks directly to this project of renewal and transformation. In these verses, Dryden predicts that London will be a city built 'on new foundations'. There are biblical resonances here, recalling imagery of the New Jerusalem in the

Book of Revelation: the perfect, heavenly city which replaces imper-
fect earthly forerunners. But 'new foundations' is also the practical,
political language of rebuilding London after the fire. Plans for rede-
signing the city were put forward by leading thinkers, including a
geometric plan, based on a grid system, published by the map-maker
Marcus Doornick, and an elegant new vision of the city, laid out
around monumental avenues and open, continental-style piazzas, by
Christopher Wren. Proposals and manifestos in print proliferated.
Stephen Primatt's *The City and Country Purchaser and Builder* (1667),
for example, put forward arguments for the rebuilding of the city
'which is now, Phoenix-like, buried in its own ashes', proposing regu-
lar and uniform styles for buildings. Even as debates about rebuilding
rage, Primatt notes that 'some noble citizens [have] scarcely recov-
ered their fiery consumption'. Feelings are running high.

Dryden's vision of the city's 'widening streets' symbolically con-
veys pomp and grandeur. But it is also a literal part of the approved
rebuilding plan. The 1666 Act for Rebuilding the City of London
was followed, in 1667, by a second Act with a focus on church build-
ings and the cathedral. Unsurprisingly, the central concern of the
1666 Act is to prevent 'great and outrageous fires' and to drive the
'speedy restoration' of the city. Legislation requires buildings to be
constructed primarily in brick, roof jetties and overhangs are banned
and streets are widened – all as precautions against future fire.

In fact, if we're being literal, post-fire London was largely rebuilt
on the foundations of previous medieval buildings. By and large,
the medieval street layout was retained. But roads did widen.
Dryden envisages the city 'opening, into larger parts she flies': a
reality realised both in the newly broadened streets, and in the rap-
idly expanding suburbs beyond the walls. In the decades following
the Great Fire, we see a sense of hope and possibility as new visions
and versions of the city emerge, as well as something of the resili-
ence we can recognise today in cities, around the world, building
back from disaster and destruction.

Dryden's image of the earlier, pre-fire city is in keeping with the
classicising 'heroick' style he claims for the poem. 'Before', he writes,

'she like some shepherdess did show, / Who sat to bathe her by a river's side'. Far from royal, or a figure of imperial majesty, London is imagined as a peasant, a rustic shepherd-girl bathing by the water of the Thames. It's apparently an image of humble simplicity – but coded with erotics, too. Picture all those Baroque paintings of female nymphs and nudes artlessly bathing, offered up to the male gaze as objects of desire. 'Now', Dryden declares, as she rises from the flames, London is a 'Maiden Queen': feminine, beautiful, regal and powerful. The image draws on the conventional associations between the enclosed, walled city and virginity, even though London has now far escaped its walled bounds. Global trade and foreign powers are reimagined as 'suitors' and 'suppliants', coming to woo their lady.

Throughout these verses, London is personified as feminine: beautiful, queenly, an object of desire. And this personified image of London appears at another key point in *Annus Mirabilis*. The work opens with a dedication – not to the king, or to a noble patron, or even to a lover, but 'To the Metropolis of Great Britain' itself: 'the most renowned and late flourishing City of London'. Here, London itself is the beloved lady to whom Dryden presents his work. It's a self-conscious twist on literary convention. Dryden reflects that 'perhaps I am the first who ever presented a work of this nature to the Metropolis of any nation'. *Metropolis* is a significant word here, too. It, too, is coded feminine through its Greek etymology – originally meaning 'mother city' or 'mother state'. While occasional uses of the term date back to the Middle Ages, it's just starting to be used more concertedly, in this period, as a term for London. It might tell us more about ambition and boosterism than the realities of London in 1667, but it marks a new vision of London as an imperial city, the centre of an empire both in the British Isles and across the globe.

The feminised London of Dryden's poem – rustic shepherdess, virgin queen, great mother – is also imagined in relation to the masculinity of King Charles II. In the poem's dedication – addressed to London herself, as well as (more pragmatically) the Lord Mayor, Aldermen and officials of the city – Dryden pictures monarch and metropolis as 'a pair of matchless lovers'. There's a well-established tradition of depicting London as the 'bride' of England's kings, conveying its loyalty but also hinting at the more precarious politics of finances, possessions and power bound up in any noble alliance. In fact, there's a long history of complicated and often uncomfortable relations between London and the crown.

Dryden is writing just a few years after the Restoration of the monarchy – after Civil War, the Commonwealth, the execution of Charles I. His Royalist agenda is concerned with consolidating a positive relationship between London and Charles II; cementing the city's gratitude to its king. We might compare Dryden's depiction of London and Charles II as 'lovers' – the maiden city rescued by the heroic king – with the relief sculpture at the base of the London Monument, constructed between 1671 and 1677. This relief, by Caius Gabriel Cibber, is an allegorical representation of the recovery and restoration of London. The city is a fainting woman, her garments falling and long hair loose, while the king is her hero and saviour. He stands firm and resolute, holding out a scroll – his plans for reconstruction.

The final stanzas of Dryden's poem return us to this imagery of the personified feminine city. Once a rustic peasant by the riverside, she is now clothed in grandeur, with the 'silver Thames' itself as her 'sweeping train'. London's waterways – its rivers and coast – are especially prominent in this last section of the poem. And this emphasis on London's maritime geography – its status as a centre for merchants and trade – connects the 'wonder' of the city's recovery from the Great Fire with another of the 'wonders' celebrated in Dryden's poem: successful naval battles in the war against the Dutch. London is a 'famed emporium', whose 'hospitable shore' attracts trade from across the world – now threatened by competing Dutch ambitions. Prompted in a large part by commercial and maritime rivalry, the Second Anglo-Dutch War plays out on the seas around England from 1665 to 1667: two nascent empires clashing in the competition for global trade and commodities. Dryden confidently predicts victory: 'Already we have conquered half the war, / And the less dangerous part is left behind' (that is, still to come).

Soon, Dryden promises, there'll be no more need to battle France or Holland: instead, 'all the world shall vindicate her [London's] trade'. Other nations shall be reduced to mere bandits, who 'Shall rob like pirates on our wealthy coast'. It's clear that celebration of London is contingent on denigration of others: other European rivers (the Tagus, Rhine and Seine) are slighted and will find their 'lustre stained and traffic lost'. Panegyric is a competitive sport.

For a poem so centred on London, the final verse of *Annus Mirabilis* drifts strangely far away, panning out into a distant, exotic world of 'Eastern wealth', beyond storms and the treacherous passage of the 'Cape' – metaphors for the struggle against the Dutch yet to come, lifted from the maps of seventeenth-century trade and navigation. Dryden uses maritime imagery to predict future victory and success, in the war against the Dutch and, implicitly, in London's wider fortunes. 'A constant trade-wind will securely blow, / And gently lay us on the spicy shore.' The poem leaves us in a far-off world of spices, balmy winds and waiting riches: an orientalist, colonialist fantasy. But, of course, this marvellous world, with its store of wealth and precious commodities, is intimately connected with London. It's the source of much of her wealth – and the prize for successfully vanquishing the Dutch. Look again at that image of London as the splendid queen visited by 'hourly suitors': 'The East with incense and the West with gold'. Deftly, the line places London at the centre of the world, looking out in one direction towards the East Indies and, in the other, towards the New World of the Americas. It's a scene derived from romance and courtship – smitten lovers willingly paying their devotion – transfiguring the reality of extractive trade and imperial exploitation into erotic terms. London's 'suppliants', Dryden fancifully imagines, are consenting lovers, not subjugated possessions.

And, most strangely of all, London itself here – the centre of growing colonial and imperial power – takes on its own magical, otherworldly properties. It mirrors, strangely, those far-flung places on the map of global trade and empire. Dryden's image of a city 'With silver paved, and all divine with gold' might recall Dick Whittington's axiom, familiar from many a Christmas pantomime, that 'the streets of London are paved with gold'. It's a place to make it big, get rich quick, claim a stake in the city's vast wealth. But Dryden points us elsewhere. The new London he sees is 'Rich as the town which gives the Indies name': that is, Mexico. Looking to the Americas for comparison, Dryden depicts London as another 'City of Gold', like those elusive mythical cities rumoured among Spanish *conquistadores* and quested for by Walter Raleigh, among many others. The new metropolis ascending from the ashes of the Great Fire will be a place of marvels, every bit as much as those exotic lands at the edges of the map, those ciphers of European desire and imagination.

In his opening dedication to London, Dryden describes his poem as both a 'History of your destruction' and a 'Prophecy of your restoration'. Here, in 1667, even as the city lies in rubble, he sees the new London in all its glory. A mythologised, eroticised vision of a global metropolis, freighted with desire and ambition. Phoenix, virgin, gold from the alchemist's crucible. A New World of wonders and miracles, rising from the foundations of the old.

Below Stairs in the Country House

Extract from 'Crumble-Hall' by Mary Leapor (around 1745)

It's the middle of the eighteenth century, and we're in a grand house on its great country estate. But we're not in the hall or the parlour, or strolling the ornamental gardens – we're in the kitchen, where the household staff are hard at work. The cook is busy making a cheesecake, while other servants prepare for dinner. Roger snores on the kitchen table – having stuffed himself with beef, cabbage and dumplings – while the lovesick maid, Ursula, reluctantly gets on with the washing up.

This is an extract from 'Crumble-Hall', a 1400-word poem by Mary Leapor, written around 1745. It's written in the tradition of the 'country-house poem': a popular genre in England through the seventeenth and eighteenth centuries, which celebrates a great house and its estate as an ideal of beauty, productivity and idealised order and governance.

But this is a country-house poem with a twist. For a start, the title, 'Crumble-Hall', hints that, rather than an immaculately kept stately home, we're visiting a dilapidated old pile. And its authorship is unusual, too. Written by a labouring-class woman, who herself worked in domestic service, this satirical poem offers a different perspective, inviting us to look in a different way at the grand country estate and to ask different questions about its workings – and its foundations.

> Hear, Artemisia, hear the Song we bring.
> Sophronia first in Verse shall learn to chime,
> And keep her Station, tho' in Mira's Rhyme;

Sophronia sage! whose learned knuckles know
To form round cheese-cakes of the pliant Dough;
To bruise the Curd, and thro' her Fingers squeeze
Ambrosial Butter with the temper'd cheese:
Sweet Tarts and Puddens, too, her skill declare;
And the soft jellies, hid from baneful° Air.

O'er the warm kettles, and the sav'ry steams,
Grave Colinettus of his Oxen dreams:
Then, starting, anxious for his new-mown Hay,
Runs headlong out to view the doubtful Day:
But Dinner calls with more prevailing Charms;
And surly Graffo in his awkward Arms
Bears the tall Jugg, and turns a glaring Eye,
As tho' he fear'd some Insurrection nigh
From the fierce Crew, that gaping stand a-dry.

O'er-stuff'd with Beef; with Cabbage much too full,
And Dumpling too (fit Emblem of his Skull!)
With Mouth wide open, but with closing Eyes
Unwieldy Roger on the Table lies.
His able Lungs discharge a rattling Sound:
Prince barks, Spot howls, and the tall Roofs rebound.
Him Urs'la views; and with dejected Eyes,
'Ah! Roger, Ah!' the mournful Maiden cries:
'Is wretched Urs'la then your Care no more,
That, while I sigh, thus you can sleep and snore?
Ingrateful Roger! wilt thou leave me now?
For you these Furrows mark my fading Brow:
For you my Pigs resign their Morning Due:
My hungry Chickens lose their Meat for you:
And, was it not, Ah! was it not for thee,
No goodly Pottage would be dress'd by me.

° harmful

For thee these Hands wind up the whirling Jack,
Or place the Spit across the sloping Rack.
I baste the Mutton with a chearful Heart,
Because I know my Roger will have Part.'

Thus she—But now her Dish-kettle began
To boil and blubber with the foaming Bran.
The greasy Apron round her Hips she ties,
And to each Plate the scalding Clout applies:
The purging Bath each glowing Dish refines,
And once again the polish'd Pewter shines.

There's a comic mis-match throughout these lines between grand, florid style and humble content. Illustrious classical names ('Sophronia', 'Colinettus') are given to servants busy with their lowly chores, just as the lines deliberately hitch together lofty rhetoric with their picture of humble 'puddens' (puddings) and pottage. It's funny: a domestic mock-heroic. The names and the high-flown style locate the poem in a particular poetic genre: the praise of an elegant country house. But this poem pulls off a witty – and radical – literary trick. It turns its gaze away from polished halls and manicured gardens, and places these 'below-stairs' staff – who wouldn't usually be in the picture at all – at the centre of the frame.

Its author, Mary Leapor, was not wealthy, learned or privileged. She received only a very elementary education, probably at her local free school in Brackley, Northamptonshire, and entered domestic service during her adolescence: first, at Weston Hall, near her childhood home, and then at Edgcote House – the model for Crumble-Hall. Her master there, Richard Chauncy, later recalled that 'her fondness for writing verses . . . displayed itself by her sometimes taking up her pen while the jack [the spit] was standing still, and the meat scorching'.

Perhaps unsurprisingly, Leapor was dismissed from Edgcote House in 1745. She returned to Brackley to care for her widowed father, where an educated local lady, Bridget Freemantle, became interested in Leapor's work, encouraging her writing and suggesting publication of an edition of her verse. But Leapor's poetry was not known beyond Brackley in her lifetime. She died of measles in 1746, at the age of twenty-four.

To unlock the meaning of Mary Leapor's poem, we first have to understand the genre it's pastiching and satirising. Ben Jonson's 'To Penshurst' (1616) is often cited as the model for the country-house poem – though it was in fact preceded by 'The Description of Cookham' by Emilia Lanier, in 1611. 'To Penshurst', though, becomes a blueprint for this kind of writing over the following centuries, setting out its conventions and ideals. Written for Jonson's friend Robert Sidney, First Earl of Leicester, it praises him on his estate Penshurst Place in Kent. 'To Penshurst' exemplifies the aims and conventions of country-house poetry. It celebrates a perfectly ordered, fertile and productive estate, under the paternal, protective care of its landholder.

The country estate is a delightful, pastoral landscape – a retreat from the city and a restful place set apart from business, commerce and labour. The human work which maintains it – which farms the fields, harvests crops, builds the house, cooks the meals – is rendered largely invisible. The stone walls of Penshurst house, Jonson writes, are 'reared with no man's ruin, no man's groan' – a delightful fiction which erases labour and effort. The poem tells how workers come gladly to pay their respects to their lord and lady:

> But all come in, the farmer and the clown,
> And no one empty-handed, to salute
> Thy lord and lady, though they have no suit.

The fruits of their labours are gifts, freely given. Workers of all kinds and ranks, from the higher-status tenant farmer to the simple 'clown' (a term used at the time for a rustic or peasant), pay grateful homage to the earl and his wife, without coercion or obligation. And, of course, the implication is that this perfect estate is England the nation in microcosm: green, arrayed with natural beauty and resources; a harmonious community in which each is in their proper place, under a benevolent master.

'Crumble-Hall' is a very different kind of country-house poem. For a start, our guide is Mira – Mary Leapor's pen-name and her own poetic persona. Not an aristocratic visitor or an honoured guest, but a servant, who gives us a different kind of tour of the estate, showing us places and perspectives we wouldn't usually see.

Here in the kitchen, Mira/Leapor's depiction of the servants' tasks is grounded in first-hand knowledge of below-stairs life – but with a brilliantly comic spin. The wise cook 'Sophronia sage' is making cheesecake – but it's described as if it's the highest, noblest art. Her 'learned knuckles' knead out the dough, while 'ambrosial butter' – an allusion to the food of the Greek gods – is mixed with the other ingredients. She's been making jellies, too, which are now kept cool in a larder so they don't melt – or 'hid from baneful Air', as the verse puts it, in comically high-flown, over-dramatic words.

Colinettus, watching the oven, suddenly rushes out to check the weather. He's 'anxious for his new-mown Hay'; concerned that the 'doubtful Day' may bring rain and spoil it before it's dried. These are the practicalities, the realities of farming life on the estate. Sadly, despite the delightful fictions of country-house poetry, the hay won't cut, stack and store itself. Roger is dozing on the table, having helped himself to kitchen leftovers or – more likely, given the humble menu of beef, cabbage and dumplings – the servants' food. The lovelorn maid, Ursula, upbraids him, fearing her devotion to him is unrequited. She declares that her deeds are all for him – much in the way that a noble heroine of classical or romance literature might do. Except, her deeds are making the soup, turning the spit to roast the meat and basting the mutton. She dedicates these mundane kitchen chores to her true love.

Ursula is still dwelling on her passion for Roger when she's rudely interrupted. The poem itself breaks and loses its thread: 'Thus she – But now her Dish-kettle began / To boil and blubber with the foaming Bran'. The water's boiled, and she must do the washing up, the 'greasy Apron' tied around her waist. (Pewter dishes were cleaned with boiling water and bran.) It's a comic moment, as Ursula's impassioned romantic speech is punctured by the whistle of the kettle. But it's telling, too. The maid's time is not her own. Her voice is silenced, and she turns to the dishes – the labour the country-house poem doesn't usually let us see.

It's not just this scene in the kitchen where 'Crumble-Hall' subverts the country-house genre, but across the entire poem. Mira/Leapor is deliberately breaking all the rules of this kind of poetry – to show us a very different kind of lived, overlooked, experience. The depiction of the house is always slightly off-key: it doesn't fit with ideals and expectations. Crumble-Hall isn't a model of fruitfulness and productivity. Even in the library, Mira tells us, the impressive collection of books is mostly unread – just rows of 'dusty Volumes'. The house is decrepit and gloomy: walking us along the corridors, Mira notes that 'Safely the Mice through yon dark Passage run'. And, in the dimness, she says, 'Along each Wall the Stranger blindly feels; / And (trembling) dreads a Spectre at his Heels'. Dark, faded and musty, it's an unsettling space, haunted rather than invigorated by its history. During Leapor's time there, the real-world 'Crumble-Hall' probably really *was* crumbling – it was knocked down and rebuilt just a few years later, in 1747–52.

Leapor seems to be anticipating this major remodelling of Edgcote House and its estate when she takes us briefly, at the end of the poem, out into the grounds. She laments that the 'rev'rend Oaks' of the park shall 'ignobly from their roots be torn' as the work of landscaping begins. Ancient trees will be felled '[t]o clear the way for Slopes, and modern Whims'. It's a glimpse into the transformation of the English countryside unfolding around Leapor and her contemporaries: the projects of agricultural enclosure, the 'improvement' of stately parks and gardens. Leapor's response hints at the impact on the lives of ordinary labouring people – especially those who lived off, and close to, the land. For Leapor, the new park will be only a 'gloomy Green', emptied of the nature, stories and memories which have dwelled within it.

But Mira/Leapor spends most of the poem indoors, and her

eye for the ridiculous – her keen sense of the comedy in bringing together the lofty country-house poem style with the banal and humdrum – is never far away. A principal room is described as 'neither long, nor round, nor square'. The poem doesn't even attempt a grandiose metaphor for its size: 'The Walls how lofty, and the Floor how wide, / We leave for learned Quadrus to decide'. In other words: you do the maths. A chimney breast is decorated with china bowls, 'Whose long Description would be too sublime' – a cheeky use of the 'ineffability topos', used poetically for subjects too awesome for words. Mira's had a busy day working: she just can't be bothered.

As she guides us through the house, Mira's informal, conversational tone punctures the typically lofty style of the country-house poem. 'Would you go farther?' she asks, then gives us the directions:

> Back thro' the Passage – up the Steps again;
> Thro' yon dark Room – Be careful how you tread
> Up these steep Stairs – or you may break your Head.

The elegant lines of poetry break up into her short, functional interjections, urging us to mind our heads as we navigate the passageways. There's a sense here that Mira is in the domain she knows well: the cramped, confined, claustrophobic geography of domestic service.

What windows does 'Crumble-Hall' open onto history? First, it reminds us of the very limited opportunities available for women, and especially for labouring-class women. Leapor's sharp, satirical verse has been compared to the poetry of Alexander Pope – widely considered one of the greatest poets of the eighteenth century. But Leapor died unknown, in relative poverty. The Brackley parish records note that she was buried 'in woollen': a humble shroud. The Second Woollen Act of 1678 had banned the use of expensive imported fabrics for burials, as an attempt to shore up the English wool industry. Breaking the law cost a fine of £5 – eminently affordable for the rich, but out of the question for the poor. Alexander

Pope has a character in one of his poems recoil in horror at the very notion of the cheap woollen burial: 'Odious! in woollen! 'twould a saint provoke!'

But Leapor's story also makes visible the world of women and their own networks and communities. As well as the informal patronage Leapor received from Bridget Freemantle, it was in Leapor's first job in domestic service, at Weston Hall, that she was able to expand her own reading and develop as a writer. Her employer Susanna Jennens (given the name 'Parthenissa' in Leapor's poetry) allowed her access to the small library of the house. In 'Crumble-Hall', the absence of a male authority figure is striking. It's Mira who interprets the house for us, not a lord, master or gentleman guest. And of all the rooms in the house, the poem pays most attention to the kitchen: the cook's domain, where 'Sophronia sage' is in charge. The country house is surreptitiously regendered, as a place of women's experience and authority.

By subverting conventions and archetypes, 'Crumble-Hall' also tells us much about ideals of the country estate – and the role of the gentry in provincial society and economy – in the early modern period. Typical country-house poetry presents a paradigm of perfect order: productivity without visible labour, hierarchy without subjection or exploitation. Leapor rejects these ideals, showing us the 'greasy pavements' and 'steaming odours' of the kitchen, as well as the ancient stone and oaken pillars. Deftly, with a comic flourish, she draws our eye to the work going on in the house: the effort and toil which underpins the estate and makes it function. But what of the other, less visible foundations? Reading the poem today, we must ask another question. What wealth – and what labour – paid for Crumble-Hall?

Edgcote House, Crumble-Hall's real-world counterpart, already had a long history by the mid-eighteenth century. Previously owned by Anne of Cleves, the estate had been bought from the Crown, in 1543, by William Chauncy, Member of Parliament and High Sherriff for Northamptonshire. By 1742, the estate had passed down to his descendant Richard Chauncy.

Richard Chauncy made a career as a successful merchant in London, trading cloth. As a textile trader, he also had an interest in East India merchant ships. He was a director of the East India Company – the joint-stock company formed in 1600 to trade in the Indian Ocean region, which by the mid-eighteenth century was already exercising military power, assuming administrative functions, and effectively forming the basis for the British Empire in India. Chauncy was Deputy Chairman of the East India Company in 1747, 1749, 1752 and 1754, and Chairman in 1748, 1750 and 1753.

The real-world Crumble-Hall estate was maintained, at least in part, by the fortune from Chauncy's East India Company ventures – and his successful trading through the company certainly provided the funds for the demolition and ambitious rebuilding of Edgcote House in 1747. While Mary Leapor was buried in plain wool, because English law banned the use of luxurious imported fabrics, Richard Chauncy was importing those very cloths – cotton, silk, fine muslin – and amassing the profits.

This story of the invisible labour – whether close to home or halfway across the world – and the resources underpinning the English country house is not unique to Edgcote or Crumble-Hall. Historians are now asking more questions about the wealth which built these great country estates, and where it came from, tracing stories of trade and empire across the globe.

Mary Leapor's 'Crumble-Hall' has a kind of modern companion in the 2013 poem 'The Doll's House', by British Nigerian poet Patience Agbabi. At Harewood House – a vast stately home in Yorkshire – the house-chef's daughter, Angelica, takes the visitor on a tour of a miniature replica of the house, sculpted from sugar. Angelica starts her tour 'below stairs, where you'll blacken your sweet tooth / sucking a beauty whittled from harsh truth'. The delicate confectionery house is delightful – a masterpiece, a treasure. The tiny bed is carved from sugarcane. The sugar-paper walls are decorated with 'hieroglyphs invisible as sweat'. Harewood's splendour, Agbabi reminds us, was built by profits from the slave trade, the labour of enslaved people on the other side of the world:

invisible but foundational to the beautiful house and its picturesque estate.

Mira/Mary Leapor and Patience Agbabi speak to each other across the centuries. Their poems both take us below stairs and ask us to look harder, to listen for the forgotten stories and to see the labour and cost beneath the landscaped grounds and stately homes of England.

15.

From Africa to New England to England: A Voice for Freedom

'To the Right Honourable William, Earl of Dartmouth' by Phillis Wheatley (1773)

Let's begin with her name. Wheatley, for the wealthy Boston merchant family who purchased her in July 1761 from slave trader John Avery: a slight and sickly girl around seven years of age, they guessed, by the gaps where she was losing her milk teeth. And Phillis after the slave ship – the *Phillis* – which trafficked her from West Africa, probably from somewhere in the region between present-day Gambia and Ghana.

This is an astonishing poem, written on the cusp of the American Revolution, by an enslaved person using her voice, and her lived experience, to address highly charged politics and a powerful political figure: Lord Dartmouth, who had become British Secretary of State for the Colonies in August 1772. Written in Boston in October 1772 and published in 1773 in London, in Wheatley's collection *Poems on Various Subjects, Religious and Moral* (the version presented here), it writes back from New England to England, speaking to a London audience and English elite. By the 1730s, Britain was the biggest slave-trading nation in the world. London in 1773, of course, was still the capital city of America.

The poem makes an impassioned case for freedom – but not necessarily in the way we might expect. These are lines from the pen of a poet who, elsewhere in her verse, in her poem 'America', imagines the people of 'New England' as still bearing 'English blood' in their 'English veins', but who advocates forcefully for independence. A young woman who writes the poem as an enslaved African Briton, but who just a few years later – alongside revolution, war and American independence – becomes a free African American. An author who navigates multiple identities: woman (or lady), enslaved person, Black African and entrepreneur. Who exploits the stylistic conventions and repertoires of classical English poetry to argue back against colonial power.

But Wheatley's poetry has puzzled and troubled some readers, too. Here, we find a poem which speaks of iron chains and bondage, but to argue for the freedom – not of enslaved people – but of the American colonies. A poem which uses the language of 'race' to describe the people of America – and not Black Africans. Verse marked by paradoxes and ambiguities, alongside Wheatley's bold advocacy and resistance. Through the poem and evidence of its early audience reception, we can glimpse London at a fraught moment towards the end of the eighteenth century: a city in which Black lives are highly present and visible, in work, culture, resistance and in political organisation, amid divergent views and intense debates around slavery, race, the colonies and freedom.

> Hail, happy day, when, smiling like the morn,
> Fair Freedom rose New-England to adorn:
> The northern clime beneath her genial ray,
> Dartmouth, congratulates thy blissful sway:
> Elate with hope her race no longer mourns,
> Each soul expands, each grateful bosom burns,
> While in thine hand with pleasure we behold
> The silken reins, and Freedom's charms unfold.
> Long lost to realms beneath the northern skies
>
> She shines supreme, while hated faction dies:
> Soon as appear'd the Goddess long desir'd,
> Sick at the view, she languish'd and expir'd;
> Thus from the splendors of the morning light
> The owl in sadness seeks the caves of night.
> No more, America, in mournful strain

Of wrongs, and grievance unredress'd complain,
No longer shalt thou dread the iron chain,
Which wanton Tyranny with lawless hand
Had made, and with it meant t' enslave the land.

Should you, my lord, while you peruse my song,
Wonder from whence my love of Freedom sprung,
Whence flow these wishes for the common good,
By feeling hearts alone best understood,
I, young in life, by seeming cruel fate
Was snatch'd from Afric's fancy'd happy seat:
What pangs excruciating must molest,
What sorrows labour in my parent's breast?
Steel'd was that soul and by no misery mov'd
That from a father seiz'd his babe belov'd:
Such, such my case. And can I then but pray
Others may never feel tyrannic sway?

For favours past, great Sir, our thanks are due,
And thee we ask thy favours to renew,
Since in thy pow'r, as in thy will before,
To sooth the griefs, which thou did'st once deplore.
May heav'nly grace the sacred sanction give
To all thy works, and thou for ever live
Not only on the wings of fleeting Fame,
Though praise immortal crowns the patriot's name,
But to conduct to heav'ns refulgent fane,
May fiery coursers sweep th' ethereal plain,
And bear thee upwards to that blest abode,
Where, like the prophet, thou shalt find thy God.

In Boston, the young Phillis Wheatley had displayed a remarkable
aptitude for the English language and for learning. The Wheatley
family fostered Phillis's talents, giving her an education in the Bible
(and baptising her into the Christian faith), as well as in English

literature, and the Greek and Latin classics – even though she continued with lighter domestic labour and remained an enslaved person. Phillis began writing verse while still a child, with her earliest compositions dating to 1766 or 1767 – astonishingly soon after her arrival in America. As her poems circulated in manuscript form, addressed to members of the Boston and New England community, her reputation gradually grew. Her first published poem, in the *Newport Mercury*, 21 December 1767, was an account of the narrow escape of two Nantucket merchants, Hussey and Coffin, from a terrible storm at sea around Cape Cod – a particularly compelling subject, perhaps, for a poet who had herself endured the horrors of the transatlantic voyage from Africa to America, as human cargo.

In February 1772, the *Boston Censor* newspaper, probably at the instigation of Phillis's mistress, Susanna Wheatley, published a proposal to print by subscription a collection of her poems. The newspaper uses the language of the time to describe Phillis's racial identity, and to underline the rarity of these compositions: they are 'by PHILLIS, a Negro Girl, from the Strength of her own Genius', written 'but a few years since she came to this Town an uncultivated Barbarian from *Africa*'. But the plan was not successful: most likely, subscriptions did not reach the 300 required for printing to be financially viable. John Andrews, a Boston lawyer, writes to his brother-in-law that this was largely because people would not believe – again, in the language of the time – 'the performance to be by a Negro'.

In October 1772, the Wheatleys were visited by Thomas Wooldridge, a former London merchant with property in Staffordshire, now in America serving in a variety of administrative colonial appointments. He already knew of Phillis Wheatley by reputation, including through the Countess of Huntingdon's support and encouragement of her work. Wooldridge spoke with Phillis and her mistress, writing later that he 'found by conversing with the African, that she was no Imposter'. Yet Wooldridge claimed to need proof of Phillis's talents. He asked her to compose a poem to William, the Earl of Dartmouth, as a test of her skill.

Was this misogyny – reluctance to believe that a woman could compose poetry of this quality? And was it racism, pure and simple? An unwillingness on Wooldridge's part to accept the abilities of an enslaved Black African? Perhaps – so disturbingly redolent of wider American and European attitudes to Black Africans in this period and beyond – this was a command to perform, to execute a trick, to provide entertainment or exhibit as a curiosity. Perhaps, the ambitious Wooldridge was exploiting an opportunity to ingratiate himself with Dartmouth and the Countess of Huntingdon and her circle, by having Phillis produce a poem for him to send. For Phillis and Susanna Wheatley, too, this may have been an expedient and welcome opportunity: the chance for Phillis's poetic gifts to be verified by a visitor with contacts and influence, setting right the gainsayers of Boston who had declined to support her book.

We know about Wooldridge's request from his own letter to the Earl of Dartmouth, recounting the event. But a second narrative, published in the *New-York Journal or General Advertiser* and published in 1773, adds a further layer of complexity. This reports that, upon Wooldridge's request, Phillis Wheatley 'told him that she was then busy and engaged for the Day, but if he would propose a Subject, and call in the Morning, she would endeavour to satisfy him'. On Wooldridge's return, Wheatley composes the poem to Dartmouth before his eyes. If we accept the *New-York Journal* account, it suggests a sophisticated and subtle ambiguity to Wheatley's response. To explain that she was already busy and engaged was the appropriate answer for an enslaved person, acknowledging that her time was not her own, and reflecting deference to the authority of her mistress and master. But, equally, Wheatley's response might suggest the decorum fitting for a lady: withdrawal and deferral, before she accepts his request. Imagine the polite young ladies of a Jane Austen novel, modestly demurring and retreating at a gentleman's advance. Already, here, we see signs of Phillis negotiating multiple identities, in her precarious place as an enslaved person accepted (conditionally) into refined white society.

Lord Dartmouth, the addressee of Wheatley's poem, had been sympathetic to the colonial cause, yet continued to support the supremacy of the British Parliament. A Methodist, he was known as a figure of faith and piety, and would have been acquainted with many non-conformist abolitionists. He had read the persuasive abolitionist autobiography of John Newton, the former slave trader and author of *Amazing Grace*, and had recommended him for ordination into the Anglican ministry. Dartmouth College, the Ivy League private university, would later be named after him. But Dartmouth took up the role of Secretary of State for the Colonies amid seething disputes and rancorous colonial politics: rebellion against the 1765 Stamp Act (a tax on printed materials and stationery in the American colonies), the 1765 Quartering Act, requiring the American colonies to provide accommodation, food and provisions for British troops, and the 'Boston Massacre' of 1770, in which British soldiers fired on a crowd of civilians.

Sent by Wooldridge direct to the Earl of Dartmouth, Phillis Wheatley's poem was also able to take advantage of the power of manuscript circulation, using the special status of coterie poetry – private, exclusive and (initially, at least) unpublished – to build patronage and gather allies. The poem plays a crucial role in opening the way for Wheatley to visit London, in 1773, and for her *Poems on Various Subjects* to be published there.

In a high classical style inspired by John Milton and Alexander Pope, Wheatley's poem begins with the rejoicing and hope brought by Dartmouth's appointment ('Hail, happy day'). The moment is imagined as a new dawn for New England, with 'Freedom' rising like a new sun, 'smiling like the morn' to light this 'northern clime'. Freedom is personified here: it is she who celebrates Dartmouth and 'congratulates thy blissful sway'. Biblical and theological language of redemption, liberation, bliss and the fulfilment of hope resonates throughout the verse. Wheatley describes 'pleasure' at the expectations for Dartmouth's tenure: 'silken reins' invoke gentle guardianship rather than tyrannical, oppressive government. The promise of freedom arrives in America at last, 'Long lost to realms beneath the northern skies'. As well as the rising sun, Freedom is also 'the Goddess long desir'd'. 'She shines supreme, while hated faction dies'.

The poem depicts the transformation of America from a state of abjection and oppression to hope, elation and anticipated freedom. 'No longer shalt thou dread the iron chain', Wheatley writes. Dartmouth's appointment promises the end of 'wanton Tyranny', which had threatened 't'enslave the land'. This is imagery from the lived experience of enslaved people, including Wheatley herself: chains, shackles, abjection and violence. But here it's transposed into a metaphor for the subjection of the British colonies. This may be powerful language, but it has troubled many readers. Wheatley presents the atrocities of slavery not as lived reality, but displaced into symbol. She uses the emblems of enslavement here to advocate not for herself and her fellow enslaved Africans, but for her captors.

The first verse of the poem, too, might confound modern-day expectations. Wheatley describes a 'race' filled with hope at the longed-for approach of freedom. Yet 'race', here, refers to the people of New England and America. Crucially, by describing the people of New England as a 'race', Wheatley reveals race itself as a construct, an invention – an abstract idea which could be applied to any particular group or nation. In the context of racialised slavery in eighteenth-century America, Wheatley's choice of words is defiant and disruptive.

Direct discussion of her own experience as an enslaved person in Wheatley's poetry is rare. In her poem to the Earl of Dartmouth, however, metaphors of enslavement move her directly to invoke her own experience as a trafficked and enslaved person. Stanza three begins as the answer to an imagined question.

> Should you, my lord, while you peruse my song,
> Wonder from whence my love of Freedom sprung . . .

What authority does Wheatley have to speak on these matters? In response, she draws on her own life. This is an explicit, radical justification of her right to speak; her status as a uniquely authoritative advocate for freedom. She looks back on her abduction from her home in West Africa:

> I, young in life, by seeming cruel fate
> Was snatch'd from Afric's fancy'd happy seat . . .

Notice 'fancy'd': imagined, supposed. Perhaps here Wheatley acknowledges the limits of her memory. But she also holds at arm's length the assumption of white abolitionists that Africa must be a place of primitive, simple happiness. She can only imagine the pain of her parents, left behind: their 'pangs excruciating' and the 'sorrows' which 'labour' in their 'breast'.

In her poem to Dartmouth, Wheatley is explicit and unequivocal in her moral condemnation of slavery.

> Steel'd was that soul and by no misery mov'd
> That from a father seiz'd his babe belov'd . . .

She imagines the moment of violence in which she was ripped from her father's embrace. The 'steel'd' soul of her abductor suggests both immoral, unfeeling coldness and hardness, as well as hinting, perhaps, at blades, weapons and violence. But then Wheatley moves to a cool, assured conclusion: 'Such, such my case'. While 'case' might just mean Wheatley's own story, the choice of language is deliberate and powerful. Wheatley speaks with the steady authority of a lawyer summing up. Her words purposefully refer to the language of eighteenth-century disputes and test cases around the legality of slavery.

Phillis Wheatley had survived the Middle Passage with her enforced childhood journey from West Africa to Boston. Now, in 1773, accompanied by Nathaniel Wheatley (John and Susanna's son), she made the voyage from America to England. In April 1773, notices (probably written by Susanna Wheatley) appeared in Boston newspapers of the plan to publish a volume of Phillis's *Poetry on Various Subjects* in London. There, Phillis Wheatley's manuscript poetry had been building a network of patrons and allies – most notably the Countess of Huntingdon – and respected figures were ready to sign an attestation to the authenticity of her verse.

Phillis Wheatley travelled to London on 8 May 1773, aboard the Wheatleys' ship, the *London*, captained by Robert Calef. Officially, the reason for her travel was ill health. Records suggest that Wheatley did indeed suffer from some kind of respiratory complaint, perhaps asthma, and sea air was believed to be a remedy. But this was also, again, about decorum and a careful performance of Wheatley's social roles. A business trip across the Atlantic would be unseemly for a lady and unfitting for an enslaved person. Nevertheless, this was a commercial venture. On the crossing, Wheatley looked both backwards and forwards: to New England and England. Her poem 'Farewell to America', penned on the eve of the voyage, bids 'Adieu, New England's smiling Meads' (meadows) and looks ahead to 'Britannia's distant Shore' and the city of London, 'Deep in a Vale', 'With misty Vapours crown'd'.

In London, Phillis and Nathaniel set about consolidating their networks of patronage and support. Phillis wrote to the Countess of Huntingdon, delicately requesting a meeting. The attestation document, authenticating her poetry, was finalised. But Phillis Wheatley was also a sightseer in a new city, visiting its attractions. She saw dancing at Sadler's Wells, visited the British Museum and Cox's Museum, went to see the paintings in the Great Hall of the Royal Hospital in Greenwich, and viewed the famous menagerie in the Tower of London. Who was her guide? The British abolitionist Granville Sharp. They were seen in public together on these excursions; Wheatley accepted one of Sharp's pamphlets. This was more than just holiday tourism.

London in the late eighteenth century – like towns and cities across Britain – was home to many Black people and other people of colour. Around 10,000 Black people, it's estimated, lived in London in this period alone, working in domestic service, trade and in the creative and cultural life of the city. The Somerset v. Stewart case of 1772 (also known as the Somerset Case or the Mansfield Judgement) would have been prominent in the minds of Wheatley and her London patrons and audience. This ruling determined that an enslaved person in England could not be forcibly removed from the country and taken overseas to be sold. It stirred concern among some in America that slavery might be outlawed there. Yet no positive law was ever passed as to whether slavery could or could not exist in England.

People of colour in domestic service were often brought from the colonies, effectively held as chattels and treated as enslaved. Hundreds of adverts in newspapers, in London and other cities across Britain, reflect the frequency with which Black servants and other servants of colour escaped and sought their freedom. A notice in the *London Gazetteer and New Daily Advertiser*, May 1772, seeks one escaped servant:

> ABSCONDED from his master, a black boy, about five feet four inches high, thin, but straight, and well made, his hair very black, and long queue or clubbed; had on when he went away a Russia drab livery frock and waistcoat, lined with yellow, and buckskin breeches, and speaks very good English.

The advert requests that 'no gentleman will entertain him, or any person harbour him', and offers a reward for any information from 'Mr. Campbell peruke [wig] maker, in Gray's-inn lane, Holborn'. Another notice seeks:

> . . . a Malabar black Boy, about 13 Years of Age, of slender Make, long black Hair, small featured, had on a blue Jacket, with Metal Buttons and red Cape and Cuffs, Waistcoat and Breeches of the same, a black Cap, snaked with Gold Twist, and a Feather . . .

The servant, the advert notes, 'speaks good English, and goes by the Name of John October'. A reward of half a guinea awaits with Captain Wilder in Frith Street, Soho. Phillis Wheatley's poetry in general, like her verses to the Earl of Dartmouth, addresses a largely white world of nobility, politicians and clergy. But eighteenth-century London as a whole was a far more racially diverse city, with people of colour engaged in daily acts of resistance and political organisation.

In the end, Wheatley's *Poems on Various Subjects* was published in early September 1773, while Phillis Wheatley was already on her return voyage to Boston. Her mistress Susanna Wheatley had been taken ill, and she was needed in New England. A frontispiece image, depicting Phillis, had been produced for the collection, possibly by the enslaved African artist Scipio Moorhead, who also lived in Boston. The portrait of Phillis Wheatley is another study in the careful negotiation of identities and fashioning of her public image. Wheatley sits at a desk, quill pen in hand, one finger resting pensively against her face in a stylised, conventional image of a writer at work. On the table next to her paper is an inkwell, and a small book which might be a Bible or prayerbook. She is dressed modestly, with a wide white collar and her hair tucked up under a white cap. She gazes upwards, as if in the moment of receiving inspiration. Her image is at once that of a pious Christian, a gifted poet and a Bluestocking intellectual. The delicate ribbon collar around her neck is her only ornament: possibly an allusion to – or deliberate subversion of – the iron or brass collars enslaved people were often made to wear at this time, as a marker of their status.

In London, Wheatley's poetry received a mixed reception. In October 1774, the *London Monthly Review* concluded that 'the poems written by this young negro bear no endemial marks of solar fire or spirit'. The review acknowledges 'many good lines' and occasionally 'one of superior character'. But its interest in Wheatley is more for her personal situation than her poetry.

> We are much concerned to find that this ingenious young woman is yet a slave. The people of Boston boast themselves chiefly on their principles of liberty. One such act as the purchase of her freedom, would, in our opinion, have done more honour than hanging a thousand trees with ribbons and emblems.

Wheatley becomes an exhibit in the case against slavery: a curiosity and talking point in London conversation and debate.

In 1778, in a private letter, the free Black British abolitionist, writer and composer Ignatius Sancho also records his response to Phillis Wheatley's poems. He comments that 'Phyllis's [sic] poems do credit to nature – and put art – merely as art – to the blush'. And he rails against the way Wheatley was paraded and lauded as a 'Genius in bondage': the darling of London society while still an enslaved person. 'It reflects nothing either to the glory or generosity of her master', he writes, 'if she is still his slave'.

Writing in 1778, Sancho did not know that Wheatley had already gained her freedom on her return to Boston in 1773. The 1772 Mansfield ruling in London had stated that no enslaved person brought to England could legally be forced to return to the colonies as a slave, and Phillis Wheatley may have returned to Boston on condition that she would be freed. Copies of her *Poems on Various Subjects* followed, from the London printer, though their arrival was delayed by the colonial rebellion of the Boston Tea Party (16 December 1773). The reception of her work in America was as mixed as in England: while George Washington, for example, praised her 'poetical genius', Thomas Jefferson, notoriously, cited her as a case in point in his treatise on the supposed inferiority of Black people in America. Along with many deeply offensive racist tropes and generalisations, he claims to identify a lack of artistic and intellectual gifts in Black people. 'Religion, indeed,' he writes, 'has produced a Phyllis Whately [sic]; but it could not produce a poet'.

Susanna Wheatley died on 3 March 1774, and John Wheatley on 12 March 1778, leaving Phillis nothing in his will. On 1 April 1778, Phillis Wheatley's intended marriage was announced: to John Peters, a free Black man, associated in tax assessment records with an eclectic range of professions, from shopkeeper to physician to lawyer. Later critics have often regarded Peters as feckless, but his patchwork of trades – and his persistent financial difficulties – may simply reflect the difficulties facing a free Black man in making an independent living in late eighteenth-century America. In October 1779, Wheatley published a new proposal for a volume of new poems and other writings, to be dedicated to Benjamin Franklin. The book never appeared. Phillis and John drop out of public records in the early 1770s. Phillis Wheatley Peters died on 5 December, 1784. Her later life suggests a marginalised, precarious existence, fêted then discarded by white American and English society.

But, in her poem to the Earl of Dartmouth, the power and assurance of Wheatley's voice rings clear. The poem's celebration of Dartmouth's appointment reads like gratitude. In fact, it's a craftily worded list of demands: those 'silken reins', and an end to 'grievance unredress'd'. There's a robust sense of expectation; an astonishing assertiveness and licence. In the final stanza, similarly, the poem simultaneously presents thanks, praise and petition. It ends with pious imagery of the earl receiving his reward in heaven, paradoxically a 'patriot' – for freeing Britain's American colonies. In reality, Dartmouth's career after 1772 was less triumphant. After the Boston Tea Party, relations between the British government and American colonies unravelled. Dartmouth continued to strive to find common ground and strategies for reconciliation. But, in 1775, he stepped down as Secretary of State for the Colonies. The American Declaration of Independence was made in 1776, and the military hostilities of the American Revolution ended in 1781, with the surrender of British forces at Yorktown, Virginia.

Wheatley's poetry shows huge sophistication in imagining its audience and engaging with the dynamics of its reception. As we've seen, her poem to the Earl of Dartmouth anticipates – and answers – queries and objections, and justifies her authority. Phillis Wheatley has sometimes been criticised for ventriloquising 'white' voices and literary traditions. Her poetry has been dogged by the accusation that it's simply not very good: a derivative assemblage of tired classical poetic conventions, from an enslaved Black author exploited by her white masters. Yet Wheatley works knowingly within the constraints of cultural conventions, reproducing tropes and deploying allusions to turn them back on the British ruling elite and London society. Her careful decorum and skill in negotiating her varied identities and roles make space for extraordinary licence.

In the third stanza of this poem, reflecting on her own experience, Phillis Wheatley imagines her reader asking:

Whence flow these wishes for the common good,
By feeling hearts alone best understood . . .

This is the moment in which Wheatley radically recentres late eighteenth-century debates about freedom, reconfiguring authority in terms of lived experience and emotion. Wheatley's own life story grants her the licence to speak; her own emotion and feeling qualify her as the authentic, indisputable authority on questions of freedom. Her prerogative comes not from politics, economics, religion or law, but from her lived experience and insight – her own identity as an enslaved Black African. In her poem to the Earl of Dartmouth, Phillis Wheatley writes to authority, *from* authority. And, even with all the prestige and weight of English literary tradition behind her verse, it's ultimately the authority of experience and emotion. Her 'feeling heart' has the last word.

Contemplation of the Dust: England in Ruins

Extract from Eighteen Hundred and Eleven by Anna Laetitia Barbauld (1812)

Ruins have always loomed large in imaginaries of England. The Old English poem 'The Ruin', in the tenth-century Exeter Book of Old English poetry, depicts the crumbling stonework of a great dominion – vast walls, towers, halls and bath houses – reminding us that what would one day become 'England' was once a postcolonial space, left in the wake of Roman withdrawal. The poem gazes in awe at the 'enta geweorc' or 'work of giants' left by this mighty civilisation, guessing at the lives of those who inhabited it and wondering at how such power and wealth were swept away. There's even an Old English word for this kind of reflection on ruin and transience: *dustsceawung*, or 'contemplation of the dust'. A few centuries earlier than these Old English texts – and just generations after the end of Roman rule – the British monk Gildas, writing from within modern-day Wales, composes his *De Excidio Britanniae* (*On the Ruin of Britain*) to warn of the dangers of increasing Saxon incursions. Addressing an early sixth-century audience, he cautions that the land of the Britons is both under attack and threatened by its own people's corruption, division and moral weakness. It risks falling into ruin.

From the very earliest texts, ruins are used to invoke other historical moments, looking both backwards and forwards in time. Ruins provoke awe and wonder; they inspire reflection on other peoples and dizzyingly different worlds – right here, on this familiar ground. They are a space of imagination: a site for envisioning history but also for dreaming speculative pasts and futures – worlds which may never have been and which may never come to pass. Most of all, perhaps, ruins are a tool to warn, to exhort and admonish.

In 1811, Britain was locked in what seemed like a Forever War against France. Since 1793, with just one eighteen-month pause, conflict had dragged on – first with the French Republic, and then with the Napoleonic Empire – pulling in nations across Europe as well as European colonies and allies across the globe. In response to Napoleon's Berlin Decree, which declared a blockade of the British Isles, and other strategies to undermine British trade worldwide, the retaliatory 1807 Orders in Council embargoed trade with any nations that traded with France. The orders ratcheted up tension between Britain and the United States, and had grim consequences at home: a collapse in manufacturing, failed merchant businesses, scarcity, shortages, high prices. Alongside the economic impacts: political repression, unrest and a doubling down against any prospect of political reform. Then, in 1811, King George III finally fell into permanent mental incapacity. At the American Declaration of Independence, in 1776, the expectation in Britain had been that the American republican experiment would quickly fall apart. But now, there was a sense that the New World was rising, while the Old World might be slipping into self-harming squabbles, decline and irrelevance.

Anna Laetitia Barbauld's *Eighteen Hundred and Eleven* was finished at the end of that year and published in early 1812. The 334-line poem is fearlessly anti-war, reformist, outspoken: an audacious intervention in contemporary politics which met, at the time, with hostile and often excoriating reviews. In this section of the poem, we time-travel to an England of the future, with 'Fancy' – the personified figure of imagination – as our guide. We find ourselves in a land of ruins: a desolate, post-apocalyptic landscape as bleak and derelict as any science-fiction dystopia. Barbauld's vision of this ravaged future England draws on contemporary Romantic and gothic aesthetics: the melancholy pleasure of ruins; the drama of speculative fiction. But hers is a bold and uncompromising prophetic voice, using England's imagined ruin to issue a moral and political warning to her readers. 'Fancy' takes our hand and leads us 'down the lapse of

years', to see Americans coming from across the Atlantic to visit the
ancient sites of England.

> Perhaps, she says, long ages past away,
> And set in western waves our closing day,
> Night, Gothic night, again may shade the plains
> Where Power is seated, and where Science reigns;
> England, the seat of arts, be only known
> By the gray ruin and the mouldering stone;
> That Time may tear the garland from her brow,
> And Europe sit in dust, as Asia now.
>   Yet then the ingenuous youth whom Fancy fires
> With pictured glories of illustrious sires,
> With duteous zeal their pilgrimage shall take
> From the blue mountains, or Ontario's lake,
> With fond adoring steps to press the sod
> By statesmen, sages, poets, heroes trod;
> On Isis' banks to draw inspiring air,
> From Runnymede to send the patriot's prayer;
> In pensive thought, where Cam's slow waters wind,
> To meet those shades that ruled the realms of mind;
> In silent halls to sculptured marbles bow,
> And hang fresh wreaths round Newton's awful brow.
> Oft shall they seek some peasant's homely shed,
> Who toils, unconscious of the mighty dead,
> To ask where Avon's winding waters stray,
> And thence a knot of wild flowers bear away;
> Anxious enquire where Clarkson, friend of man,
> Or all-accomplished Jones his race began;
> If of the modest mansion aught remains
> Where Heaven and Nature prompted Cowper's strains;
> Where Roscoe, to whose patriot breast belong
> The Roman virtue and the Tuscan song,
> Led Ceres to the black and barren moor
> Where Ceres never gained a wreath before

With curious search their pilgrim steps shall rove
By many a ruined tower and proud alcove,
Shall listen for those strains that soothed of yore
Thy rock, stern Skiddaw, and thy fall, Lodore;
Feast with Dun Edin's classic brow their sight,
And visit 'Melross by the pale moonlight.'
   But who their mingled feelings shall pursue
When London's faded glories rise to view?
The mighty city, which by every road,
In floods of people poured itself abroad;
Ungirt by walls, irregularly great,
No jealous drawbridge, and no closing gate;
Whose merchants (such the state which commerce brings)
Sent forth their mandates to dependant kings;
Streets, where the turban'd Moslem, bearded Jew,
And woolly Afric, met the brown Hindu;
Where through each vein spontaneous plenty flowed,
Where Wealth enjoyed, and Charity bestowed.
Pensive and thoughtful shall the wanderers greet
Each splendid square, and still, untrodden street;
Or of some crumbling turret, mined by time,
The broken stair with perilous step shall climb,
Thence stretch their view the wide horizon round,
By scattered hamlets trace its antient bound,
And, choked no more with fleets, fair Thames survey
Through reeds and sedge pursue his idle way.

'Fancy' is speaking here, and that opening 'Perhaps' is crucial: an acknowledgement that this is a speculative glimpse of one possible future, which may or may not come to pass. The poem paints a moment far-off in time, after 'long ages past away'. Right away, we're confronted with imagery of decline. The sun has set on England's greatness ('set in western waves our closing day'); power is passing to the west, to America and the New World. We're faced with a future world in which 'England, the seat of arts' is now 'only known / By the gray ruin and the mouldering stone'. Once great, England is now a realm of ruins and decay.

The future Europe 'in dust' is compared to 'Asia now': an expansive geographical area in the early nineteenth-century imagination, encompassing the modern-day Middle East and some of North Africa, too. Perhaps Barbauld is thinking in particular of the ruins of ancient Egypt, just beginning to enthral European travellers, writers and artists with their crumbling grandeur. Soon, the watercolour painter David Roberts will be publishing his hugely popular lithographs of ancient Egyptian sites: temples, pyramids, monuments in the desert; the sand-blown ruins of Thebes and Alexandria. The lost civilisation of ancient Egypt will emerge as a major theme in nineteenth-century art: from the decadent fallen world of Pharaohs and tyrants to the scenes of Old Testament stories.

And, of course, the aesthetic taste for ruins in Barbauld's period extends far beyond ancient Egypt. Young aristocrats make the Grand Tour to explore the cradles of European culture: Greek temples, Roman ruins, the traces of classical origins and traditions. Back in England, stately homes acquire their own ruins, invented by obliging landscapers and architects. Painshill Park in Surrey has its ruined gothic abbey (1772). Castle Howard (North Yorkshire) has its own pyramid, obelisks and classical temples (all eighteenth-century creations). Thomas Whately's *Observations on Modern Gardening, and Laying out Pleasure-grounds, Parks, Farms, Ridings etc.* (1770) comments that 'at the sight of ruins, thoughts of variability, destruction and devastation naturally come to mind, and behind them stretches a long string of other images, slightly tinged with melancholy, which the ruins inspire'. There's a melancholy frisson and pleasure in reimagining the solid, familiar geography of England as the mysterious, romantic ruins of the future.

In Barbauld's poem, this future England is itself the destination for curious travellers, intent on discovering the evocative ruins of ancient culture and glory. The tourists, specifically, are 'ingenuous youth' visiting England from North America, their imagination fired 'With pictured glories of illustrious sires'. This is the future Grand

Tour – the fashionable gap year for the moneyed classes – as they travel 'From the blue mountains' (in Pennsylvania) 'or Ontario's lake'. This is more than just a pleasure trip, but a 'pilgrimage' which they undertake with 'duteous zeal'. Just as the young men of Barbauld's time make their way to the storied ancient sites around the Mediterranean, these future visitors come 'With fond adoring steps to press the sod / By statesmen, sages, poets, heroes trod'. They come to walk in the footsteps of the greats of the past, in the hallowed places of their long-vanished splendour.

The itinerary of these imagined future visitors is centred on England (as Barbauld explicitly signals), though also touches on places across Britain. There are 'Isis' banks', a reference to the River Thames in Oxford, and the 'Cam's slow waters' where they flow through Cambridge: two great universities and seats of learning, now only 'silent halls' where 'shades' (ghosts) and 'sculptured marbles' congregate. 'Avon's winding waters' allude to Stratford-upon-Avon, birthplace of William Shakespeare, with the 'knot of wild flowers' a reference to his 'natural', untutored genius. The imagery may be of ruin, but it's also pastoral and strangely beautiful: a regreening of England's pleasant land in the wake of its fallen might and grandeur.

The tour includes Runnymede, where, in 1215, Magna Carta was sealed. It takes in places associated with more recent great figures in English history: the campaigner for abolition of the slave trade, Thomas Clarkson (1760–1846), the linguist and scholar and political radical Sir William Jones (1746–94), the poet and abolitionist William Cowper (1731–1800) and the lawyer, politician and historian William Roscoe (1753–1821), another opponent of the war with the French. Roscoe had also helped to reclaim and cultivate the land of Chat Moss in Lancashire, showing that moorland could be productive for agriculture. This is referenced cryptically in the poem, in the note that he 'Led Ceres' – the classical goddess of fertility – 'to the black and barren moor'.

This is Barbauld's new pantheon: a hall of fame of the great and good, the men of learning, culture and science – all, emphatically, aligned with her own political convictions. Strikingly, her poem rejects a more typical patriotism founded on militarism. Only one of the great 'British worthies' Barbauld lists in *Eighteen Hundred and Eleven* is a soldier: the 'gallant' John Moore, killed while protecting his army in a retreat during the Peninsular War. There's barely a mention of Nelson in the entire poem. This is a different kind of patriotic poetry, written by an anti-war poet. And its itinerary through future Britain is framed by regret and loss, rather than triumphalism. This is a catalogue of absence; an elegiac map of past virtues and achievements.

The tour moves on to Skiddaw and Lodore, a mountain and waterfall in the Lake District – that landscape being celebrated so passionately by Barbauld's Romantic contemporaries, notably William Wordsworth. Moving across the Scottish border, Dun Edin (a poetic name for Edinburgh) presents another dramatic topography, while 'Melross by the pale moonlight' depicts the romantic ruins of Melrose Abbey – also painted by Turner – through a quotation from Walter Scott. Again, Romantic aesthetics and sensibilities come to the fore. Even as the poem seeks to shock us with this desolate future Britain, its wild and rugged beauty becomes more striking.

The visitors to future England reach London – and here the poem prepares us for its most intense and visceral contrast.

> But who their mingled feelings shall pursue
> When London's faded glories rise to view?

The once 'mighty city', in this future timeline, is ruined and decaying. Streets once bustling with the world's diversity ('where the turban'd Moslem, bearded Jew, / And woolly Afric, met the brown Hindu') are unpeopled and empty. It's an astonishing, dystopian vision of a derelict future London – every bit as arresting as the post-apocalyptic landscapes we might recognise from present-day film and science-fiction. But, remarkably, this narrative of future travellers visiting a ruined London wasn't new.

In October 1775 – barely a generation before Barbauld writes her poem – the *London Evening Post* was preoccupied with tensions and

unrest in the American colonies, threats to trade and political scuf-
fles. But the front page of the 10–12 October edition is dominated
by one major story: 'Remarks, which is supposed will be made in
this kingdom by two North American travellers, in the year one
thousand nine hundred and forty-four, published originally in 1769'.
Alongside the newspaper's factual reporting, here's a speculative
piece of future history, recording an American visit to London in
nearly 200 years' time.

Written in the first person, in the style of a journal, the article
records the Americans' trip, in 1944, 'to find this once imperial city . . .
the capital of Europe'. The travellers discover 'this ancient, and once
most august city, now fallen to a similar decay and ruin with Balbec,
Persepolis, Palmira, Athens, and Rome'. In 1944, London is merely
a relic of past glories, like these famed ruins of antique civilisations.

There's an obvious satirical intent to the newspaper story. Wan-
dering the 'depopulated streets' of the city, the American visitors
find the Houses of Parliament standing vacant by a field of turnips.
The crumbling Mansion House – formerly the residence of Lon-
don's mayor – is now the site of a makeshift barber's shop. The Bank
of England has vanished, 'scarce one stone left upon another', as it
'had not a firm basis to stand on'. South-Sea House in Threadneedle
Street, once the headquarters of the South Sea Company and an
emblem of empire and trade, is now 'jakes' – outdoor latrines. The
end of the article is clear: England's ruin can be traced back to its
long-ago mishandling of the 'great disturbances' from its Ameri-
can colonies – that is, today's news, reported across the rest of the
paper. This despatch from the ruins of London in 1944 is an acerbic
warning to readers in 1775.

The vision of a future London in *Eighteen Hundred and Eleven* is
more elegiac in tone, but no less satirical in intent. The streets –
once the centre of global trade – are now empty and 'untrodden'.
Where 'spontaneous plenty flowed, / Where Wealth enjoyed, and
Charity bestowed', the city is now barren. It's not hard to trace
Barbauld's political message here. This desolate, vacant city is the
spectre of the inevitable long-term impact of the Orders in Council,

protracted war and other foreign policy failures: a gradual slide into poverty and irrelevance.

The poem imagines the American travellers climbing 'some crumbling turret, mined by time', ascending a 'broken stair' to look out over the city and its surrounds. The extent of the once-vast capital is now marked merely by 'scattered hamlets'. The Thames is 'choked no more with fleets' – no longer full of the ships and barges of trade and commerce. The visitors watch the river 'Through reeds and sedge pursue his idle way'. It's a breathtaking image of this once-bustling waterway now reclaimed by nature; reabsorbed into wetlands and estuary. An unintended and awesome rewilding, as London sinks back into clay and silt.

Perhaps you've already been thinking of Percy Bysshe Shelley, and his poem 'Ozymandias', published just a few years later than *Eighteen Hundred and Eleven*, in January 1818. There's an affinity, certainly, in their use of ruins to inspire wonder and melancholy, and to evoke a moral message.

> I met a traveller from an antique land,
> Who said—'Two vast and trunkless legs of stone
> Stand in the desert . . . Near them, on the sand,
> Half sunk a shattered visage lies, whose frown,
> And wrinkled lip, and sneer of cold command,
> Tell that its sculptor well those passions read
> Which yet survive, stamped on these lifeless things,
> The hand that mocked them, and the heart that fed;
> And on the pedestal, these words appear:
> My name is Ozymandias, King of Kings;
> Look on my Works, ye Mighty, and despair!
> Nothing beside remains. Round the decay
> Of that colossal Wreck, boundless and bare
> The lone and level sands stretch far away.'

Shelley takes inspiration from the same stories and images of ancient Egypt, and, like Barbauld, presents material ruins as traces of past splendour, pomp and pride. 'Ozymandias' is sometimes read as a direct comment on Napoleon – a satire on his vanity and hubris. But it reflects more generally, as does Barbauld's poem, on transience, impermanence and the futility of human ambition.

The depiction of a ruined future England in *Eighteen Hundred and Eleven* is of its time: it reflects its cultural context and contemporary tastes and aesthetics. Barbauld's future England is wreathed in 'Night, Gothic night' – inviting us to read this as a gothic tale, a fireside ghost story to frighten and thrill. The poem's picturesque but haunting ruins are straight from Horace Walpole or Walter Scott. We might look further, too, to other works depicting the collapse of civilisation or post-apocalyptic futures written around this time. Lord Byron's 1816 poem 'Darkness' imagines the end of the world. Mary Shelley's dystopian novel *The Last Man* (1826) is narrated by the last survivor of a global pandemic, making his way through an empty, desolate Europe.

But the vision of the future in *Eighteen Hundred and Eleven* isn't about indulging a gothic mood or aesthetic for its own sake. It's satire, deeply engaged with its own present moment. These words are weaponised, seeking to make a political impact. Barbauld's opposition to the French war, and her reformist politics, are the driving force behind the poem.

1812: Barbauld's poem is published and the reviews are in. An anonymous review in the March issue of the *Universal Magazine* observes that Barbauld's entire poetic output displays 'the same cold regularity, the same frigid observance of what is right without any thing that is very good'. While Barbauld wrote widely, across poetry, essays and literary criticism, there's a sense here that her famous early works for children – the *Lessons for Children* books and *Hymns in Prose for Children*, which earned her the Victorian epithet 'good Mrs Barbauld' – are being used against her. A hint that, as a woman writer, she's being derided for daring to step out of her place.

In these early months after publication, the political context is changing around the poem: fevered and reactionary, but also dangerously revolutionary (this is the moment of the Luddites, for instance). In May, during an inquiry into the Orders in Council, Prime Minister Spencer Perceval is shot and killed in the lobby of the House of Commons by a desperate merchant. The assassination ignites fears of an uprising. The Orders in Council are repealed in June, amid ongoing political rancour and division – but Barbauld's words already look too risky, too incendiary.

John Wilson Croker, in the June issue of the *Quarterly Review* (published August 1812), dismisses 'Mrs Barbauld' as a lady writer meddling out of her depth. In a backhanded compliment, he acknowledges that her 'former works . . . although they display not much of either taste or talents, are yet something better than harmless'. But, he continues, 'we must take the liberty of warning her to desist from satire, which indeed is satire on herself alone'. Some friends and allies lend qualified support in private, but other prominent Romantic figures – Wordsworth, Coleridge and Robert Southey – distance themselves from her and her politics.

William Roscoe – the same man honoured by Barbauld in *Eighteen Hundred and Eleven* as one of the pantheon of greats visited by the future American pilgrims – writes to her privately, praising 'your very beautiful poem'. His words acknowledge the danger of such powerful and uncensored satirical verse: 'I really fear it is but too prophetic of the doom which awaits this infatuated country'.

A prophet in her own land, Anna Laetitia Barbauld's vision of a future England is dismissed, critically eviscerated and mocked by contemporary readers. But how does her prophecy stand up? How far has her vision of England's future come true? It's a mistake, of course, to read Barbauld's poem as a prediction. Instead, it's a conversation with its own historical moment. Its depiction of the desolate England of the future is a message for readers – politicians, opinion-makers, thinkers – in her own present. Like writers before her, she exploits the image of the ruin to caution and admonish, to present a provocative alternative vision of England – and to challenge her audience to action.

But there is prescience there, too. Long after Barbauld's lifetime, wealth and influence have indeed moved westwards, from Europe to America. Her poem dares to imagine an afterlife beyond the acme of England's global power. A land of ghosts and shades, haunted by its 'mighty dead', romancing ruins and memory. An England of pilgrims and shrines, of hallowed paths and storied hills. A land with a gift for *dustsceawung*, contemplation of the dust.

Under the Wheels of Progress

Extract from 'The Cry of the Children' by Elizabeth Barrett Browning (1842)

On 4 July 1838, in South Yorkshire, it rained and rained. Not a typical summer downpour, but a freak, violent storm: thunder, lightning, torrential rain and hail. At Elsecar, a certain George Walton was struck by lightning while sheltering in a doorway, and left unable to speak until the next day. At Wentworth Castle, massive hailstones shattered windows and broke the cupola, smashing the glass in the greenhouses and flattening shrubs and trees. The *Sheffield Independent* put the cost of the damage to the estate at £500. But the real devastation that day was under the ground, in a coal mine just outside the village of Silkstone Common, near Barnsley.

At Huskar Pit, the heavy rain put out the boiler fire of the steam-powered winding engine, so the wheel could not turn and workers underground could not be lifted out of the mine. A message was conveyed: they were to wait at the pit bottom until they could be brought out. But, in the darkness and confusion underground, the message unravelled. There were rumours of a fire or gas. Some mistook the distant rumble of thunder for explosions. A group of children decided to make their own way to the surface, by walking up a shallow 'drift tunnel' or dayhole, which led back above ground.

What happened next couldn't have been foreseen. A small stream above ground was inundated with rainwater, which rushed down the drift tunnel into the mine. Giving evidence later, the Underground Steward, Benjamin Mellor, said that he was 'quite certain that the stream had never overflowed before'. Indeed, it was 'very small and dry nine months out of twelve'. Water flooded the drift tunnel, knocking the children off their feet and pushing them back against a ventilation door, where they drowned.

Twenty-six children were killed: the oldest, seventeen, and the youngest just seven. The age of one lad, John Simpson, is given, with the heartbreaking precision of a child or a doting parent, as '9½'. As their bodies were dug out of the mud and silt of the tunnel, local tragedy quickly turned into national outrage. The devastating accident brought the working conditions of Victorian industry to renewed attention – and, most especially, the conditions of the thousands upon thousands of child labourers, often doing the most dangerous, degrading and brutal jobs.

The Huskar Pit disaster was a key trigger for the Royal Commission on the Employment of Children and Very Young People in Mines and Factories, which reported its findings in 1842. The report was compiled by the writer Richard Henry Horne – a friend of the poet Elizabeth Barrett Browning (at that time, prior to her marriage, Elizabeth Moulton-Barrett), who followed the commission's progress, and read its documentation, with serious interest.

A protest poem – a rallying cry against social injustice, and a call to action – 'The Cry of the Children' received widespread attention in Victorian England, playing a powerful role in public revulsion at the use of child labour, and in processes of change and reform. But its author, Elizabeth, was a sickly young woman, from a comfortable background, whose own experience barely reached beyond the walls of the family home in Wimpole Street, London. What did Elizabeth know of the horrors of child labour, and how far was she able to write them?

The poem, first published in *Blackwood's Edinburgh Magazine* in August 1843, opens with a direct question: 'Do you hear the children weeping'? The first verse imagines the youth and freshness of nature: lambs 'bleating', birds in the nest 'chirping', fawns 'playing' and new flowers 'blowing'. Only the sound of the 'young, young children' is discordant and unnatural, 'weeping bitterly' during the 'playtime of the others'. The poem asks why these children are crying – and, in the extract here, the children are giving their answer.

'True,' say the children, 'it may happen
   That we die before our time!
Little Alice died last year—her grave is shapen
   Like a snowball, in the rime.
We looked into the pit prepared to take her—
   Was no room for any work in the close clay:
From the sleep wherein she lieth none will wake her,
   Crying, "Get up, little Alice! it is day."
If you listen by that grave, in sun and shower,
   With your ear down, little Alice never cries;
Could we see her face, be sure we should not know her,
   For the smile has time for growing in her eyes,—
And merry go her moments, lulled and stilled in
   The shroud, by the kirk-chime!
It is good when it happens,' say the children,
   'That we die before our time!'

Alas, the wretched children! they are seeking
   Death in life, as best to have!
They are binding up their hearts away from breaking,
   With a cerement from the grave.
Go out, children, from the mine and from the city—
   Sing out, children, as the little thrushes do—
Pluck you handfuls of the meadow-cowslips pretty
   Laugh aloud, to feel your fingers let them through!
But they answer, 'Are your cowslips of the meadows
   Like our weeds anear the mine?
Leave us quiet in the dark of the coal-shadows,
   From your pleasures fair and fine!

'For oh,' say the children, 'we are weary,
   And we cannot run or leap—
If we cared for any meadows, it were merely
   To drop down in them and sleep.

Our knees tremble sorely in the stooping—
    We fall upon our faces, trying to go;
And, underneath our heavy eyelids drooping,
    The reddest flower would look as pale as snow.
For, all day, we drag our burden tiring,
    Through the coal-dark, underground—
Or, all day, we drive the wheels of iron
    In the factories, round and round.

'For all day, the wheels are droning, turning,—
    Their wind comes in our faces,—
Till our hearts turn,—our heads, with pulses burning,
    And the walls turn in their places
Turns the sky in the high window blank and reeling—
    Turns the long light that droppeth down the wall,—
Turn the black flies that crawl along the ceiling—
    All are turning, all the day, and we with all!—
And all day, the iron wheels are droning;
    And sometimes we could pray,
"O ye wheels," (breaking out in a mad moaning)
    "Stop! be silent for to-day!" '

Ay! be silent! Let them hear each other breathing
    For a moment, mouth to mouth—
Let them touch each other's hands, in a fresh wreathing
    Of their tender human youth!
Let them feel that this cold metallic motion
    Is not all the life God fashions or reveals—
Let them prove their inward souls against the notion
    That they live in you, or under you, O wheels!—
Still, all day, the iron wheels go onward,
    As if Fate in each were stark;
And the children's souls, which God is calling sunward,
    Spin on blindly in the dark.

Now tell the poor young children, O my brothers,
    To look up to Him and pray—
So the blessed One, who blesseth all the others,
    Will bless them another day.
They answer, 'Who is God that He should hear us,
    While the rushing of the iron wheels is stirred?
When we sob aloud, the human creatures near us
    Pass by, hearing not, or answer not a word!
And we hear not (for the wheels in their resounding)
    Strangers speaking at the door:
Is it likely God, with angels singing round Him,
    Hears our weeping any more?'

The children's words are shocking. The imagined collective voice of thousands of child labourers speaks of a life so brutal that early death would be a welcome release. Though ' "it may happen / That we die before our time" ', the children say, this would be a merciful end to their misery. We have the story of 'Little Alice', who died prematurely but now, at last, has the chance to 'sleep'. At last, 'the smile has time for growing in her eyes'; now, only in death, 'merry go her moments, lulled and stilled, in / The shroud, by the kirk-chime'. It's an emotive image: the tolling of church bells her only lullaby, and the grave-wrappings like the comforting swaddling she barely knew in life. The words are shocking: ' "It is good when it happens," say the children, / "That we die before our time!" '.

The bold imagery continues. The children 'are binding up their hearts away from breaking / With a cerement from the grave'. This is a metaphor of living death, the children bandaging their broken hearts with the 'cerement' or waxed cloth of the shroud. The poem's speaker urges them to go out 'from the mine and from the city' and instead to

Sing out, children, as the little thrushes do—
Pluck you handfuls of the meadow-cowslips pretty
Laugh aloud, to feel your fingers let them through!

These are the more familiar pictures of Victorian childhood: those ideals of innocence, simplicity and playfulness being shaped in art and literature of the period – even as less fortunate children are put to work in mines and factories.

But the children's answer is puzzled and uncomprehending, asking ' "Are your cowslips of the meadows / Like our weeds anear the mine?" ' The original published version of 'The Cry of the Children', in *Blackwood's Edinburgh Magazine*, includes a footnote here, which is usually removed from modern editions. It notes that 'A commissioner mentions the fact of weeds being thus confounded with the idea of flowers'. Elizabeth is responding directly to a point in the Report of the Children's Employment Commission, finding particular poignancy in the idea that working children cannot tell the difference between weeds and flowers.

We're not used to footnotes as a part of poetic style, but there's another, further into 'The Cry of the Children', too. Later in the poem, following this extract, the children comment that their prayers consist of two words only, repeated like 'a charm'. ' "We know no other words, except, 'Our Father' ". The footnote adds: 'The report of the commissioners represents instances of children, whose religious devotion is confined to the repetition of the two first words of the Lord's Prayer', because they have had no further schooling or religious teaching. The footnotes drop out of most modern editions of the poem – perhaps a casualty of a sense that poetry should be timeless, or should speak for itself without the need for glosses and explanations. But they show how Elizabeth is writing directly in response to the Report of the Children's Employment Commission, reflecting on specific details and imagining the implications for individual lives.

Despite this close engagement with the work of the Royal Commission, the poem transposes the findings of the report into a completely different register. Instead of the objective reporting of witness testimonies, the statistics and tabular displays of information, 'The Cry of the Children' transforms the realities of child labour into emotive imagery, and imagined vignettes designed to elicit empathy, pity and tears. Yes, the poem is undeniably sentimental, its depiction of the weeping children designed to tug at the heart strings. But it's not mawkishness for its own sake. Rather, it's a kind of activist sentimentality, seeking to rouse the better instincts of middle-class Victorians by appealing to their compassion.

The poem then turns to the daily misery of children's lives as labourers. Again, there's little here of the concrete factual information collected in the Report of the Royal Commission. There, the testimonies of individual children, and their parents, give detailed insights into realities of life in mines and factories. In the report on South Wales collieries, a Mrs Mary Lewis, herself a worker at Waterloo Colliery, explains that 'My youngest boy, Lewis, was taken down at five years and three months old, and has been down ever since'. William Richards of Buttery Hatch Colliery, aged just seven and a half, speaks for himself. 'I have been down about three years. When I first went down, I couldn't keep my eyes open; I don't fall asleep now; I smokes my pipe; smokes half a quartern a-week'. The commissioner interviewing adds that 'this little fellow was intelligent and good-humoured; his cap was furnished with the usual collier candlestick, and his pipe was stuck familiarly in his button-hole'.

Children were typically five times cheaper to employ than adults. They undertook a range of jobs in mines: as drammers, hurriers or coal-putters, pushing and pulling carts of coal to the surface; as trappers, opening ventilation doors; as drivers, leading horses pulling wagons, and sometimes also as getters or colliers' helpers, cutting the coal itself from the seam. Their smaller size made them useful for many tasks in confined spaces. Children interviewed by the commission tell of regular beatings in the course of their work, including being hit with sticks or pick handles. But the job presented many other dangers.

The report lists 'the chief accidents to which persons employed in coal mines are exposed', including 'falling down the shaft', 'the breaking of the rope or chain', 'being crushed by a mass of coal', 'suffocation', 'burning', 'drowning' – as with the children at Huskar Pit – and more. The commission covered Wales, Scotland and Ireland, too. In Glamorganshire (Wales), the commission spoke to a Philip Phillips, who was nine years old. He told of a life working in the mine since the age of seven. He had been burned by 'fire-damp' – flammable methane gas – nine months previously: 'expected to die', he had nevertheless made a remarkable recovery over five months' convalescence, and was now back in the pit. 'I was carried home by a man', he remembers. 'The fire hurt me very badly; it took the skin from my face'. The report adds, in quiet parenthesis: '(Face quite disfigured)'.

'The Cry of the Children' doesn't set out to do this same work of compiling evidence and testimony. Instead, it translates the detail of individual lives and experiences into its collective picture of 'the children', and powerful, abstracted imagery of labour, toil and suffering. In the poem, the children speak of their daily work in 'the coal-dark, underground', or driving 'the wheels of iron / In the factories, round and round'.

And now, something powerful and terrifying happens. A machine in the poem's imagery grinds into motion: the cogs of a metaphor which turns, drives and builds momentum, until it completely takes over the verse. ' "For all day," ' say the children, ' "the wheels are droning, turning" '. The next lines pivot around the word 'turn':

> 'Till our hearts turn,—our heads, with pulses burning,
>   And the walls turn in their places
> Turns the sky in the high window blank and reeling—
>   Turns the long light that droppeth down the wall,—
> Turn the black flies that crawl along the ceiling—
>   All are turning, all the day, and we with all!'

Turning, turning in every line: a vertiginous, dizzying circling around that repeated word, as the monotonous, claustrophobic routines of the children's lives mimic the turning of the wheels in factories and mines. Wheels become the central, dominating metaphor: the 'cold metallic motion' of the children's existence; the suffering of those who 'live in you, or under you, O wheels!'; the relentless drive of industry as 'the iron wheels go onward' while the children's souls 'spin on blindly in the dark'. In their despair, the children have lost all hope that even God himself can hear them, above 'the rushing of the iron wheels' and 'the wheels in their resounding', which drown out the sound of their tears.

Later, the poem offers a damning comment on religion – or those who profess to be religious. The children look up, but see only a God whose '"image is the master / Who commands us to work on"'. God, it seems, is just another foreman, driving their brutal existence like the daily taskmasters in the factory or the mine. In heaven, the children say, '"Dark, wheel-like, turning clouds are all we find!"' Everywhere, only wheels, machines and turning: the inexorable cogs of modernity and their lives trapped in between.

It's a powerful image. But what did Elizabeth Barrett Browning know of the conditions in mines and factories? How authentic is her depiction of the plight of child labourers? When she wrote 'The Cry of the Children', Elizabeth was an unmarried woman, living in the family home in Marylebone, London. The family wealth, passed down from Elizabeth's maternal grandfather, derived from land-holdings, as well as industry (including mills and glassworks), and sugar plantations in Jamaica – though the family's fortunes had fluctuated. Elizabeth became ill in adolescence, suffering from multiple medical problems (probably including tuberculosis) and dependent on the pain-killing drug laudanum (opium) from an early age. As an invalid, her horizons were necessarily narrow and her direct experience limited. But she wrote poetry from the age of eleven, and was a lifelong campaigner on a range of issues, including the abolition of slavery.

It's clear, from clues throughout 'The Cry of the Children', that the poem's context is other writing, rather than direct, real-world experience. We've seen, already, the footnotes which link the poem directly to the Report of the Children's Employment Commission and the work of Elizabeth's friend, Richard Henry Horne. Later editions also follow the poem's title with a reference to another text: the ancient Greek tragedy *Medea*, by Euripides.

Pheu pheu, ti prosderkesthe m ommasin, tekna

(Alas, alas, why do you gaze at me with your eyes, my children)

It's an astonishing and chilling analogy. In the ancient Greek play, Medea speaks these words before she murders her two children with a knife. Elizabeth draws a parallel between this monster of ancient tragedy and the mundane, quotidian sacrifices and cruelties of Victorian life, as mothers send their sons and daughters into mortal danger and society condemns a whole generation of labouring-class children to misery and death.

'The Cry of the Children' also has a direct textual forbear in an earlier poem written by Elizabeth Barrett Browning herself: 'The Cry of the Human', first published in *Graham's American Magazine* in 1842. More abstract and ornate than 'The Cry of the Children', this earlier poem focuses more broadly on the pity of the human condition, and, in particular, the 'plague of gold' or 'curse' of wealth, capitalism and social inequality. Far less well known, the poem nevertheless contains germs of familiar imagery, such as the suffering of humankind while 'the cloud-wheels roll and grind'.

'The Cry of the Children' was widely read in the years after its publication, building public awareness of the appalling working conditions of children and contributing to continuing processes of reform. Its depiction of the weeping children elicited powerful reactions and helped to stir change. But its portrait of 'tender human youth' is shaped by other texts, secondhand reports and sentimental tropes, rather than authentic or observed reality – a fact seized upon by some contemporary critics.

By 1854, 'The Cry of the Children' was well-known enough to be quoted without attribution in an article, 'Ground in the Mill', by Henry Morley, in Charles Dickens' *Household Words* magazine. At the very beginning of the article, Morley takes issue with Barrett Browning's verse. ' "It is good when it happens" – say the children, – "that we die before our time." Poetry may be right or wrong in making little operatives who are ignorant of cowslips say anything like that. We mean here to speak prose.'

There's a sense of irritation, even anger, here – a backlash against the sentimental, perhaps naive, depiction of working children in Barrett Browning's poem. Morley is critical of the way 'The Cry of the Children' instrumentalises the 'little operatives' themselves, putting them to work as ventriloquist's puppets for middle-class fantasies of suffering innocence. And he's dismissive of poetry in general, suggesting that its sentimental tropes and metaphors aren't up to the job of this subject matter: only prose can confront this horrifying material head on.

In particular, Morley contends with that particular line: the children's declaration that it's good and welcome 'that we die before our time'. His reply is caustic. 'There are many ways of dying. Perhaps it is not good when a factory girl, who has not the whole spirit of play spun out of her for want of meadows, gambols upon bags of wool, a little too near the exposed machinery that is to work it up, and is immediately seized, and punished by the merciless machine that digs its shaft into her pinafore and hoists her up, tears out her left arm at the shoulder joint, breaks her right arm, and beats her on the head.' He describes further horrifying, violent accidents, in visceral detail – a boy whose leg is cut off in an engine, another caught in a machine and spun to death – then asks, 'Why do we talk about such horrible things? Because they exist, and their existence should be clearly known'.

In his response to Elizabeth Barrett Browning, Morley rejects what he sees as the softening opiate of poetry: the sentimental imagery of cowslips and meadows, the carefully crafted pathos and poignant words put into the mouths of imagined children. And it's not easy to answer his charge: 'The Cry of the Children' is indeed a text existing in a textual world, not immediate reportage from the factory floor or the mine shaft. It deals in the sentimental and symbolic, and converts the authentic into metaphor – but with a huge and transformative impact for its readers and for middle-class Victorian views on employment practices and the rights of the child. It helped to make a difference.

Change was already coming: the Factory Act of 1844 had banned the employment of children younger than nine, and the Royal

Commission on the Employment of Children led to the Mines Act (1842), raising the starting age for colliery workers to ten; the Factory Act of 1878 then prohibited work before the age of ten and applied to all trades. The 1880 Education Act, followed by further amendments, meant that, by the end of Victoria's reign, most children were in school until the age of twelve.

Wheels are everywhere in the machinery and rhetoric of the Victorian age. Pit wheels, mill wheels, the wheels of carts and carriages, then of steam and locomotion; flywheels, the wheels of factory machinery, the spinning jenny and the power loom; the pulley wheels at Huskar Pit and so many other mines. And beyond: the wheels of industry, wheels of progress, the wheels of empire. Wheels the engine of the Victorian capitalist and imperial imaginary; the cogs driving the lexicon of modernity. 'The Cry of the Children' confronts the central metaphor which powers an economy and a culture. And it shows us those who are crushed beneath those wheels, as they turn relentlessly onwards.

You'll Be a Man, My Son

'Rules and Regulations'
by Lewis Carroll (Charles Lutwidge Dodgson) (1845)

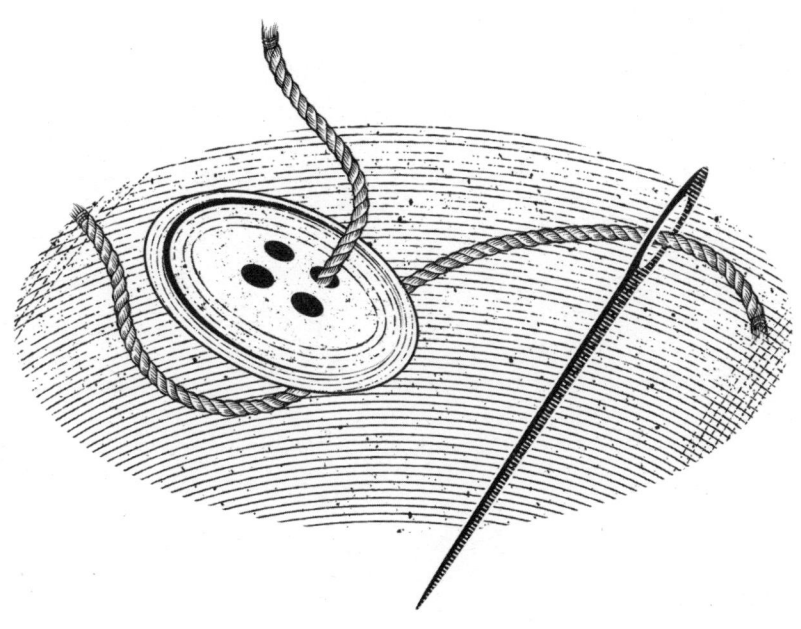

If this were a different kind of book – an anthology of England's twenty-five favourite poems, perhaps, or a 'best-loved' round-up – it would likely include a certain poem by Rudyard Kipling. Kipling's 'If' regularly tops lists of the nation's favourites: a BBC poll in 1995 saw it win, gathering twice as many votes as the runner-up; it triumphed again in 2005 and 2009. Published in 1910, in Kipling's book for children *Rewards and Fairies*, but written in 1895, 'If' reflects distinctly Victorian sentiments and morality, with its series of prescriptions for manliness: 'If you can keep your head when all about you / Are losing theirs and blaming it on you', and so on . . . The enduring popularity of the poem is unavoidable: posters, inscriptions, quotations so well-known they've slipped into aphorism or adage. The lines 'If you can meet with Triumph and Disaster / And treat those two impostors just the same' are written on the wall of the players' entrance to Centre Court at Wimbledon. Even in Kipling's lifetime, the text was ubiquitous – in the poet's own words, 'anthologised to weariness'. But the poem's blueprint for stoic, virtuous masculinity is bound up with Kipling's imperialist and racist beliefs. Those familiar final lines, holding up the reward if such manly virtue is achieved, are grounded in axioms of white male dominion, possession and entitlement: 'Yours is the Earth and everything in it, / And – which is more – you'll be a Man, my son!'

Lewis Carroll's 'Rules and Regulations' is in this book instead of Kipling's 'If'. Written at the age of thirteen by Charles Lutwidge Dodgson – before he'd adopted his more famous pen-name – it

deals in the same kind of maxims and instructions for proper con-
duct as Kipling's poem – but with some significant twists. 'Rules and
Regulations' is a poem written by a child, at the receiving end of
education and discipline, rather than by a master dispensing lessons.
It allows us to hear the authentic voice of a child amid all those
adults, over the centuries, speaking for English history and identity.
And, in a fashion which hints already at the ground-breaking fan-
tasy writing Carroll will produce as an adult – including the books
Alice's Adventures Under Ground (or *In Wonderland*) and *Through the
Looking Glass* – the poem folds together the stern language of the
schoolroom with whimsy and exuberant nonsense.

In later life, Carroll's own relationships with children and child-
hood were complicated, not least in his obsessive interest in little
girls, including Alice Liddell – inspiration for his most famous child
character. But here we have the voice of a thirteen-year-old child,
writing a poem to entertain two of his younger siblings. It mocks
conventions of writing for children, and turns rubrics of Victorian
conduct on their head.

Stiff upper lip, English fair play, pluck and grit, the 'playing fields
of Eton' . . . Young Charles's poem gives us an alternative way into
a model of Englishness forged through the nineteenth century –
and which lingers in archetypes of national character still invoked
today. Charles's poem suggests something of the experience of
all middle- and upper-class children in the nineteenth century, but
most especially the education of boys, shaped through England's
public schools. It points us towards doctrines of ruling-class mascu-
linity and training for the future leaders of empire: Victorian values
viewed through the carnival mirror of wit and whimsy.

> A short direction
> To avoid dejection:
> By variations
> In occupations,
> And prolongation
> Of relaxation,

And combinations
Of recreations,
And disputation
On the state of the nation
In adaptation
To your station,
By invitations
To friends and relations,
By evitation
Of amputation,
By permutation
In conversation,
And deep reflection
You'll avoid dejection.

Learn well your grammar,
And never stammer,
Write well and neatly,
And sing most sweetly,
Be enterprising,
Love early rising,
Go walk of six miles,
Have ready quick smiles,
With lightsome laughter,
Soft flowing after.
Drink tea, not coffee;
Never eat toffy.
Eat bread with butter.
Once more, don't stutter.
Don't waste your money,
Abstain from honey.
Shut doors behind you,
(Don't slam them, mind you.)
Drink beer, not porter.
Don't enter the water

Till to swim you are able.
Sit close to the table.
Take care of a candle.
Shut a door by the handle,
Don't push with your shoulder
Until you are older.
Lose not a button.
Refuse cold mutton.
Starve your canaries.
Believe in fairies.
If you are able,
Don't have a stable
With any mangers.
Be rude to strangers.
Moral: Behave

'Rules and Regulations' is written in young Charles's little book *Poems Useful and Instructive* – one of his many home-made publications or 'domestic magazines', as the adult Lewis Carroll later remembered them. He recalled that this one was 'clumsily bound up in a sort of volume'. The manuscript still survives, in Charles's handwriting with simple pen drawings, and was published in print in 1954. In later life, Carroll gave the book's date of composition as 1845, which would make him thirteen years old when he penned the poem. The verses were written to entertain his younger siblings, Wilfred Longley Dodgson (aged seven) and Louisa Fletcher Dodgson (five). Even the title of the little handwritten pamphlet is a parody of the improving books and conduct manuals for Victorian children.

It seems that Charles Dodgson had a generally happy childhood. His poem 'Faces in the Fire', published in 1860, looks back with affection on his childhood home, 'That happy spot where I was born'. By 1845, the Dodgson family was living at Croft Rectory, near Darlington. The third child of eleven siblings, Charles was the oldest boy.

At age twelve, Charles was sent to board at Richmond Grammar School. School reports comment on his 'very uncommon share of genius', painting a portrait of an 'ingenious', 'gentle, intelligent, and well-conducted boy'. There are hints here, already, of the studious, brilliant, but unconventional man he would grow up to be: the Fellow in Mathematics at Christ Church, Oxford, master logician, writer of children's fantasy and nonsense – but also an outsider, with eccentric habits and all-consuming obsessions. Charles's letters home give glimpses into some of the 'character-building' trials of school life. In one, to his siblings, he describes how 'the boys have played two tricks upon me', but he also lists more quotidian catastrophes.

> I have had 3 misfortunes in my clothes etc. 1st, I cannot find my tooth-brush, so that I have not brushed my teeth for 3 or 4 days. 2nd, I cannot find my blotting paper, and 3rd, I have no shoe-horn.

Another letter home, to a younger brother, adopts the same playfully didactic tone as 'Rules and Regulations': 'My dear Skeff, – Roar not lest thou be abolished. Yours, etc . . .'

What are little boys made of? Slugs and snails, and puppy-dogs' tails, of course, as any book of nursery rhymes can tell you (though the oldest versions, from the early nineteenth century, replace 'slugs' with 'snips' or 'snigs' – a Cumbrian dialect word for a little eel). While their labouring-class peers toiled in mines and factories, a comfortable middle-class Victorian childhood was about moulding these slippery raw materials into a decent, social adult. Even girls, made out of 'sugar and spice, and all things nice', required firm education.

Charles Dodgson's poem plays with the conventions of conduct books and improving literature for the young. In some ways, the poem is an extended linguistic joke, concerned first and foremost with its own internal, nonsense logic. In the first verse, every single line (all twenty of them!) ends with a word ending '-tion'. It's a virtuoso bit of comic wordplay, but undoubtedly also mimics and mocks the hooky rhymes of mnemonic verse and schoolroom didactic poetry.

Some instructions surely recall the exhortations and proscriptions of the Victorian nursery. 'Sit close to the table. / Take care of a candle. / Shut a door by the handle.' Other advice is perfectly sensible, but

rendered ridiculous by the poem's form. 'Don't enter the water /
Till to swim you are able' is undercut by stilted word order to fit the
rhyme scheme. Is there also a hint here of thirteen-year-old Charles
mocking a pompous adult voice? Did he have a particular teacher or
authority figure in mind? And some instructions strike particularly
close to home for Charles. 'Learn well your grammar, / And never
stammer' is reinforced by the later repetition 'Once more, don't stut-
ter'. In an otherwise happy early childhood, Charles Dodgson's own
speech impediment was a source of humiliation and misery.

Other admonitions are more eccentric. The poem's audience
may 'avoid dejection' 'By evitation / Of amputation'. *Evitation*, for
'avoidance', is an archaic, obsolete term: vocabulary pushed into an
esoteric, laughable register by Charles's extended rhyming game.
Avoidance of amputation? Sound advice, but rather beyond the
usual remit of nursery conduct books.

In 1847, Charles entered Rugby School, by then recognised as
one of the pre-eminent public schools of England, alongside Eton,
Winchester, Westminster, Harrow, Shrewsbury and Charterhouse.
Charles kept no diary for these years, but looking back on his time
at Rugby School, in 1855, he writes that 'During my stay I suppose
I made some progress in learning of various kinds'. However, 'I
cannot say that I look back upon my life at Public School with any
sensations of pleasure, or that any earthly considerations would
induce me to go through my three years again'.

The ethos of Rugby School in the mid-nineteenth century was
shaped profoundly by its headmaster from 1828 to 1841, Dr Thomas
Arnold: a widely influential figure who cast himself as a visionary
reformer of public school education. Arnold's emphasis was on inner
virtue and discipline as well as outward shows of obedience. His phil-
osophy of Christian manliness helped to underpin the precepts of
'muscular Christianity' valorised in the second half of the nineteenth
century and beyond: a combination of patriotism, athleticism, discip-
line, morality, duty and self-sacrifice, which formed the ideal for boys
as they were moulded into young men of the nation and empire.
Elements of this emerging doctrine are imprinted already on 'Rules

and Regulations': 'Be enterprising, / Love early rising, / Go walk of six miles, / With lightsome laughter, / Soft flowing after'. Exacting demands of athleticism, virility and virtue wryly linked together with the deceptive ease of rhyming couplets.

Thomas Arnold's sermons in the chapel of Rugby School, published and read widely, cast boyhood as a dangerous time of temptations, immaturity and moral weakness. He reminds his pupils that 'whatever you are doing, God ever sees you', and explains the purpose of school rules and regulations. They are not enforced 'out of a petty love of power or moroseness', he declares, 'but are intended solely to train and accustom you to do what a few years hence you would be ashamed not to do'. The aim of the public school, according to Arnold, is to produce 'decent and useful men' of the future; men of good character and Christian virtue, unashamed of doing their duty.

School served to produce the moral, manly citizens of tomorrow's nation and empire. Unruly, wayward boys needed taming and training. Rudyard Kipling's own book of school stories, *Stalky & Co*, caused a stir with its depiction of a naughty gang of boys, at a minor English public school, doing their best to evade rules and discipline. But in the last chapter of the book, we meet the boys again, now grown men, as officers in India. ' "India's full of Stalkies – Cheltenham and Haileybury and Marlborough chaps" ', a character declares. Yesterday's public schoolboys are holding the empire together. Boys made of slugs and snails are the future rulers of the world.

Rugby headmaster Dr Thomas Arnold may have been an influential figure in nineteenth-century public school education, but he's eclipsed by the fame of Rugby's most celebrated pupil: the fictional Tom Brown, of the novel *Tom Brown's School Days* by Thomas Hughes. Published in 1857, the book draws on the author's own experiences at Rugby School from 1834 to 1842, reflecting the ethos of the Thomas Arnold years. Tom Brown, the novel tells us, is a 'hearty, strong boy from the first, given to fighting with and escaping from his nurse'. Before Rugby, he plays with the village boys at home in Oxfordshire. 'Prisoner's base, rounders, high-cock-a-lorum, cricket, football – he was soon initiated into the delights of them all; and though most of the boys were older than himself, he managed to hold his own very well. He was naturally active and strong, and quick of eye and hand, and had the advantage of light shoes and well-fitting dress, so that in a short time he could run and jump and climb with any of them.'

At Rugby, Tom Brown is a natural at the school's distinctive version of football, learning, with his peers, to 'play your games and do your work manfully'. There are squabbles and brawls, of course, but Hughes reassures his readers that 'Fighting with fists is the natural and English way for English boys to settle their quarrels'. If done from 'true Christian motives', then it's right to 'fight it out; and don't give in while you can stand and see'.

When asked by a younger boy about his ambitions – what he wants to achieve in his time at school – Tom Brown answers sincerely. ' "I want to be A1 at cricket and football, and all the other games, and to make my hands keep my head against any fellow, lout or gentleman. I want to get into the sixth before I leave, and to please the Doctor [Thomas Arnold]; and I want to carry away just as much Latin and Greek as will take me through Oxford respectably. There, now, young un; I never thought of it before, but that's pretty much about my figure. Ain't it all on the square? What have you got to say to that?" '

An instant success, *Tom Brown's School Days* remained hugely popular into the late twentieth century, with numerous editions and reprints, and a clutch of screen adaptations, before falling out of fashion in more recent years. In an early review, in May 1857, the *Spectator* magazine expressed its approval of Tom Brown as 'a thoroughly English boy. Full of kindness, courage, vigour and fun – no great adept at Greek and Latin, but a first rate cricketer, climber and swimmer, fearless and skilful at football, and by no means adverse to a good stand-up fight in a good cause'. Tom Brown is the archetype of hearty English manliness, forged through the character-building experience of the English public school. 'Gentle' Charles Dodgson, with his bookish ways and eccentric, fastidious habits, would never quite fit the mould.

Looking back to this idealised 'Golden Age' of English public schools in the mid-nineteenth century, an article in the *Strand Magazine*, 1905, asks 'Has the Public Schoolboy deteriorated?' Dr Joseph Wood, headmaster of Harrow, is one of the leading educationalists to offer a response. 'Like all the rest of the world', he observes, 'boys have more luxury now than fifty years ago. But this does not seem to disagree with them or make them soft. Within the last year I have seen a boy stand to have a dislocated shoulder reduced, and never move a muscle or utter a sound . . . In courage and kindliness and frankness of character English public schoolboys seem as good as they ever were.' There's a familiar insistence, here, on the positive attributes of English schoolboys – the English men of the future. A portrait of a distinctively English character: stoicism, honesty, duty, stiff upper lip.

A sense of English exceptionalism appears throughout Victorian writing on character and conduct. From the late 1860s, the popular *Cassell's Household Guide* offered advice on 'The Rearing and Management of Children': from feeding and diet to clothing and, most seriously, 'Moral Influence'. The section on 'Truth' emphasises the paramount importance of instilling honesty in children – with an aside commenting that this is especially crucial 'where schoolboys are concerned'. Implicitly, these are English moral values and superior English standards. 'In nations where a high sense of honour does not prevail', *Cassell's* notes, 'truth is disregarded, and cleverness in lying is accounted a virtue.'

But young Charles Dodgson's poem punctures this loftiness. In 'Rules and Regulations', the sternness and pomposity of schoolroom admonitions meet nonsense and absurdity. The poem is peppered with random, bizarre instructions: 'Drink tea, not coffee; / Never eat toffy', 'Abstain from honey', or 'Refuse cold mutton'. Again, most of these peculiar dietary requirements seem to derive from the logic of the rhyme scheme rather than any moral or nutritional purpose. The final line of the poem – 'Be rude to strangers' – is a complete inversion of proper, courteous conduct: a model of good behaviour turned on its head. The moral at the end – simply 'Behave' – is so brief and general that it's funny. Perhaps we might imagine it intoned under the breath of an irate parent or governess. Other verses in *Poems Useful and Instructive* come with their own morals, in imitation of so many improving books for children. They range from 'Change your conduct' and 'Keep your wits about you', to the more abstract 'Don't dream' and the certainly surprising 'Woo the yellow moon' and 'Don't stew your sister'. There's a bit of a paradox here, though. Thirteen-year-old Charles is subverting the conventions of Victorian education and conduct training. But he's also conforming to the playful and rebellious spirit which would have been expected – indeed, admired – in a healthy, hearty young boy. Think of Tom Brown running away from his nursemaid, or disappearing off to play with the village children. That's the pluck and mettle that will, with a firm hand from school, make a man of him. For Charles Dodgson – Lewis Carroll – however, the story played out in a less conventional way.

Written by a precocious schoolboy, 'Rules and Regulations' is also an early flowering of the Victorian nonsense tradition which would burgeon over the later years of the century. Edward Lear's *Book of Nonsense* – a collection of comical limericks and accompanying drawings – was first published in 1846, a year after Charles had written his *Poems Useful and Instructive*, if the adult Carroll's memory was correct. Lewis Carroll's own later books for children – the magical adventures of Alice – hold up a mirror to the absurdity and arbitrariness of polite behaviour and decorum, in a fantasy world governed only by principles of whimsy and nonsense logic. If 'English fair play' and stiff upper lip are often invoked as markers of national character, then whimsical, surreal and absurd humour is cited almost as often, traced in a lineage from Victorian nonsense to the Goons, Monty Python and beyond.

One other line in Charles's poem stands out: 'Believe in fairies'. It seems an appropriate exhortation for the young Charles – later to become Lewis Carroll – to make, urging his fellow children to trust their imagination, to follow it into worlds of dreams and fantasy. But it's poignant and bittersweet. It's an abrupt, curt instruction, in the same tone as admonitions requiring the poem's addressees to

'Lose not a button' and mind their Ps and Qs. In the context of the poem, 'Believe in fairies' is just another mandate imposed by Victorian adults on their children: these middle- and upper-class offspring are required to be innocent believers in magic and wonder (their labouring-class peers in coal mines and cotton mills, of course, have no such obligation). But it's a necessarily temporary condition. From Charles Dodgson's own letters home, to *Tom Brown's School Days*, to Dr Arnold's sermons, all the evidence points to the move to public school as the moment when childhood dreams and illusions crumble. There's a sense of distance in the poem already: aged thirteen, Charles passes this directive down to his younger siblings, even as the innocence of childhood is slipping through his fingers. It's something he will pursue all his life, through his writing and imagination, and in his obsessive, all-consuming interest in young girls and their company.

'Rules and Regulations' represents establishment Victorian values, voiced by a child and refracted through parody. But the version of English masculinity the poem points us towards – the model of English manliness and character – looms far larger than a single historical moment. It echoes still today in a hallowed national self-image as well as in caricature, in the stories we tell ourselves about the past: sacrifice, honour, the grit that can 'force your heart and nerve and sinew / To serve your turn long after they are gone'. From the playing fields of England to the furthest outposts of empire, to the trenches of Ypres and the Somme and beyond, that ethos of English manliness plays out its inexorable logic: stiff upper lip, fair play, duty, 'fight it out; and don't give in'.

Queen Victoria's Book: Science, Nature and Faith

Extract from In Memoriam A.H.H. by Alfred, Lord Tennyson (1850)

The morning of Monday, 14 April, 1862. Victoria, Queen of England, is at her residence Osborne House, on the Isle of Wight. In her room, the table is laden with beautifully wrapped packages, parcels and toys. She clasps a little posy of flowers, gathered from the Osborne gardens, tied neatly with ribbon: wild daffodils from the meadows, perhaps, or the earliest lily of the valley, or orange blossom from the glasshouse. Before breakfast, darling 'Baby' – Princess Beatrice – is brought in, her hair dressed in plaits for the special occasion. Victoria wraps the child in her arms and wishes her the happiest fifth birthday. It's a day for joy and family celebration – but, as Victoria writes in her diary later, one marred by the 'agony' of grief and overshadowed by loss. Albert, Victoria's beloved husband, is barely four months dead. There's a dark, unbearable absence at the heart of the festivities.

After lunch, Victoria has a meeting – perhaps a strange one to follow a child's birthday party. She has requested an audience with Alfred, Lord Tennyson, the poet laureate. She's struck, as she notes in her diary, by his 'peculiar' looks and 'odd' dress; the 'long black flowing hair' and beard. But these trifling details don't matter. The monarch and poet speak of Albert's memory and shed tears together. Victoria tells Tennyson how much comfort she has found in his poem *In Memoriam*: a long collection of reflections on grief, loss and faith.

In Memoriam was published in 1850, over ten years earlier. And – despite the consolation Victoria found from it – it's not an assemblage of platitudes or comfortable reassurances lifted from Christian teaching. In the poem, Tennyson wrestles with the devastating loss of his friend Arthur Henry Hallam, at the age of just twenty-two, in the face of seismic shifts in scientific knowledge, and a changing understanding of humankind's place in the universe.

Giant prehistoric lizards, cut from the cliffs of southern England, are being studied and named. Microscopes are revealing teeming kingdoms of infinitesimal life, or the monumental architecture of an insect's wing. And scientists are developing new ideas about the origin and purpose of life itself. Tennyson is searching for meaning in a senseless loss – but can the old certainties of heaven and eternity hold? *In Memoriam* doesn't shy away from the complexities of faith and religion in this changed world, charting a path through doubt, despair, loss and grief.

In this extract from the poem, Tennyson imagines a conversation with Nature, about humankind's place among the many 'types' or species which have lived, died and passed into extinction.

'So careful of the type?' but no.
　　From scarped cliff and quarried stone
　　She cries, 'A thousand types are gone:
I care for nothing, all shall go.

'Thou makest thine appeal to me:
　　I bring to life, I bring to death:
　　The spirit does but mean the breath:
I know no more.' And he, shall he,

Man, her last work, who seem'd so fair,
　　Such splendid purpose in his eyes,
　　Who roll'd the psalm to wintry skies,
Who built him fanes of fruitless prayer,

Who trusted God was love indeed
      And love Creation's final law—
      Tho' Nature, red in tooth and claw
With ravine, shriek'd against his creed—

Who loved, who suffer'd countless ills,
      Who battled for the True, the Just,
      Be blown about the desert dust,
Or seal'd within the iron hills?

No more? A monster then, a dream,
      A discord. Dragons of the prime,
      That tare each other in their slime,
Were mellow music match'd with him.

O life as futile, then, as frail!
      O for thy voice to soothe and bless!
      What hope of answer, or redress?
Behind the veil, behind the veil.

In this conversation with Nature, Tennyson tries to make sense of humankind's place in the world. In the previous verses, he has been reflecting that Nature seems concerned only with the survival and success of entire species, or 'types', and is 'careless of the single life'. A life such as Hallam's, in other words, is apparently insignificant and expendable – however precious to his loved ones. But here, in this imagined dialogue, Tennyson confronts even darker thoughts. As the latest Victorian science is revealing, it's not just individuals who die and pass into oblivion, but entire species which vanish into extinction. Set against such a vast scale of annihilation, he asks, 'What hope of answer, or redress?'

In Memoriam might seem an odd choice when looking for history in a Tennyson poem. A far more obvious contender might be a text like 1854's 'The Charge of the Light Brigade', with its famous account of the doomed British cavalry advance at the Battle of Balaclava during the Crimean War. Published just days after the event, and later distributed in printed copies to soldiers in the Crimea, Tennyson's poem celebrates the 'glory' and courage of the 'noble six hundred' British soldiers, despite their catastrophic losses and the 'blunder' of those in command.

In Memoriam, by contrast, seems at first a more personal, introspective work; less concerned with public events and more a meditation on private loss and grief. Tennyson and Arthur Henry Hallam had become close friends while undergraduates at Cambridge. As their friendship deepened, Hallam fell in love with Tennyson's sister, Emilia, and they became engaged. Tragically, in July 1833, on a trip to Europe with his father, Hallam died suddenly of a cerebral haemorrhage, or stroke. When Tennyson received word, in a letter from Hallam's uncle, he broke the news to his sister and caught her as she fainted. Later, Tennyson reflected that Hallam was 'as near perfection as mortal man could be'.

Although the poem itself runs to 131 sections and 2,916 lines, *In Memoriam* captures the rawness of bereavement in sparing, powerful verse, such as the scene in which Tennyson stands outside his friend's former home. The realisation hits him anew:

> He is not here; but far away
> The noise of life begins again,
> And ghastly thro' the drizzling rain
> On the bald street breaks the blank day.

But *In Memoriam* isn't merely the account of an individual journey of loss and grief. In its struggles with Christian belief and faith, and its search for answers to fundamental questions about the purpose and value of life, the poem confronts the changing ideas and shifting worldviews which were reshaping Victorian thinking. Tennyson's moments of crisis and despair dramatise the profound transformations – and ruptures – in mid-nineteenth-century science and religion, as emergent theories around prehistoric life, natural selection and evolution entered the public consciousness.

If you don't know *In Memoriam*, you certainly know some of its lines. Phrases from the poem have entered the language – even if they've become disconnected from their source. Reflecting on the pain of grief, Tennyson reflects that 'Tis better to have loved and lost / Than never to have loved at all'. And here, in this extract, we find the familiar depiction of nature as 'red in tooth and claw': in its ferocity, ruthless competition and survival of the strong by preying on the weak. In traditional elegiac poetry, nature is a source of consolation, with its comforting imagery of continuity, rebirth and renewal. But here, nature itself is the brutal challenge to Tennyson's faith and hope.

In this extract, the verses present a dizzying recalibration of perspective and scale. Moving from Tennyson's grief over the loss of his beloved friend, they open out to a vertiginously long view of time, nature and the life and death not of individuals, but of whole 'types' or species. Nature cries out 'From scarped cliff and quarried stone', to make the devastating declaration: 'A thousand types are gone: / I care for nothing, all shall go'. From beneath England's green pastures, the voice of Nature, strange and terrible, speaks out of rock and earth; through geology, fossils and the newly discovered traces of deep time.

In early nineteenth-century 'Natural Theology', nature had been understood as a kind of living scripture, which pointed the way to an omnipotent creator and a benevolent God. The clergyman and philosopher William Paley articulated this mode of thinking through comparison with a watch and its maker – a widely influential argument still known today as the 'watchmaker analogy'. Paley imagines walking across a beach and finding a watch upon the ground. If he were asked how the watch happened to be in that place, how would he reply? He answers that he would inspect the watch, and observe its perfectly shaped and ordered parts, the transparent face showing the movement of the hands, and the regulated motion of the mechanism. He would conclude, he writes, that 'the watch must have had a maker'. To be so exactly and precisely constructed, the watch must have been designed by someone 'who formed it for the purpose'. Paley extrapolates: in nature, an 'intelligent designing mind' must be responsible for the 'forms which organised bodies bear'.

For Paley, nature reveals God the creator. Yet, throughout *In Memoriam*, Tennyson struggles and fails to read God in the natural world. Later in the poem, he confesses: 'I found Him not in world or sun, / Or eagle's wing, or insect's eye'. From the vastness of the cosmos to the awe-inspiring minutiae being revealed by the microscope, Tennyson seeks the evidence of God's existence in vain. And the verses in this extract are even more disturbing. If nature is to be read as a mirror reflecting its creator, then what does it mean to find it 'red in tooth and claw'? What truths does this brutal world – with its deaths, extinctions and annihilations – tell about God?

This crisis in the perceived relationship between creation and the Creator is famously captured a few years later by Charles Darwin, writing in 1860 (a year after the publication of *On the Origin of Species*, in 1859) on *Ichneumonidae* or parasitic wasps. These wasps typically inject their eggs into the body of a host – in this case, moth caterpillars – and, after hatching, consume the host's body while it's still alive. Today, we know even more about the life cycles of various parasitoid wasps, including the ways in which they can manipulate and control the behaviours of their hosts, effectively 'zombifying' them to serve better as a source of food or even defence for their own larvae. Darwin writes with horror: 'I cannot persuade myself that a beneficent and omnipotent God would have designedly created the Ichneumonidae with the express intention of their feeding within the very living bodies of caterpillars'.

The living book of nature is no longer testament to a just and merciful Creator. Instead, it tells a story of violence and extravagant cruelty. As Tennyson writes his poem, astonishing new scriptures are being read from the rock beneath his feet: the strata of unimaginable aeons, the fossils of strange and colossal creatures, the traces of lost worlds and 'types' swept away by time.

The 'Dragons of the prime' Tennyson refers to here are the huge fossil lizards which have only recently, in 1841, been given the name *dinosauria* or 'dinosaurs'. Palaeontologist Richard Owen coins the name in a 'Report on British Fossil Reptiles' for the British Association for the Advancement of Science, composing the term from the Greek words for 'terrible' and 'lizard'. 'Terrible' was intended to resonate in multiple ways: not just the horror of gigantic teeth and claws, but also the – perhaps even more profound – awe and terror that these colossal creatures could have vanished so absolutely into oblivion: the dread of extinction and erasure.

Dinosaurs are prominent in the public consciousness as Tennyson writes his poem, and as it is read by its first readers. Life-size models of dinosaurs are made (with the advice of Richard Owen) for the Great Exhibition of 1851, and later commissioned as a long-term exhibit in Crystal Palace Park. Mary Anning – the 'fossil finder' of Lyme Regis, Dorset, who died in 1847 – still holds national celebrity. An 1865 article about Anning, published in Charles Dickens' literary magazine *All the Year Round* (but drawing on material from an earlier Lyme Regis guidebook by Henry Rowland Brown) makes an explicit connection between her fossil-collecting and the reflections on deep time in *In Memoriam*. 'Gradually the truth dawned on her mind', writes the author, 'which our Laureate has so beautifully expressed':

> There rolls the deep where grew the tree;
> O earth, what changes thou hast seen!
> There, where the long street roars, hath been
> The silence of the central sea.

So: in the context of this vast, unknowable chronology, what's special about a single human life? And, indeed, what's special about humankind as a species? Tennyson imagines 'Man, her [Nature's] last work, who seem'd so fair'. But the certainty of humanity's special place in the universe – ordained by God to Adam, in the Garden of Eden – collapses in ruins. These lines teeter close to the brink of despair or apostasy – complete rejection of religious faith. Tennyson sees the 'fanes', or temples, of 'fruitless prayer'; he hears the voices who 'roll'd the psalm to wintry skies'. All those words of praise and supplication disappearing up into the earth's cold atmosphere, emptied of its God and heaven.

There's a burning rage in these verses: that humankind 'trusted' in God and 'loved', and 'suffer'd' – but all for nothing. The logical conclusion is truly terrible: the horrific primordial lizards or 'dragons' would be 'mellow music' compared with a human. Tennyson presents us with an appalling, awful provocation: humankind is the true 'monster'. Dinosaurs ruled the earth and then passed into extinction. But only humans have lived – and will surely die – in such hubristic delusion, self-deceit and futility. Tennyson's line of argument turns the world upside down. Those ferocious dragons excavated from the bedrock hold no terror compared to the horror of humanity itself.

With these verses, we leave Tennyson at a low ebb, near to total despair. But the final line suggests a glimmer of hope. In answer to his own question 'What hope of answer, or redress?' Tennyson replies: 'Behind the veil, behind the veil'. It's a deliberately religious image, recalling the veil in the Jewish temple, used in Christian writing as a metaphor for the unknowability of God, hidden from sight. There are answers, Tennyson is suggesting – but beyond the view or understanding of humankind.

Logic has taken Tennyson to a dark, desperate place. Ultimately, in *In Memoriam*, it's not logic or reasoning which helps him find his way out – but a trust in feeling and instinct above intellect and argument. Towards the end of the poem, as he moves towards acceptance of his loss and welcomes new beginnings in his life, he gives his response to doubt and despair. 'Like a man in wrath the heart / Stood up and answer'd "I have felt." ' Tennyson corrects himself in the next stanza: 'No, like a child in doubt and fear' who cries and reaches out for his father. He writes of the comfort of faith in embodied, physical terms: he senses 'what I am beheld again' – the idea of being seen, known and understood, articulated in the tactile language of embrace.

But this imagery of childlike feeling and trust belies the complex intellectual conceit which unfolds through the poem. Having confronted the challenges of scientific thought, Tennyson folds the emergent theories of natural selection and evolution back into his religious beliefs. He concludes that 'the man, that with me trod / This planet, was a noble type / Appearing ere the times were ripe'. In other words, Hallam was the forerunner of a more perfect species of human yet to evolve. And the very final word of the poem labours to harmonise science and faith. Tennyson returns to God 'To which the whole creation moves'. Narratives of evolution and progress now align, rhetorically, with the idea of a divine plan, providence, the advent of a more perfect world. Yes, the world changes and 'moves' – but it moves *towards* something greater than itself.

Long after that first meeting, on Princess Beatrice's fifth birthday, Queen Victoria meets Tennyson privately for the last time on Tuesday, 7 August, 1883. The morning at Osborne House begins with thick mist blown in from the Solent, but the warm summer sun burns through and the day turns fine. In the morning, Victoria drives out in the pony chair – a small carriage – and then sits in the garden. In her mid-sixties now, she's no longer the young mother with a family at her knee. Dressed in black, as always, she's every inch the 'Widow of Windsor', derided, at times, in the press for her stubborn fidelity to mourning.

After lunch, Tennyson arrives. Victoria sees the change in her visitor, noting in her diary that 'he is grown very old, his eyesight, much impaired, and he is very shaky on his legs'. They speak of friends lost, and their shared hope of 'another world, where there would be no partings'. If not, they agree, God 'would be far more cruel than a human being'. Victoria tells Tennyson again of the comfort *In Memoriam* has always brought to her, in her long widowhood. She's astonished when he reveals the countless letters of abuse he's received, in response to the poem, over the years. They discuss 'unbelievers and philosophers' and those who try to 'explain everything away'.

Tennyson leaves, and *In Memoriam* is returned to its treasured place on Victoria's bookshelf, next to the Bible. She sees the swifts soaring outside, over the lawns and the treetops. The myrtle is blooming, down by the terrace walls and in the little garden Albert planted for the children. She is going out to tea.

The History of a Moment

'Adlestrop' by Edward Thomas (1917)

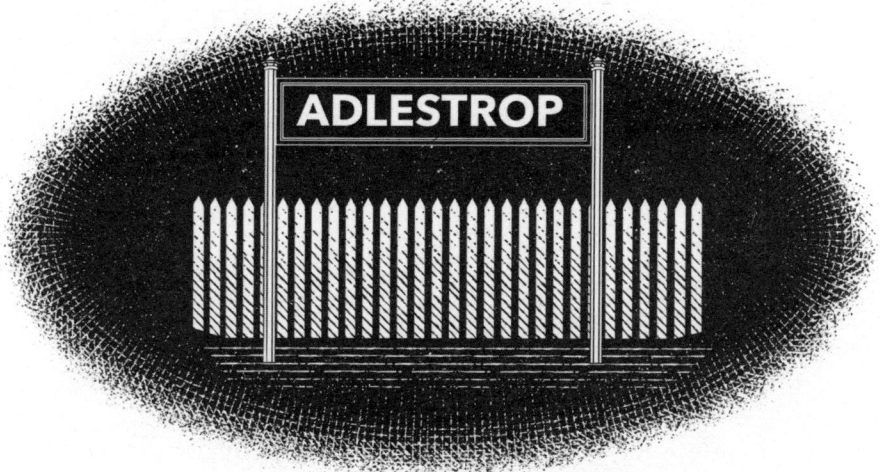

A history of England in *moments*: what might that look like? A history made of the littlest, most ephemeral fragments; the tiniest particles of time? A crown being placed onto a bowed head, perhaps, or the iron point of an arrow meeting an eye. A statue toppling, or a bomb dropping from the open hatch of a Heinkel over a sleeping city. And what about those moments that slip through the fingers of history? The glimpse of a swallow returning after a hard winter. Evening light slanting through a window onto an open book. The first glow of dawn on the morning of battle; the sharp intake of breath before going over the top.

The poem 'Adlestrop' by Edward Thomas captures one fleeting, ephemeral moment in time. An unexpected halt at the eponymous station on a train journey: an in-between fragment, a space in which, apparently, nothing happens; a brief pause amid the clamorous events of history. Inspired by a train journey on 24 June 1914, the poem 'Adlestrop' was written over six months later, on 8 January 1915, while Thomas was convalescing with a sprained ankle. In those months, the world had changed radically, torn apart by the Great War. 'Adlestrop' was eventually published in the magazine *The New Statesman* in April 1917, just days after Second Lieutenant Edward Thomas, Royal Garrison Artillery, was killed in the first hours of the Battle of Arras.

Today, we might think of Edward Thomas as a nature writer or place writer, with a passion for the natural world and a keen interest in the personalities of places. Much of the work Thomas has left is in prose: he was only finding his voice (and confidence) as a poet in the very last years of his life. Thomas's ancestry was Welsh: his father had left Tredegar, in the south Wales valleys, in his teens, and the family were settled in Battersea, south London. Throughout his life, Thomas retained a deep connection with, and affection for, Wales, with regular visits to family, writing on Welsh places (including a lively essay on Swansea), and even a journey to the 1906 Eisteddfod in North Wales. But he was intrigued by the elusive idea of England and Englishness, pursued in his writing across prose and verse. In his writing, Thomas declares his affinity with what he calls the 'little things' – and 'Adlestrop' embodies that commitment to the smallest, often humblest fragments of experience and memory. Yet the poem depicts a moment at the edge of enormous, cataclysmic historical change: from that last summer of Edwardian innocence to the brutality and horror of the Great War. And it opens up questions about what England actually is, and where we might find it.

On 24 June 1914, Edward Thomas and his wife Helen set off by train to visit their friend, the poet Robert Frost, in Gloucestershire. The account in Thomas's notebook that day describes 'tiers and tiers of white cloud' over Battersea Park as they left his parents' home. It continues:

> . . . then at Oxford tiers of pure white with loose large masses above and gaps of dark clear blue above haymaking and elms
>
> Then we stopped at Adlestrop, through the willows could be heard a chain of blackbirds songs at 12.45 and one thrush and no man seen, only a hiss of engine letting off steam.
>
> Stopping outside Campden by banks of long grass willowherbs and meadowsweet, extraordinary silence between the two periods of travel – looking out on grey dry stones between metals and the shining metals and over it all the elms willowy and long grass – one man clears his throat – a greater than rustic silence. No house in view Stop only for a minute till signal is up.

Thomas's account reflects his eye for moments: his attention to detail, acute perception and sensory engagement with the world around him, and his aliveness to the extraordinary, even amid the most mundane and everyday.

Vivid moments in time – animated by lived experience and sensory detail – abound across Thomas's work. In his 1906 book *The Heart of England* he distils other, likely many and monotonous, journeys through suburbia by train into a compelling image of 'the hundreds of streets parallel or at angles with the railway – some exposing flowery or neglected back gardens, bedrooms half seen through open windows, pigeon-houses with pigeons bowing or flashing in flight, all manner of domesticities surprised'. Beauty is transfigured out of the grubby ordinariness of views glimpsed from the train window. But it is in moments of encounter with the natural world that Thomas's writing – across his notebooks, letters, prose and verse – is most alive. For example, his essay 'This England', written in autumn 1914 for *The Nation*, and later gathered in a posthumous collection of his essays, *The Last Sheaf*, begins by recalling a sequence of moments, that same year, in the area around the Gloucestershire–Herefordshire border.

In April here I had heard, among apple trees in flower, not the first cuckoo, but the first abundance of day-long-calling cuckoos: here, the first nightingale's song, though too far-off and intermittently, twitched away by gusty night winds; here I found the earliest may-blossom which by May Day, while I still lingered, began to dapple the hedges thickly, and no rain fell, yet the land was sweet. Here I had the consummation of Midsummer, the weather radiant and fresh, yet hot and rainless, the white and the pink wild roses, the growing bracken, the last and best of the songs, blackbird's, blackcap's. Now it was August, and again no rain fell for many days; the harvest was a good one, and after standing long in the sun it was gathered in and put up in ricks in the sun, to the contentment of men and rooks. All day the rooks in the wheat-fields were cawing a deep sweet caw, in alternating choirs or all together, almost like sheep bleating, contentedly, on until late evening.

An account of almost a whole year, sweeping from spring to autumn, yet gathered from unmistakably real, almost tangible, moments of experience. A kind of rustic almanac or Shepherd's Calendar of the seasons, made out of the precise, authentic sights, sounds and scents of Thomas's walks in place. The year 1914 written in the littlest things: an account that reads today almost as a radical counter-history, defiantly contrasting with the too-familiar textbook accounts: European militarisation, the assassination of Archduke Franz Ferdinand, the chain reaction of political alliances and pacts. Thomas's eye for the beauty of moments – his ability to parse their minute details and qualities – continues in his diaries and letters, even right until the end in Arras.

It's clear from Thomas's notebook that his train journey, with Helen, that day in June 1914, involved not one stop but several. And his notebook account gives no hint that the stop at Adlestrop was unexpected, as the poem depicts. While the poem recalls a journey by 'express-train', which halts 'unwontedly', train timetables from 1914 suggest that it's more likely Thomas and his wife were on a slow train all along, and the various stops on the route were all scheduled. But Thomas's poem is not a documentary. Instead, 'Adlestrop' conflates several moments, recorded in Thomas's notebook on 24 June, into one. Fragments of experience and memory from that slow train journey through the west of England are transfigured into one moment of luminous experience.

Yet the poem begins as naturally as an overheard conversation. The first line even seems to be the answer to a silent question.

> Yes. I remember Adlestrop –
> The name, because one afternoon
> Of heat the express-train drew up there
> Unwontedly. It was late June.

The language is disarmingly colloquial, informal. The first stanza is halting, stop and start, with short sentences and phrases broken over lines. Perhaps the mental effort of the speaker piecing together fragments of memory. Or the discomfort, and even frustration, of that unexpected stop, in the sultry heat of the end of June. In this conversational, colloquial idiom, the word 'unwontedly' stands out: more elaborate, more self-consciously literary, more precise. Perhaps there's a deliberate double meaning here: the train's stop is 'unwonted' – out of the ordinary, unusual – but also 'unwanted' – undesired, a mild irritation or annoyance. And the reason for Thomas's insistence on the 'express-train' comes into focus. While his original version of the poem simply describes it as a 'steam train', the contrast between the express – the rush of travel, of busyness, of time speeding ahead – and the silent halt at Adlestrop is powerful.

The second stanza continues the short, staccato phrases of the first verse: brief impressions, and that same sense of an uncomfortable interruption.

> The steam hissed. Someone cleared his throat.
> No one left and no one came
> On the bare platform. What I saw
> Was Adlestrop – only the name

The language insists on emptiness, nothing. The repetition of 'no one' in the second line, the 'bare' platform, the sight 'only' of the name of the station, no more.

While the language of the first two verses of 'Adlestrop' seems so naturalistic, even colloquial, Thomas's draft of the poem, held in the British Library, shows the labour in achieving this effect. The first stanza, in particular, is a tangle of scribbles, crossings-out and replacements, with the entire verse written out again – with further changes – in the right-hand margin. A previous alternative for 'unwontedly' was 'against its custom'. Thomas plays with minute details: the difference between 'It was June' and 'It was late June', between 'At least the name' and 'The name, because . . .' These lines may convey the sense of pure, immediate experience, and direct encounter with a lived moment. But they are forged from the poet's sweat and toil. Elsewhere in his writing, Thomas describes the labours of his prose composition as 'chaos cut up into beds and borders and fountains and rusticwork like a garden'.

But the second half of 'Adlestrop' is different.

> And willows, willow-herb, and grass,
> And meadowsweet, and haycocks dry,
> No whit less still and lonely fair
> Than the high cloudlets in the sky.
>
> And for that minute a blackbird sang
> Close by, and round him, mistier,
> Farther and farther, all the birds
> Of Oxfordshire and Gloucestershire.

From those halting, hesitant stanzas, the poem opens out into lush, luminous description. The second two verses flow freely, carrying the reader with them into that moment. There's the list of trees and flowers by the side of the railway. Nothing special – these are the weeds and stragglers of waste ground, of in-between places. The 'haycocks' are the conical haystacks of the summer harvest. But they're all transfigured by poetic language and form. The repetition of 'and' creates a rushing sensation, the feel of abundance. The poetic word order in 'haycocks dry' elevates this mundane rural sight: a fact of agricultural life nudged into the register of landscape art. The haycocks are compared to the clouds above, in a kind of mirroring or symmetry: 'No whit less still and lonely fair / Than the high cloudlets in the sky'. Again, poetic word order lifts the scene, while 'No whit' moves beyond the conversational register and perhaps plays an extra lexical trick, suggesting the whiteness of the clouds in the sky. The word 'cloudlets' is formed with a diminutive suffix or ending – denoting something small, but often more familiar from terms of endearment and affection. It also forms a rhythmical skip, a kind of miniature leap of delight. This is a moment of joy. In the final stanza, the poem expands further, its horizons broadening. 'Adlestrop' starts with a little thing, and opens wide.

The poem deftly – deliberately – conveys the sense of a single exquisite moment of direct and unmediated experience. But this idea of the moment in art and literature has a complex and controversial pedigree in late nineteenth- and early twentieth-century art, as Edward Thomas well knew. In 1915, when he wrote 'Adlestrop', Thomas was just stretching his legs as a poet. But he was well established as a prose essayist and literary critic. In 1912 he had published a book on the poet Charles Algernon Swinburne and in 1913 a book on Walter Pater. Both writers were associated with the nineteenth-century Aesthetic movement and later – whether justly or not – with the literary and artistic trend known as 'Decadence', often condemned by social and cultural critics for its perceived excesses and moral dereliction.

Walter Pater imagines human lived experience as a succession of intense 'moments' of sensory perceptions and impressions. In his monumental work *The Renaissance: Studies in Art and Poetry* (1877), he writes that 'Every moment some form grows perfect in hand or face; some tone on the hills or the sea is choicer than the rest; some mood or passion or insight or intellectual excitement is irresistibly real and attractive for us – for that moment only'. Pater finds these moments of intensity not only in high art, but also in the most mundane and ordinary. 'A sudden light transfigures trivial things: a weathervane, a windmill, a winnowing flail, the dust in the barn door.' Aestheticism privileged beauty and the sensory effect of art over meaning, or its didactic or moral message. Pater was no liver of a decadent life: Thomas describes him as 'a man of no great passion, no great wealth or activity'. But the Aesthetes' valorisation of the moment is an important literary and cultural antecedent for 'Adlestrop'.

What is 'Adlestrop' actually about? Does it have any meaning, or does it simply evoke a moment of sensory experience? The final lines seem to gesture towards some kind of secular revelation or epiphany. But this is never defined. While Thomas took pains to distance himself from the Aesthetic movement, is his most famous poem, in fact, merely an empty moment of beauty, devoid of meaning? Perhaps, if the poem is indeed a kind of epiphany – if Thomas does approach any larger meaning or realisation in these moments at Adlestrop – then the almost-encounter is with the idea of England itself. And, in the context of Thomas's wider work, it's unsurprising that this England remains elusive, fugitive, always just beyond reach.

In another essay, 'England', also included in the collection *The Last Sheaf*, Thomas sets out in search. What does England mean? Where might we find it? Writing after the start of the Great War, he observes that 'patriotic' words and phrases are not much used or scrutinised in times of peace. 'Trouble changes this.' He recalls over-hearing a woman speaking, in those early months of the war (again, tellingly, a little and accidental moment of experience). 'I heard a woman say: "I don't quite know what they mean by England. Some-times I feel proud, but more often ashamed, though certainly I can't say there is any other country to which I would rather belong".' He reflects on the limits of capturing the idea of England in any kind of language. 'And I am not sure that love of country can go much farther in words, except under the influence of alcohol or a crowd; that is, among those who only stand and wait.'

Thomas's mistrust of jingoism and patriotic language is, in part, a reaction to the nationalist propaganda all around him in the first years of the Great War. Lord Kitchener's iconic 'Your Country Needs YOU' poster, first published in September 1914. St George slaying the (German) dragon. And, in 1915, as the necessity of con-scription approached, Savile Lumley's famous poster mobilising shame as a motive for service to the nation: two children on their father's knee asking 'Daddy, what did YOU do in the Great War?'

Edward Thomas finds England, instead, in what he describes as the 'little things' in history: not in grand narratives and the great icons of patriotism, but at the smallest scale. In 'England' he gives examples of the two 'little things' in early English history which sug-gest the most vivid sense of England to him. 'One is a very stunted hawthorn round which the battle of Ashdown clashed', between the Danes and King Æthelred with his brother Alfred. The other is 'the hoar apple tree where Harold's host met the Conqueror near

Hastings'. In both cases, histories of power, conquest and territory are folded back into the timeless natural landscape of England itself. Love of country, Thomas argues later in the essay, can really only be love of place, of the local, of home. That may occasionally connect with a 'more fitfully conscious love of the island, and glory in its glories'. But the intimacy of place, individual memory and belonging is what matters.

In January 1915, as he wrote 'Adlestrop', Thomas was wrestling with what to do: how to play his part in the Great War. At the age of thirty-six, and married, he was not a candidate for conscription, he had a family to support, and doubted how useful he could be in the front-line warfare of the trenches. A poem written for Thomas by his friend Robert Frost, 'The Road Not Taken', played a significant part in his deliberations. While written as an affectionate joke – apparently Thomas was a notoriously indecisive walking companion – Thomas increasingly read it as censure or provocation, its call to take 'the road less travelled by' a charge to make the courageous choice and enlist. In the poem 'Adlestrop' we also glimpse something of Thomas's process of reflection and reckoning, as he revisits that moment in June 1914 from the perspective of a changed world.

One moment, according to Thomas's published account in 'This England', made up his mind. It's evening, the end of a day which 'had begun wet' but 'turned warm and muggy, and at last fine but still cloudy'. Thomas watches a new moon rise. 'The sky was banded with rough masses in the north-west, but the moon, a stout orange crescent, hung free of cloud near the horizon.' The moment hits Thomas with meaning.

At one stroke, I thought, like many other people, what things that same new moon sees eastward about the Meuse in France. Of those who could see it there, not blinded by smoke, pain, or excitement, how many saw it and heeded? I was deluged, in a second stroke, by another thought, or something that overpowered thought. All I can tell is, it seemed to me that either I had never loved England, or I had loved it foolishly, aesthetically . . .

This ephemeral moment becomes a blow of realisation. Thomas rejects purely 'aesthetic' experience and draws the line from this moment of sublime beauty to the moral response it (in his view) demands. He interprets the moment as a call to action.

Thomas enlisted in the Artists Rifles in July 1915. He was promoted to corporal, and in November 1916 was commissioned into the Royal Garrison Artillery as a second lieutenant. In his private war diary, he describes his arrival at Le Havre at 4 a.m. on 30 January 1917:

> Light of stars and windows of tall pale houses and electric arcs on quay. March through bales of cotton in sun to camp. The snow emptying its castor of finest white.

Life in France on the Front is hard, physically demanding and uncomfortable. Thomas's fellow officers are much younger men and he struggles to connect with them. But in the midst of the horrors of the war, Thomas's diary and letters continue to capture vivid moments of experience – and even beauty. On 11 March 1917, after a heavy night of shelling, Thomas describes a moment of peace at 6.15 a.m.: 'all quiet and heard blackbirds chinking'. His letters to Helen, in particular, reflect their shared passion for the natural world, which he cherishes even in the blasted landscape of northern France. On 24 March 1917, he describes signs of spring in his dug-out, in an old chalk pit.

> It is almost a beautiful spot still and I am sitting warm in the sun on a heap of chalk with my back to the wall of the pit which is large and shallow. Fancy, an old chalk pit with moss and even a rabbit left in spite of the paths trodden almost all over it. It is beautiful and sunny and warm though cold in the shade. The chalk is dazzling. The sallow catkins are soft dark white.

Most of all, fragments of birdsong echo through the letters. On 1 April, for example, he writes to Helen that 'Blackbirds began to sing at 6 and a yellowhammer'. On 5 April, he writes to his mother of his pleasure to 'hear the wrens in the copse'. In his last letter home, to Helen, on 7 or 8 April 1917, he captures a scene of appalling destruction – and the anticipation of future death and devastation in the offensive soon to come – wrapped up with details of beauty in the spring landscape around him, and the enduring cycles of the natural world as the seasons change.

> The pretty village among trees that I first saw two weeks ago is now just ruins among violated stark tree trunks. But the sun shone and larks and partridges and magpies and hedgesparrows made love and the trench was being made passable for the wounded that will be harvested in a day or two.

Edward Thomas was killed on Easter Monday, 9 April 1917, in the early hours of the Battle of Arras, while still in the Observation Post, by a direct hit through the chest.

Edward Thomas's 1915 poem presents Adlestrop as a remembered moment, a relic of a lost world, a source of comfort and, perhaps, a challenge to action. Looking again at the last stanza of the poem, we can see how the moment it depicts is already receding, even at the point of experience. The scene becomes 'mistier'; the birds sing 'farther and farther' into the distance. That last line invokes the county names 'Oxfordshire and Gloucestershire' almost as words of magical power: the evocative language of the shires, the map and identities of England stretching back into the deepest history. Yet, as Thomas writes in 1915 – and for the poem's first readers in 1917 – perhaps there are newer, sadder resonances here: the names of regiments, the epithets of Pals Battalions, and a new geography of national loss and mourning.

'Adlestrop' evokes a cherished moment, captured and preserved but never fully held. A sense of a lost England which can never be fully defined. That imagined moment at the railway station in June 1914 slips through the fingers. An echo of remembered birdsong, through misty trees.

Yes. I remember Adlestrop –
The name, because one afternoon
Of heat the express-train drew up there
Unwontedly. It was late June.

The steam hissed. Someone cleared his throat.
No one left and no one came
On the bare platform. What I saw
Was Adlestrop – only the name

And willows, willow-herb, and grass,
And meadowsweet, and haycocks dry,
No whit less still and lonely fair
Than the high cloudlets in the sky.

And for that minute a blackbird sang
Close by, and round him, mistier,
Farther and farther, all the birds
Of Oxfordshire and Gloucestershire.

Modernity, Mourning and the Shadow of War

'Funeral Blues' by W. H. Auden (1936 and 1937)

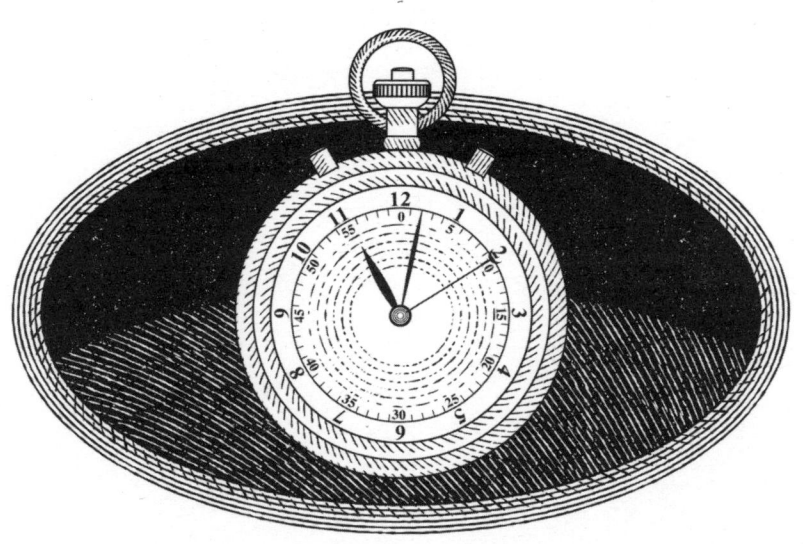

Stop all the clocks, cut off the telephone,
Prevent the dog from barking with a juicy bone,
Silence the pianos and with muffled drum
Bring out the coffin, let the mourners come.

Let aeroplanes circle moaning overhead
Scribbling on the sky the message 'He is Dead'.
Put crepe bows round the white necks of the public doves,
Let the traffic policemen wear black cotton gloves.

He was my North, my South, my East and West,
My working week and my Sunday rest,
My noon, my midnight, my talk, my song;
I thought that love would last forever: I was wrong.

The stars are not wanted now; put out every one,
Pack up the moon and dismantle the sun,
Pour away the ocean and sweep up the wood;
For nothing now can ever come to any good.

It's a poem we think we know well. Many of us have been consoled
and comforted by its words about love and loss; have taken refuge
in its lines at times of mourning and pain. It's probably best known
from the scene in the 1994 British romantic comedy *Four Weddings
and a Funeral*, when the character Matthew (played by Scottish actor
John Hannah) reads the poem at the funeral of his partner Gareth.

Such was the public impact of this moving recital that Faber rushed out a new Auden anthology, *Tell Me the Truth about Love*, including 'Funeral Blues' as well as nine other poems. The book was an instant smash hit; a rare poetry blockbuster. 'Funeral Blues' continues to be cherished by a wide readership. It's often read at funerals and memorials. It speaks to many of us at moments of grief.

But the original version of Auden's poem is very different, in a wildly different dramatic context. It appears in the play *The Ascent of F6: A Tragedy in Two Acts*, which Auden co-wrote with Christopher Isherwood: published in 1936 and first staged in 1937. In the play, those familiar Auden verses are not a sincere, moving expression of personal grief, but instead bitterly satirical and ridiculous: a parody of mourning with the fraught politics of the 1930s firmly in its sights.

The original published version of Auden's poem tackles 1930s patriotism and nationalism, the cult of the 'Great Man' and its tipping points into totalitarianism. It regards the trappings of modernity with cool scepticism, and examines language and performance themselves as sites of manipulation and control. In its original form, the poem speaks very specifically to an England in the wake of the Great Depression, gripped by a decade-long economic slump. But this is also an England of growing affluence, consumer culture and rising standards of living. Extremist threats loom at home and abroad, and the gathering clouds of the Second World War are already on the horizon.

Let's look, briefly, at the play which provides the first context for Auden's poem. In *The Ascent of F6*, a fictional mountaineer, Michael Forbes Ransom, is coerced, for political reasons, into attempting the first climb to the summit of F6, a mountain in contested territory on the border of the fictional 'British Sudoland' and 'Ostnian Sudoland'. It's an explicitly nationalist endeavour, seeking to consolidate British control of the region (and to beat a rival Ostnian expedition) and to provide morale-boosting grist to the media mill back home. Local legend that a demon lives at the peak of the mountain is dismissed as primitive superstition.

As Ransom makes his ascent of F6, his companions die one by one, and he begins to accept the existence of the demon. When he reaches the summit, he encounters the demon in the form of his mother (yes, it's all rather Freudian and confusing) and dies. Early critics were quick to point out that the ending of the play is incoherent and puzzling – probably at least in part due to the many revisions made by Auden and Isherwood, often independently of each other. The action of the play is observed by an unusual kind of dramatic chorus: 'Mr and Mrs A' – an ordinary suburban couple, back home in England, who follow this great patriotic adventure through the wireless and the newspapers. They seize on it as an escape from their humdrum, disappointing lives. In the play, 'Stop All the Clocks' is the poem performed to mark the death of the great hero Ransom: the tragic emblem of English pride and glory, demanding a dutifully patriotic display of grief.

The absurdity of the poem in the play is marked unmistakably. At the start of the scene, stage directions note that the characters – Stagmantle, the General and Isabel, all instigators of the patriotic F6 expedition – 'jostle each other, jump on each other's shoulders to get a better hearing and behave in general like the Marx brothers'. The poem is sung by Stagmantle and Isabel, to a blues setting for two pianos and percussion, by Benjamin Britten. The two performers are vying to outdo each other in an exaggerated display of grief. The first two verses are exactly the same as those from 'Funeral Blues' which we know so well. But the next three, in the play, become outrageously ridiculous and absurd, as the speakers gabble over Ransom's dead body:

Hold up your umbrellas to keep off the rain
From Doctor Williams while he opens a vein;
Life, he pronounces, it is finally extinct.
Sergeant, arrest that man who said he winked!

Shawcross will say a few words sad and kind
To the weeping crowds about the Master-Mind,
While Lamp with a powerful microscope
Searches their faces for a sign of hope.

And Gunn, of course, will drive the motor-hearse:
None could drive it better, most would drive it worse.
He'll open tip the throttle to its fullest power
And drive him to the grave at ninety miles an hour.

There's no mistaking this for a sincere elegy or authentic expression of grief. The play's poetic eulogy for the great man, Ransom, collapses into comic profanity and insult.

So, where are the traces of that 1930s performance in the version of 'Funeral Blues' we know today? The poem is widely loved for its moving account of loss. But what happens if we read against the grain and look for clues to its political, satirical origins? Auden was working on his alternative version of the poem as early as 1937, bridging from those bitterly satirical opening stanzas into something apparently rather different: a genuine expression of personal grief. Rewritten for performance as a cabaret song, Auden's revised version of the poem cuts references which would only make sense within the narrative of the play. But it remains, perhaps, poised between satire and elegy, between comedy and consolation.

The first two stanzas of 'Funeral Blues' – retained word-for-word from Auden and Isherwood's play – present grief as a choreographed public performance. To be fair, elegy – and especially eulogy – is often a public form. Think of Matthew speaking at the funeral service for Gareth in *Four Weddings*, standing up in front of family and friends. But Auden's poem pushes this to extremes. It gives us grief as something staged and manufactured – like a civic pageant or municipal show. Look at the first verse. The first word of each line is an imperative, a command: 'Stop', 'Prevent', 'Silence', 'Bring'. It's a curt list of instructions or orders: a bureaucratic checklist for the correct display of communal grief.

And what kinds of display are being required? While the tradition of stopping the clocks after a death goes back centuries, the other observances here are rather less familiar. And, if we're honest, they're rather less plausible as genuine rituals of heartfelt mourning. They tip the poem's tone beyond a conventional elegiac register into something jarring, even ludicrous. With 'Prevent the dog from barking with a juicy bone' we're a long way from the traditional sombre language and poetic decorum of elegy. Aeroplanes sky-writing 'the message "He is Dead"' is just exaggerated and over-the-top: a spectacular display which has more to do with corporate advertising stunts popular in the 1920s and 30s than sincere public mourning. 'Put crepe bows round the white necks of the public doves'? It's a ridiculous image – before we even think about the absurd notion of 'public doves', at the service of civic, patriotic duty. 'Let the traffic policemen wear black cotton gloves' is a jolting collision between the pomposity of staged municipal grief and the banality of its details: the uniform on hands waving cars and lorries along the road.

The comic awkwardness – even unseemliness – of these lines also comes from somewhere else: their direct and uneuphemistic engagement with the trappings of modernity. Elegy – a poetic lament for the dead – typically deals in more timeless, universal imagery, such as the natural world or changing seasons. But here, the poem locates its performative grief very precisely in an urban or suburban 1930s world. With its aeroplanes, cars and traffic policemen, it offers up a bustling new landscape of modernity. And we shouldn't forget that the telephone (which must be decorously 'cut off') is, also, a new technology, finding a place in many households for the first time. Perhaps we might imagine solemnly intoning 'Set your notifications to silent' in a serious piece of elegiac poetry today.

But these uncomfortable references to modernity aren't just a stylistic joke. They're pointers to England's economic and social situation in the 1930s. It's a decade often associated primarily with the worldwide repercussions following the Great Crash of 1929. In 1930s Britain, never fewer than one million people were out of work, reaching a peak in 1932 with almost 3 million unemployed. Two million people remained workless in 1935. The Labour government of Ramsay MacDonald, elected in 1929, found itself unable to deal with the international economic crisis. A new 'National' government – a coalition of a small group of Labour MPs along with Conservatives – was formed in August 1931 and elected with a landslide majority later that year. But the economic effects of the global slump continued to be felt, and unemployment continued to rise.

Economic misery was spread unevenly around the country. The old industrial areas were hardest hit, especially those associated with the pre-war boom industries like coal, cotton, steel and ship-building. Images of the 1936 'Jarrow Crusade' remain potent in the popular imagination: men trudging with weary dignity through the rain, carrying their banners and petition to London to protest against unemployment and poverty. Soup kitchens, ragged children, the dole.

In the play *The Ascent of F6*, the ordinary suburban couple, Mr and Mrs A, watch the action from the edge of the stage, using it to escape the drudgery of daily life. Together, they describe in verse the state of England in the grip of economic depression.

Let the eye of the traveller consider this country and weep,
For toads croak in the cistern; the aqueduct chokes with leaves:
The highways are out of repair and infested with thieves:
The ragged population are crazy for lack of sleep;
Our chimneys are smokeless; the implements rust in the field
And our tall constructions are felled.
Over our empty playgrounds the wet winds sough;
The crab and the sandhopper possess our abandoned beaches;
Upon our gardens the dock and the darnel encroaches;
The crumbling lighthouse is circled with moss like a muff;
The weasel inhabits the courts and the sacred places;
Despair is in our faces.

This is England's green and pleasant land gone to ruin: stagnating, rotting, overgrown with weeds and crumbling. It's the language of rancour and corruption: the fertility of the island garden turned to waste and misery.

But the 1930s were a time of tensions and contradictions. While mass unemployment blighted many communities and regions, the majority of the population remained in work. The decade saw, for many, growing affluence and rising standards of living. Consumer goods and new technologies were in reach for the first time – like the 'telephone' of Auden's poem. J. B. Priestley's 1934 account of his travels in England, *English Journey*, pictures a land of

> arterial and by-pass roads, filling stations and factories that look like exhibition buildings, of giant cinemas and dance-halls and cafés, bungalows with tiny garages, cocktail bars, Woolworths, motor coaches, wireless, hiking, factory girls looking like actresses, greyhound racing and dirt tracks, swimming pools, and everything given away for cigarette coupons.

This is a world of mass entertainment and consumption; a population in search of escape, pleasure, purpose.

And this new technology might also telegraph something else to audiences of 'Stop all the clocks'. There's a disturbingly clear line from the glossy trappings of modern consumer culture in the 1930s to visions of shiny new futures: political promises to sweep away the dirty, dusty past and replace it with something radically different. In 1930, the MP Bill Allen – on the brink of defection from the Unionists to join Oswald Moseley's New Party – writes to *The Times* about the values of a (British) fascist future. '[W]e have no respect for the grey hairs, grey theories, methods and traditions' of the pre-war generation, he asserts. Instead, the world heralded by Moseley and his fellow fascists is one of 'aeroplanes, wireless, talkies, speedboats, of all things new and wonderful'. The promised future is all technology, machines and engineering: modernity pushed to its ultimate realisation.

The play *The Ascent of F6*, from which Auden's poem comes, is inherently concerned with the idea of the great hero or 'superman' – the 'Master-Mind' eulogised by Stagmantle and Isabel in their crazy final verses. Through its character of Michael Forbes Ransom, it interrogates the patriotic and nationalist agendas which fuse around the Great Man. And it's no accident that it does this through a story of a heroic expedition. Exploration – and especially

mountaineering – is an explicitly nationalist endeavour in the dec-
ades after the First World War: a context in which Britain's imperial
supremacy is beginning to look precarious. A series of Everest
expeditions throughout the 1920s and earlier 30s included the heroic
adventure of 1924, in which George Mallory and Andrew 'Sandy'
Irvine both lost their lives near the peak. The endeavour attracted
enormous media interest: Mallory and Irvine were fêted as patriotic
heroes.

T. E. Lawrence – better known today in the public imagination
as 'Lawrence of Arabia' – was a more particular inspiration for the
great hero of *The Ascent of F6*. Lawrence died in 1935, and Winston
Churchill's eulogy for his friend was published widely in the British
press. 'In Colonel Lawrence', Churchill declared, 'we have lost one
of the greatest beings of our time. [. . .] No such blow has befallen
the Empire for many years as his untimely death. The personal
sorrow which all who knew him will feel is deepened by national
impoverishment'. In Auden and Isherwood's play, the death of
mountaineer Ransom on the summit of F6 attracts a similar eulogy.
Just moments before the 'Stop all the clocks' verses, the character
Stagmantle proclaims that 'the whole of England is plunged into
mourning for one of her greatest sons; but it is a sorrow tempered
with pride, that once again Englishmen have been weighed in the
balance and not found wanting'. This isn't just a private, personal
loss, but national grief and nationalist glory. Auden's poem is the
logical – and absurd – extension to its performance.

Heroes and supermen are rising across Europe: Franco in
Spain, Mussolini in Italy, Hitler in Germany, and, at the other end
of the political spectrum, Stalin in the Soviet Union. The cultish
adoration of Great Men is dangerous, with potentially disastrous
consequences. There's a dark subcurrent to the exaggerated public
performances of grief and duty in Auden's poem. We might detect
in it a fear, or revulsion, at the state co-opting private emotion, con-
trolling feelings.

The final verses in the original *Ascent of F6* version of the poem are
simultaneously even more ludicrous and sinister. As Stagmantle and

Isabel jostle over the body of Ransom and declare him dead, they order 'Sergeant, arrest that man who said he winked!' The character Lamp uses a 'powerful microscope' to examine the gathered crowds (the play's audience?) and 'Searches their faces for a sign of hope'. It may be mocking and comic, but this is about surveillance and scrutiny; the pressure to conform and show an adequate display of patriotic devotion and grief – as well as appropriately boosted morale. It's Orwellian, ominous.

The chorus in the play are tuned into heightened tensions across Europe through their wireless. Mrs A refers, frustratedly, to –

Talk in Westminster, talk at Geneva, talk in the
lobbies and talk on the throne;
Talk about treaties, talk about honour, mad dogs
quarrelling over a bone.

We can recognise, here, the 1930s language of politics and uneasy diplomacy. For ordinary Mrs A, all it adds up to is words piled on words: an endless barrage of 'talk'. Both Mr and Mrs A agree that Ransom's expedition to F6 is essential for England's pride and glory.

Mr A: England's honour is covered with rust.
Mrs A: Ransom must beat them! He must! He must!
Mr A: Or England falls. She has had her hour
And now must decline to a second-class power. .

Yet, while Mrs A is captivated by the idea of a heroic death, Mr A remembers all too clearly the bodies he saw torn apart on the battlefields of the Great War.

I've watched men writhing on the dug-out floor
Cursing the land for which they went to war;
The joker cut off half-way through his story,
The coward blown involuntary to glory.
The steel butt smashing at the eyes that beg.

The stupid clutching at the shattered leg.
The twitching scarecrows on the rusty wire;
I've smelt Adonis stinking in the mire.

The horror of war in Europe looms, again, at the end of the decade. And Auden was one of the poets most occupied with documenting its advance.

The Ascent of F6 received mixed reviews. The *Manchester Guardian* noted that it 'is played against the background of our sick civilisation, and its sharp satire cuts, among other things, at imperialism, patriotism, war'. But its incoherent and incomprehensible ending proved a problem. The poem we know today has slipped its confines in the Auden and Isherwood play, and, in its new version, has found rich and varied afterlives. It's shed those extravagantly absurd, outrageous final verses, and instead has two more stanzas, added by Auden so the poem can stand alone as a 'song'. So, how has a piece of vicious and absurd political satire transformed into a much-loved reflection on personal grief and loss?

The third stanza of the poem does lots of work, shifting from that public register and focus – aeroplanes, sky-writing, traffic policemen and 'public doves' – to something far more personal. Suddenly, the poem pivots into a direct, first-person account of grief. The word 'my' is repeated nine times in this verse alone; 'I' appears twice. In fact, the stanza still uses public, even civic imagery, but brilliantly transposes it into an acutely personal meaning. 'He was my North, my South, my East and West' sets out the points of the compass and suggests that, while this might not actually be a public loss, for the poem's speaker, he was the whole world. The line 'My working week and my Sunday rest' looks, again, beyond the private to the outward-facing realms of work, organised religion and social decorum. But that repeated 'my' makes it personal. It becomes clear that the public imagery of the poem should be understood not literally, but as metaphor.

In the last stanza, we're back to those instructions again, mirroring the first verse of the poem. But they're now doing something rather different. This is beyond even the absurd over-reaching of civic ceremonial we imagined at the start of the poem. Here, the entire landscape of the earth and the heavens should be boxed up and moth-balled. It's no longer relevant or necessary. The last stanza is perhaps even more exaggerated than the first (though, significantly, it deals in timeless symbols rather than the consumerist trappings of modernity). But it lands differently. We've moved now into the register of the personal, aching with the agony of loss and despair.

So, given its satirical origins, why does this poem work as a genuine reflection on grief? How does it speak so powerfully to so many of us at times of mourning and pain? It's not just that everyone knows it from that scene in *Four Weddings*. The final stanza makes new sense of the first verse. We recognise there, and in the poem as a whole, something of the self-conscious, helpless absurdity of grief. Our outrage that life carries on as normal. Our sense of indecorum and affront that, for everyone else, it's business as usual. How dare the world keep turning? The poem imagines the rage and anguish of our grief as a great dictator, stopping the world in its tracks. Why can't we cut off the telephone and put out the stars? Why isn't our loss written in the sky for all to see, marked by the council and the government, tied around the necks of the public doves?

The version of Auden's poem we know and love still bears traces of its satirical, political purpose in 1930s England, taking a vicious swipe at nationalism, the rising tide of totalitarianism, modern consumer culture, political and media manipulations. But, removed from the original play, and with the later revisions, 'Funeral Blues' becomes something more: an achingly honest poem about the realities of loss, voicing the outrage and absurdity of grief in ways that aren't usually spoken. Auden, both then and now, tells us the truth.

22.

Poetry after Auschwitz

'September Song' by Geoffrey Hill (1968)

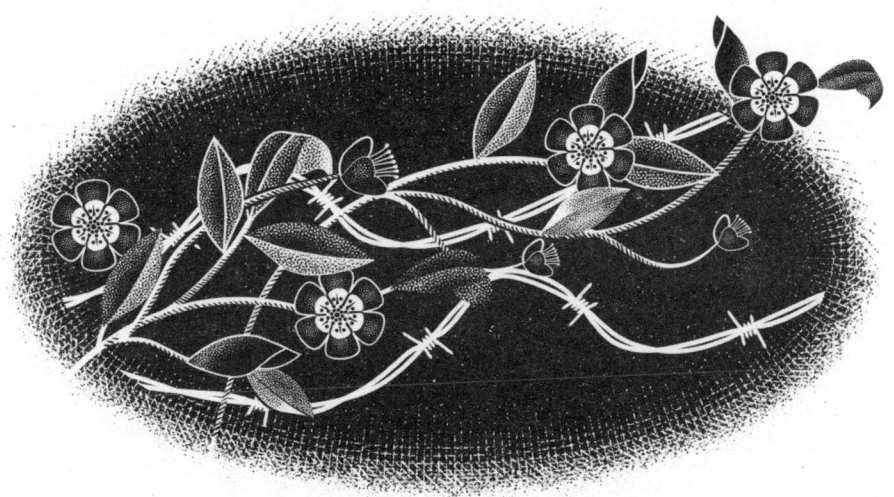

Is it possible to write about the Holocaust if you weren't there? Whose history is it to tell? We might go back to the assertion of German philosopher Theodor Adorno in 1949 (often misquoted and misunderstood) that 'to write poetry after Auschwitz is barbaric'. Can there be poetry after Auschwitz? Are there moments in history when poetry fails?

In one sense, the Holocaust is not England's history. It is, first and foremost, the history of the six million Jewish people, across Europe, murdered as part of a systematic programme of genocide, alongside the persecution and murder of millions of others from minorities and groups targeted by the Nazi state. But the Holocaust is also the world's history, everyone's history. The history of England is not separate, insular, cut off from global – or even, in this case, European – events. Boundaries drawn on a map are irrelevant: England is involved and connected with the Holocaust, and with its memorialisation.

In 'September Song', published in 1968, the English poet Geoffrey Hill (1932–2016) wrestles with questions around writing the Holocaust, including his own relationship to it, the legitimacy of his voice and poetic form, and the limits of poetry itself. Can poetry always engage meaningfully with history? What have literary aesthetics got to do with genocide and atrocity? What is the ethical purpose of poetry and imagination alongside facts and evidence? Hill's poem gives us an alternative way into England's place in the Second World War: the Home Front, the perspective of children, public reactions to Nazi atrocities and the fraught process of re-evaluating history, identity and responsibility.

born 19.6.32 — deported 24.9.42

Undesirable you may have been, untouchable
you were not. Not forgotten
or passed over at the proper time.

As estimated, you died. Things marched,
sufficient, to that end.
Just so much Zyklon and leather, patented
terror, so many routine cries.

(I have made
an elegy for myself it
is true)

September fattens on vines. Roses
flake from the wall. The smoke
of harmless fires drifts to my eyes.

This is plenty. This is more than enough.

Geoffrey Hill lived through the Second World War not as a sol-
dier, but as a child, and 'September Song' is an unusual kind of war
poetry. Born in 1932, Hill grew up in Worcestershire – a part of the
border region between England and Wales known as the Welsh Mar-
ches. He describes a rural and apparently idyllic childhood: exploring
the local countryside, reading and composing poetry in the midst
of nature. This poem brings childhood into focus, asking us to
think about memory, voice and responsibility. 'September Song'
imagines a child murdered in the Holocaust: their date of birth and
date of deportation given beneath the title. This is the first of the
poem's negotiations with history – an adjustment of scale: the vast,
unimaginable horror of genocide represented with a single life.

The first line twists on the irony of 'untouchable': shunned and
cast out by society, the child is not beyond the reach of its violence.

Not 'passed over at the proper time': the language echoes the Jewish festival of Passover, the celebration of the Exodus of the Israelites from Egypt, their children 'passed over' and spared by the Angel of Death while the first-born sons of Pharaoh and their Egyptian enslavers are killed. There is no such deliverance here.

The second stanza moves into a different register: rather than language of religion and ritual, it's the vocabulary of genocide on an industrial scale. The child dies 'as estimated'. The process is 'sufficient'. The poem itself becomes a miniature inventory of 'Zyklon and leather'; the terror of the victims is 'patented' – a manufactured product; their horror 'so many routine cries' – a banal quota, logged and tallied. For four lines, the poem tries out the language of the industrialised Final Solution: words as collaborators, so readily complicit and compliant, just like so many ordinary people who played their part in the Nazi genocide machine.

How to write – or speak – about the Holocaust? From the very start, following the liberation of the western concentration camps, reports and media coverage in Britain struggled with this problem. The liberation of Bergen-Belsen, in April 1945, was covered widely in British media, including the Pathé news film screened in cinemas, making a huge impact on the public consciousness. Belsen was not itself an extermination camp, and housed not only Jews but many other prisoners, including prisoners of war. But by 1945, tens of thousands of Jewish men, women and children had been brought there. Conditions at the end of the war were horrific, with disease, starvation and exhaustion rife. Early reports were beset with anxieties about what could be shown and how it should be told. The Ministry of Information documentary assembled in early summer 1945 under the working title 'German Atrocity Film' was instead released as the 'German Concentration Camps Factual Survey', muting the language of horror and instead emphasising facts, evidence and objectivity.

Yet even facts have their limits. Richard Dimbleby's report for the BBC from Belsen in April 1945 was not broadcast until several days later, his bosses initially refusing to believe that the horrors he described were real. Dimbleby's report opens with an assurance that he has waited to be 'absolutely sure of the facts now available', and he notes again, at the end, that each fact has been 'verified'. 'Here', he begins his account, 'unadorned are the facts', running through statistics which convey the sheer, horrifying scale of death and suffering in the camp. But facts themselves fail. Dimbleby comments: 'Those are the simple horrible facts of Belsen. But horrible as they are, they can convey little or nothing in themselves.' Throughout his landmark report, Dimbleby wrestles with the inadequacy of facts to represent what he has seen in Bergen-Belsen, to communicate both the vast magnitude and the intense individual suffering of the Nazi genocide.

Among the thousands of people watching the Pathé footage of Bergen-Belsen in the cinema was Nella Last, a middle-aged Lancashire housewife, who kept a diary for the Mass Observation Archive – a project to document the experiences and feelings of ordinary people in Britain – from 1939 to 1966. She's sometimes known today as 'Housewife, 49', after the heading of her first diary entry and the dramatisation of her diaries for television by Victoria Wood. Last describes initially avoiding 'the Belsen horror-camp pictures', feeling that the photos in the paper were 'quite dreadful enough'. But the film is shown again in her local cinema – apparently the result of a special request – and Last is deeply affected. 'I looked in such pity', she writes, 'marvelling how human beings could have so clung to life'. The Pathé footage triggers a series of bewildered, anguished questions for Last – but, crucially, she is not satisfied with a purely emotional response. Her diary entry continues with a robust, critical reappraisal of Britain's role, and the responsibility of nations beyond Nazi Germany. She used to have 'a deep aversion to interference,' she writes, explaining that she previously felt countries should be allowed to 'develop their own way' and get on with their own affairs. Belsen changes all that. 'No power can be left so alone that, under a veil of secrecy, *any*thing can happen.'

Children were watching the newsreel of Bergen-Belsen, too, and we know its impact from the testimony of some who saw it.

The author Alan Garner, who grew up in Cheshire, recalls the horror of the Belsen films. 'Although children were forbidden entry, we had always known the free way in. I saw the films four times. The not-dead corpse in the black skull-cap, picking over his shirt and grinning at the camera that had come too late; the bulldozer ploughing its graceful, hideous choreography into the mass grave.' Garner reflects, like Dimbleby in his dispatch from Belsen, that facts are not enough. 'I knew a lot of facts', he says, 'but could not give them a context. Then, within minutes, the facts came together and I was violently wise.' Suddenly, he explains, he understood the war which had formed the constant backdrop to his childhood: 'It was about the ovens and the people inside'.

Despite the horror of Last and Garner, however, wartime Home Intelligence reports show concerns about rising anti-semitism in Britain, even as the full scale of the Nazi genocide became apparent. Anti-Jewish sentiment emerged particularly in talk around black marketeers and profiteering, and avoidance of military conscription, with evidence, in some cases, that it was 'deliberately organised and fostered'.

The place of children on the Home Front, too, was more complicated and ambivalent than popular memory often allows. While Geoffrey Hill's own wartime childhood in Worcestershire was safe and privileged, others had different experiences. We're familiar with images of city evacuees boarding trains to the countryside, as well as children sent away from Europe in the Kindertransport. Many children took on roles helping with the war effort, from agricultural labour to helping with civil defence and assisting Air Raid Precaution teams. But Home Intelligence reports show concerns about juvenile behaviour and delinquency, especially with children often away from home and parental supervision, with many more women, including mothers, working, and young people tasting new-found independence with paid jobs. 'September Song' refocuses our attention on childhood, raising questions about innocence, knowledge and responsibility.

Alan Garner's recollection of the Belsen films suggests that knowledge of the Holocaust brought the brutal arrival of adult wisdom and the loss of childhood innocence. But Geoffrey Hill's wider work reflects on something more disturbing, refusing to sentimentalise childhood as a pre-lapsarian, innocent idyll. Hill's 1971 poetry collection *Mercian Hymns* weaves together early English history with the landscapes of his upbringing and autobiographical elements. In one episode, he overlays the life writing of a mid-twentieth-century childhood with names and echoes from early medieval history. A boy (perhaps an imaginary version of Hill?) lets his friend, Ceolred (a deliberately archaic, Saxon name) play with his treasured toy biplane – and it's lost through a hole in the classroom floorboards.

> . . . After school he lured Ceolred, who was sniggering
> with fright, down to the old quarries, and flayed
> him. Then, leaving Ceolred, he journeyed for hours,
> calm and alone, in his private derelict sandlorry
> named Albion.

In this imagined episode, boyhood play and squabbles spill over into extravagant violence – the brutality of a barbaric medieval king. (The sand-lorry 'Albion' also reminds us that the poem is interleaving stories of individual and nation here.) Hill points to an inherent human capacity for violence, resisting and rejecting the notion of childhood innocence or immunity. Alan Garner, too, hints at something similar in his remembered response to the Belsen films. 'It was right for us to see this, to remind us that what we children were playing was being played better by adults, because they were bigger and had more toys.' Though Geoffrey Hill was still a child during the war, the context of 'September Song' within his wider work suggests that he is nevertheless implicated, like everyone, in the violence and brutality of the Holocaust.

The 'Little England' of Hill's childhood, also, is more ambivalent than the 'green and pleasant land' of poetic tradition. In the beautiful countryside of his childhood Hill traces the scars of violence and conflict across the centuries – from Offa's Dyke to the present. Pastoral undercut with brutality; England's green seeded over blood and bodies. Hill's poetry reflects a complicated, torn nostalgia for England's past and the mythologisation of history. But there's an acute awareness that England is not different or exceptional – not a paragon of virtue and principle. It shares in shameful histories of violence, subjugation and atrocity.

The dates under the title of 'September Song' are significant. Born on the 19th of June 1932, this nameless child almost shares a birthday with Hill – born just the day before him. This proximity is key to Hill's sense of personal connection – and perhaps an uncomfortable awareness of his privilege and the other child's devastating fate. But it's more than just a sense of similarity or connection. Hill pauses in the midst of the poem and turns aside, in parenthesis: 'I have made / an elegy for myself it / is true.' Imagining the Holocaust, he's actually somehow writing about himself. The poem fractures around this moment of confession: an acknowledgement that this account of the Holocaust from Hill's vantage-point of safe, privileged Englishness is an act of appropriation. Does Hill's voice have any legitimacy or authority here? The poem's stumble, bracketed off from the rest of the text, presents an ethical crisis. Is this story really Hill's to tell? And what about the pleasures of making an 'elegy': the aestheticised mourning, the emotional indulgence, the comforts of tradition. Does Hill deserve these consolations?

'September Song' presents the ethical dilemma of meeting the Holocaust with the beauty and carefully crafted aesthetics of poetry. The poet's eloquence is potentially dishonest, dangerous, anaesthetising the horrors of genocide. At best, the attempt of this English poet to write the Holocaust could be considered naive, hubristic. At worst, his poetical imagining of Auschwitz is an act of deceit.

Can Hill only cope with the Holocaust through metaphor, poetry? The poem brims with evasive and euphemistic language. 'Things marched' suggests the phrase 'the march of history' – a kind of weary falling back on cliché – but 'things' is indirect and vague, avoiding direct attention to the actual forces and actions – and people – which cause the death of this child. In his September garden, Hill enjoys 'the smoke of harmless fires'. The ovens and incinerators of Auschwitz are there only in his peripheral vision, displaced from direct representation or confrontation.

After the initial footage of Belsen, British media coverage tended to shrink away from such direct confrontation with the horrors of the camps. The first history of what would later be called the Holocaust written by a British author – Gerald Reitlinger's *The Final Solution* – was not published until 1953. Books on the Holocaust were published throughout the post-war decades, but with significant gaps and silences, and wider interest only gathering from the 1970s onwards.

Early publications grapple uneasily with questions of form, register and audience. The autobiographical account of Ida Cook (well known as romance author Mary Burchell), detailing her rescue of Jews from Nazi Germany during the 1930s, was published in 1950 as *We Followed Our Stars* – by the romance publishers Mills & Boon. Marketed as a memoir of Ida and her sister's love of opera, and their visits overseas to meet opera stars, the story of their work with Jewish refugees is tucked discreetly in the second half of the book. Only much later was the book retitled *Safe Passage*, with further material added on the sisters' efforts, and, in 2016, a subtitle added: 'The Remarkable Story of Two British Sisters Who Rescued Jews from the Nazis'.

John Castle's eyewitness account of Auschwitz in his wartime autobiography *The Password Is Courage* (1954) is romanticised as 'the man who broke into Auschwitz' – a rollicking story of heroism and adventure, released as a 'light-hearted' film by MGM in 1962, starring Dirk Bogarde. Even the entertainment industry magazine *Variety* was bewildered by the choice of mood, remarking in its review that the film suffers from 'an overdose of slapstick humour'. The sequence set in Auschwitz was removed for television release.

While some of these early portrayals might, to us, seem inexplicably crass or misjudged, they reflect a working through of the unprecedented challenge of how to represent this appalling recent history. If facts themselves are not adequate, then how might the Holocaust be shaped into story and narrative? What genre is appropriate? How much truth can the audience cope with? Can the public be expected to look directly at the horrors of Bergen and Auschwitz?

'September Song' views the Holocaust through the filters of literary tradition and aesthetics. Its title, 'Song', signals that we're in the realm of poetics rather than the domain of factual reporting. The poem situates itself in the long tradition of poetry about autumn: the pleasures of goldening, ripening nature, the delights of harvest, the comfort of the familiar signs and rituals of the turning season.

In fact, the poem might specifically recall one other, famous, text: John Keats' ode 'To Autumn' (published in 1820) – learned by rote by many a schoolchild of Hill's generation. The last stanza of 'September Song' speaks back to Keats' 'Season of mists and mellow fruitfulness' as a kind of textual forebear, acutely aware of its place in literary tradition. If Keats helps us make sense of the aesthetics and conventions of Hill's poem, then 'September Song' also potentially changes how we read 'To Autumn'. Phrases in Keats' poem, describing the bees in the hive which have 'o'er-brimmed their clammy cells', and are now 'drowsed with the fume' (the sleepy scent of poppies), the gentle wind which 'lives or dies', and 'barred clouds' (in the sky at sunset) take on disturbing, uncanny new resonances. Perhaps reading Keats' poem after Auschwitz helps us to surface ambivalence and darkness which were always there: some critics have suggested that 'To Autumn' is Keats' own political response to the 1819 Peterloo Massacre. Or perhaps the imagery of 'To Autumn' after the Holocaust is forever changed, marred, tainted. Can we go back to poetry after Auschwitz?

Throughout, Geoffrey Hill's 'September Song' is marked with the language of measure. 'Sufficient', 'just so much', 'plenty': the quantitative vocabulary of ledgers, records and tallies – the Final Solution – but also the vocabulary of poetic decorum: metre, counts of syllables, rhythms and words. The last words of the poem hint at those mechanics of poetic craft: 'This is more than enough' – the lines have done their work and mustn't slip into superfluity or excess. There's also a hint, of course, that this is 'more than enough' for Hill to cope with: even the 'harmless fires' with their indirect allusion to Auschwitz are almost too much for him to take.

There's also another echo in those last words: the language of politicians, apologists, historians, reporters. A hint of clubbable, affable reassurance and absolution. Responding to questions in the 1960s about whether the British government had done enough to intervene in Europe and potentially halt the atrocities of the Holocaust, Prime Minister Harold Macmillan concluded that he was 'satisfied that everything possible was done'. The poem leaves us with questions about what constitutes 'enough', and whether poetry can ever be enough to write the histories of Auschwitz. It also leaves us with a stark challenge in our own historical moment. We make and read poetry in a world which continues to tolerate massacre or genocide: in the 1990s in the Balkans and Rwanda, for instance, and today in Myanmar, Sudan, Gaza . . . What is our responsibility as a nation and as individuals? Is everything possible done to intervene and save human lives? When, the poem compels us to ask, is enough?

23.

North–South Divide

'England's Glory' by Fleur Adcock
(1986)

A line from the Severn to the Wash? The threshold of the three English regions of the north-east, Yorkshire and the Humber, and the north-west? Or anywhere beyond the Watford Gap? There's no consensus on where to draw the boundary. But England's north–south divide is as old as the nation itself. In Margaret Thatcher's Britain of the 1980s, these divides became ever more visible and acute, in the context of de-industrialisation in the north, the banking and finance boom in London and the south-east, and, perhaps most emblematically of all, the bitter and protracted miners' strike of 1984–5.

'England's Glory' is a poem by Fleur Adcock, a New Zealand poet of English and Northern Irish ancestry, who lived in England for eight years as a child, and returned as an adult. Published in her 1986 collection *The Incident Book*, the poem imagines the 'England's Glory' matches preferred in the north of England in contrast with the Bryant & May 'safety matches' more popular in the south. It's a wry, humorous look at England's perennial north–south divide, written with the arch distance and detached observation of an outsider. It's funny, playing on familiar stereotypes, laughing at the petty rivalries and snobberies of (geographically speaking) next-door neighbours. It doesn't pick a side.

But the poem isn't detached from the politics of 1980s Britain. *The Incident Book* also includes a group of poems called 'Thatcherland', looking at life in Thatcher's own constituency of Finchley, North London. Adcock notices the small stories unfolding across the country in these years of social and economic change. She's interested in divisions and inequalities wherever they're found.

And, behind 'England's Glory', the backdrop of the miners' strike looms large.

Red-tipped, explosive, self-complete:
one you can strike on the coal-face, or
the sole of your boot. Not for the south, where
soft men with soft hands rub effete
brown-capped sticks on a toning strip
chequered with coffee-grounds, the only
match for the matches, and any lonely
stray (if they let them stray) picked up
from a table or found loose in a pocket
can't, without its container, flare
fire at a stroke: is not a pure-
ly self-contained ignition unit.

'Security' proclaims the craven
yellow box with its Noah's ark,
'Brymay' Special Safety's trade-mark
for southern consumption. That's all right, then:
bankers can take them home to Surrey
for their cigars, and scatter the odd
match-head, whether or not it's dead,
on their parquet floors, without the worry
of subsequent arson. Not like here
where a match is a man's match, an object
to be handled with as much respect
but as casually as a man's beer.

You can't mistake the England's Glory
box: its crimson, blue and white
front's a miniature banner, fit
for the Durham Miners' Gala, gaudy
enough to march ahead of a band.
Forget that placid ark: the vessel

this one's adorned with has two funnels
gushing fat blue smoke to the wind.
The side's of sandpaper. The back
label's functional, printed with either
holiday vouchers, a special offer
on World Cup tickets, or this month's joke.

Somewhere across England's broad
midriff, wanderingly drawn
from west to east, there exists a line
to the north of which the shops provide
(catering for a sudden switch
of taste) superior fried fish, runnier
yogurt, blouses cut for the fuller
northern figure; and the northern match.
Here England's Glory begins; through all
the vigorous north it reigns unrivalled
until its truce with Scottish Bluebell
round about Berwick and Carlisle.

It's OK to laugh: it's a funny, playful poem and northerners and southerners alike will assure you they can take a joke. Adcock contrasts the 'strike anywhere' 'England's Glory' matches of the north with the safety-conscious Bryant & May (or 'BryMay') matches more common in the south, which can only be lit by striking on the box ('the only / match for the matches', as the poem quips). The yellow Bryant & May box bears the image of Noah's Ark: that symbol of protection and safety which preserved the animals, two by two, from the dangers of the Flood, familiar from Sunday School stories and toys on the nursery floor. 'England's Glory', on the other hand, shows a battleship (the nineteenth-century HMS *Devastation*) in full steam, surrounded by decorative flourishes in red, white and blue.

As much as a ribbing of England's regions, the joke's on poetry, too. 'England's Glory' is a title which promises patriotic grandeur, in the long tradition of praise to the nation – but turns out to be a mock-heroic paean to a matchbox. The verse is patterned with intricate rhymes and half-rhymes, only for the words to contort and convolute themselves to fit. The end of the first stanza pushes language to (or perhaps beyond) its limits. The BryMay safety match –

> can't, without its container, flare
> fire at a stroke: is not a pure-
> ly self-contained ignition unit.

Fussy, finnicky word order, and a word split over a line break. A knowing joke, perhaps, about the trick of conjuring a humble box of matches into highbrow praise poetry?

The poem plays on the idea that northerners are tough, hard, full of grit, while southerners – represented here by the 'bankers' of 'Surrey' – are 'soft men with soft hands', anxious about safety and nervous about damaging their 'parquet floors'. The south is a world of 'coffee-grounds' and 'cigars'. Even the matches are 'effete', with their 'craven' yellow box – a timid accessory for wimps. The poem mocks southern softness. But its teasing humour looks both ways. It seems to speak from the north, celebrating northern tradition and grit. 'Not like here', the second verse sneers, looking down at that yellow BryMay box, 'where a match is a man's match, an object / to be handled with as much respect / but as casually as a man's beer'. It's exaggerated – a spoof of a certain kind of self-congratulatory masculine pride: hints of the 'Four Yorkshiremen' made famous by Monty Python, with its competitive hardship and toughness. Look again at the poem's first line. 'Red-tipped, explosive, self-complete'. Is it the matches we're talking about, or are these cheeky epithets for the northerners themselves? Socialist (red) leaning, quick to passion and hardily self-sufficient?

What's also clear is that – both north and south – this is a poem inhabited by men. Adcock's outsider identity – as a New Zealander – means she can get away with her teasing observation and gentle mockery. But her gender, here, makes her an outsider, too. She's dealing in stereotypes and traditions – but specifically masculine ones. She stands back and satirises male tribalism and self-mythologising just as much as any regional differences. The northern world of the poem, it's also worth noting, is a very white one. The diverse South Asian communities of Bradford or Leeds, for example – present since the 1940s – are not visible here.

'England's Glory' derives its comic energy from those well-worn stereotypes of north and south. Those clichés like northern muck and brass versus the gentle hills of the Home Counties and privet hedges of southern suburbia. Short 'a's, flat caps and butties, against bankers, pin stripes and Received Pronunciation. None of this is new in the 1980s, but a set of long-established tropes and caricatures evolved over centuries. In 1937, in his book *The Road to Wigan Pier*, George Orwell lines up some of the stock images of the north: industry, pollution, filth and (for some) money. Travelling by train, he passes through pockets of countryside, then all too quickly again 'the outer slums, and then the slag-heaps, belching chimneys, blast-furnaces, canals, and gasometers of another industrial town'. Orwell also portrays what he calls 'a curious cult of Northernness, a sort of Northern snobbishness', which chimes with the stereotype Adcock lampoons in 'England's Glory'. Orwell writes that:

> A Yorkshireman in the South will always take care to let you know that he regards you as an inferior. If you ask him why, he will explain that it is only in the North that life is 'real life', that the industrial work done in the North is the only 'real' work, that the North is inhabited by 'real' people, the South merely by rentiers and their parasites. The Northerner has 'grit', he is grim, 'dour', plucky, warm-hearted and democratic; the Southerner is snobbish, effeminate and lazy – that at any rate is the theory.

Like Orwell, Adcock picks up (and parodies) that supposed northern doctrine that people in the south are soft, delicate, feeble, nesh.

So, how far back can we trace that great north–south divide? Possibly as far back as the ninth century, when Viking raiders began to settle in the north of England, eventually building a wide region of control, extending down into the Midlands and East Anglia, known as the 'Danelaw'. Traces of Viking language and culture are still there today in the Old Norse origins of northern place names, and in some local dialect. Or perhaps we might look to moments in history when the north has rebelled or stood firm against southern aggression and control. The Harrying of the North in 1069–70, when William the Conqueror waged campaigns to subjugate the north of England. Or the sixteenth-century Rising of the North, when Catholic nobles revolted against the Protestant Queen Elizabeth I.

The groundbreaking English printer, William Caxton, tells an iconic story, at the end of the fifteenth century, about how northerners and southerners can't even understand each other. In the preface to his printed English edition of the *Aeneid*, published in 1490, he narrates how some merchants from the north of England try to buy eggs from a woman in the south. But they ask for 'egges' – derived from Old Norse – while she can only offer 'eyren' – after the Old English word. The bewildered woman protests that she doesn't speak French, and a total breakdown in communication ensues.

Tropes of north and south continue and develop over the nineteenth century. Benjamin Disraeli's 'Two Nations' may refer to the divide between rich and poor, but it comes from his novel *Sybil* and emerges after a character's visit to manufacturing towns in the north. Charles Dickens' depiction of 'Coketown' in *Hard Times* reinforces the image of a dirty, ugly, 'severely workful' north. And Elizabeth Gaskell's novel *North and South* sets up a central crisis of difference between the pastoral, rural (but perhaps rather soft) south and the harsher, industrious north – rather too neatly resolved by the southern Miss Hale and northern Mr Thornton falling in love. The north–south divide, it seems, is as old as England itself.

Fleur Adcock plays with the north–south divide again in her poem 'The Genius of Surrey', also in her collection *The Incident Book*. She recalls the southern English landscape of her childhood, which 'lacked factories' – a (curious and unusual) framing as a deficit or defect. She remembers the countryside of the Home Counties as placid, tame, insipid, contrasting it with Yorkshire mills and the stark hills and factories of Westmorland. Even the local sewage works were known, euphemistically and prettily, as 'Surridge Hill'. 'Surrey's genius', she concludes, 'was found to be for the suburban'. A place of gentle snobbery and softness.

'England's Glory' may caricature northern self-mythologising, but it also offers glimpses of the rich and precious culture of the north of England, at a time when it's under serious threat. The last verse presents a humorous list of cultural markers of northernness – from 'superior fried fish' to 'runnier / yogurt' and 'blouses cut for the fuller / northern figure' – but fondly and with affection. And the resplendent iconography of the England's Glory matchbox is imagined as 'a miniature banner, fit / for the Durham Miners' Gala'. It's 'gaudy / enough to march ahead of a band'. Even the England's Glory match itself is one 'you can strike on the coal-face, or / the sole of your boot'. The industrial heritage and tradition of the north of England – and most especially its mining heritage – are to the fore.

We can't read 'England's Glory', published in 1986, without placing it in the immediate wake of the 1984–5 miners' strike. It's difficult to summarise, in a few lines, such a complex historical context: many other published histories and personal testimonies offer accounts. In 1984, 173 coal mines were operating in the UK, down from 1,000 in the early twentieth century. Around 231,000 people remained employed in the coal-mining industry in the decade to 1982. Ian MacGregor, head of the National Coal Board, had declared many pits 'uneconomic' and announced a plan to close twenty collieries, with a loss of around 20,000 jobs. The leader of the National Union of Miners (NUM), Arthur Scargill, always maintained that this figure was an under-statement: secret papers released thirty years later by the National Archives show that a figure of seventy closures was considered, while another file suggests that the final plans were to close around forty to fifty pits.

There was no national ballot for strike action, but regional branches of the NUM made their own decisions. The strike began in March 1984: almost universally observed in Yorkshire and north-east England – as well as, beyond England, in south Wales and

Scotland, and in Kent in the south. There was less support for the strike in Nottinghamshire, Leicestershire, south Derbyshire, north Wales and the West Midlands, with the majority of miners continuing to work, but acute tensions within many local communities. Could that 'self-contained ignition unit' of the England's Glory match, in Adcock's poem, be a knowing nod to the particular militancy of the Yorkshire coalfields? More militant NUM leaders like Mick McGahey, who opposed a national ballot, did indeed hope that strikes in the Yorkshire coalfields would ignite wider support and a concerted national campaign. But that was not to be.

At the NUM conference in 1984, after eighteen weeks of the strike, Arthur Scargill described the 'intense hardship' experienced by striking miners and their families, honouring their 'incredible determination and courage'. He went on:

> Not only have they faced deprivation and hunger – they have found themselves in the front line facing the most massive assault on civil liberties and human rights ever launched against trade unionists in this country. On the picket lines, riot police in full battle gear, on horseback and on foot, accompanied by police dogs, have been unleashed in violent attacks on our members.

Party politics polarised and fractured around the dispute. Margaret Thatcher used her Conservative Party Leader's speech at Brighton in 1984 – the morning after the IRA bombing in Brighton's Grand Hotel – to condemn the 'violence' of 'an organised revolutionary minority'. Deploring the miners' demands, she invokes early English history and the world of the Old English poem *The Battle of Maldon*, with its Viking Danegeld. She quotes Rudyard Kipling: 'We never pay anyone Dane-geld, no matter how trifling the cost; / For the end of that game is oppression and shame, and the nation that plays it is lost'.

While Neil Kinnock told the Labour Party Conference at Blackpool in 1984 that he found 'the case for coal compelling, and the case for the communities overwhelming', he and some of his allies were hugely uncomfortable with Scargill's tactics, including the failure to ensure broad support for the strike through a national ballot. In 1984, the Durham Miners' Gala was cancelled and a rally held instead. Photos show Kinnock and Scargill together, deceptively suggesting solidarity. But, when Kinnock stood to address the crowd, some miners, angered by what they saw as his half-hearted support, turned their backs.

But Kinnock joins his voice with Scargill and others in accusing Thatcher of ignorance and contempt for the north. In his Labour Leader's speech in Bournemouth in 1985, Kinnock rails at the government's intransigence and refusal to offer concessions. 'All we get', he observes, 'is a fleeting visit to what the Prime Minister thinks of as "the North" . . .' In an interview with the *News of the World* (a strongly anti-strike paper) published on 20 May 1984, Margaret Thatcher dismisses the possibility of a deepening north–south divide. She 'turned on her opponents who claim Government policies are creating a divide between North and South', the report states. Thatcher is quoted:

'A lot of heavy industry was concentrated in the North and a lot of the business has been moved away from this country. But now we are getting a much wider variety of work in the North', she says.

'It gave me a tremendous fillip as well as the North-East, when Nissan said they were going to build their new car plant there. It boosted the whole morale of the area.

'But it does grieve me greatly when I see coal orders for Durham not being taken up. I know there's a feeling that the North hasn't been thought about but that is simply not true.'

Thatcher speaks of boosts to local morale as new industry arrives. But, in most mining communities, no major new industry replaced the traditional employment and community focus of the pit. The heritage and pride evoked by the England's Glory matchbox – the customs and culture of galas, banners, marches, bands; all the rich identity built over generations around the coal industry and its towns – was crumbling.

While north–south contrasts and inequalities deepened – across health, life expectancy and wealth – London and the south-east were in the midst of a banking and finance boom. The pull of London had never been greater: its concentration of national power and decision-making, as regional powers were lessened; its building and expansion, with attendant pressures on housing for ordinary working people. In September 1987, Lord Young of Graffham, Secretary of State for Trade and Industry, argued that it was simply the 'turn' of the south to enjoy wealth and prosperity.

> Until 70 years ago the North was always the richest part of the country. The two present growth industries – the City and tourism – are concentrated in the South. I try to encourage people to go North; that is where all the great country houses are because that's where the wealth was. Now some of it is in the South. It's our turn, that's all.

With the irony of hindsight, we now see how little time there was before the bubble of that southern boom burst with the recession of the early 1990s. Yet the south of England, on many measures and indices, remains significantly better off in the long term.

We might compare Fleur Adcock's witty, sardonic outsider's voice in 'England's Glory' with poetry written in the 1980s in and from the north, in northern voices. The Leeds poet Tony Harrison, perhaps, whose poems brim with anger and resentment as well as tender memories of ordinary family life. Poems which rail against the exclusion of northern accents and northern experiences from the literary canon. Personal stories of disenfranchisement and marginalisation. And Harrison's great poem *v.* – which takes a quote from Arthur Scargill on the importance of words and learning as its epigraph – written in response to graffiti sprayed by football fans on gravestones in the cemetery where his parents are buried. First published in 1985 and written during the miners' strike, the poem rages at deepening social divisions and conflicts: working class v. the Establishment; black v. white; north v. south – and Leeds United v. the world. Yet, where Adcock is arch and wry, Harrison is furious and heartbroken.

Adcock reminds us, though, that north–south isn't the only way to look at divisions and inequalities in England in the 1980s. *The Incident Book* includes a group of poems titled 'Thatcherland', focused on Margaret Thatcher's own parliamentary constituency of Finchley, London, where Adcock also lived. In 'Street Scene, London N2', Adcock describes a pair of young men smashing a piano for fuel. In 'Post Office', she depicts elderly locals queuing for their pensions and sharing memories, evoking a rapidly changing community, loss of belonging and social fragmentation.

And the north doesn't have a monopoly on heroic narratives of worker organisation and industrial action. Perhaps the yellow box of Bryant & May matches reminds us of the matchgirl strike of 1888, based around their factory in Bow, east London – an early landmark in the British labour movement. The strike led not only to the banning of white phosphorus in matches – which had impacted so devastatingly on the health of factory workers – but also formation of the Union of Women Matchmakers. Not all union militancy is either male, or northern.

It's always more complicated. As the last verse of Adcock's poem hints, identities are interleaved and messy. 'Somewhere across England' is as precisely as Adcock can pin down that north–south dividing line. The poem ends with a wry reference to the Scottish border and another, equally proud, identity represented by 'Scottish Bluebell'. England's Glory matches were originally made in Gloucester by S. J. Moreland and Sons, which became a subsidiary of Bryant & May in 1913, moving into full ownership by BryMay in 1938. Only later, production of the matches moved to Bryant & May's Garston factory in Liverpool, from where England's Glory were sold mainly to the north of England and the Midlands. Matches made by the very same company in Glasgow were marketed in Scotland as 'Scottish Bluebell'. A small island, but tightly drawn identities, rivalries, differences and overlapping geographies of national and regional pride.

Adcock's collection *The Incident Book*, in which 'England's Glory' appears, takes its title not from the world of high literary culture, but from industry. Like an incident book at a coal mine, on a factory floor, or in a workshop, it logs accidents, injuries, near misses, damage. A workaday, diligent archive of the small details and impacts it's imperative to record. But what about the miners' strike itself? Where does that appear in 'England's Glory'? Is it strange that this major context plays out entirely off stage? Adcock's poem may be witty and comic, but that doesn't mean it's without political drive and heft. It offers a striking depiction – albeit fondly teasing – of a way of life under threat. With the strike of a match, tiny details of northern culture and tradition are illuminated, just for a moment. The second line of the poem centres that image of the match 'you can strike on the coal-face'. 'Strike' is the key to the whole poem: folded into the language, into the deep seam running through its lines. The miners' strike is there all along, hiding in plain sight; the poem lit with a flame of pride, compassion and empathy from the beginning to the end.

24.

Winds of Change

'Hurricane Hits England' by Grace Nichols (1996)

15 October 1987. After the BBC One O'Clock News, Michael Fish comes on with the weather forecast. 'Earlier on today, apparently', he tells viewers, 'a woman rang the BBC and said she heard there was a hurricane on the way. Well, if you're watching, don't worry, there isn't!' (In the interests of historical accuracy, it's only fair to note that Fish did say the weather would be 'windy', and the map clearly indicated 'gales'.) As Fish spoke, an area of low pressure was moving from the Bay of Biscay towards the UK. It developed overnight into a violent storm, an exceptional weather event with wind speeds of up to 100 m.p.h.: 15 million trees felled, ships wrecked, structural damage to buildings and 18 people killed. The worst of the impact was in the south of England, especially coastal areas and the 'Home Counties'. Although not technically a hurricane, as the storm didn't originate in the tropics, the term quickly took hold in the popular imagination, and the label stuck.

Grace Nichols' poem 'Hurricane Hits England' is an intensely personal response to the Great Storm of 1987. Born in 1950 in Guyana (then the colony of British Guiana), Nichols migrated to Britain in 1977 and lived for a short time in London before moving to Sussex and the countryside of the South Downs. In the poem, she lies awake through the night, listening to the Great Storm buffet the landscape around her. The idea of a hurricane striking England – something with the power of a tropical storm making landfall on English soil – connects Nichols' home in England with her Caribbean heritage. She has described 'Hurricane Hits England' as 'a bridging-poem between the two cultures': a deeply personal exploration of migration, diaspora and hybrid identity.

Beyond Nichols' own unique experience, her poem also opens a window onto wider stories of twentieth-century migration to Britain, including the landmark arrival of the *Empire Windrush* in 1948. Indeed, the name 'Windrush' hovers only a semantic sidestep away from the 'hurricane' of Nichols' title. While Black people have been part of English places and communities since at least as far back as Roman times, the second half of the twentieth-century brought mass migration and more rapid change. New negotiations of 'Englishness' and identities, new voices and traditions enriching and enlarging British and English culture, diverse communities carrying their own diasporic heritage. But the wider context of Nichols' poem is also one of gradually tightening laws around citizenship and immigration, eventually reaching Theresa May's 'hostile environment' and the horrors of the so-called Windrush Scandal. Grace Nichols' poem refocuses this vast and complex migration history through the intensity and immediacy of individual experience, one stormy night in 1987.

It took a hurricane, to bring her closer
to the landscape.
Half the night she lay awake,
the howling ship of the wind,
its gathering rage,
like some dark ancestral spectre,
fearful and reassuring.

Talk to me Huracan
Talk to me Oya
Talk to me Shango
and Hattie,
my sweeping, back-home cousin.

24: Winds of Change

Tell me why you visit
an English coast?
What is the meaning
of old tongues
reaping havoc in new places?

The blinding illumination,
even as you short-
circuit us
into further darkness?

What is the meaning of trees
falling heavy as whales –
their crusted roots
their cratered graves?
O why is my heart unchained?

Tropical Oya of the Weather,
I am aligning myself to you.
I am following the movement of your winds
I am riding the mystery of your storm.

Ah, sweet mystery,
come to break the frozen lake in me,
shaking the foundations of the very trees
within me.
Come to let me know –
that the earth is the earth is the earth.

The opening lines hint at dislocation or disconnection – an uncertainty around belonging. 'It took a hurricane, to bring her closer / to the landscape'. Immediately, the poem is animated by a sense of in-betweenness, dealing in a series of tensions, paradoxes and ambivalences. Listening to the clamour of the storm, Nichols is poised between terror and a strange feeling of comfort. Its raging force is both 'Fearful and reassuring'. The image of the wind as a 'howling ship' invites associations with voyaging, oceans, journeys – but also, more disturbingly, with the cries and howls of people packed into 'slavers' as human cargo. The storm's presence as a 'dark ancestral spectre' opens up connections to heritage and ancestry, as well as the traumatic history of transatlantic African enslavement. This is a dreadful, unlooked-for, yet strangely consoling haunting.

The storm becomes a mystical experience. In the second verse, the repetition of 'Talk to me', beginning the first three lines, beats a deliberate rhythm: a steady and building incantation, invoking old gods and ancestors. 'Huracan' is a Carib word for the storm (hurricane). Then the poem summons gods and divine spirits from African traditions, brought to South America and the Caribbean by enslaved people. 'Oya' is the Yoruba name for an Orisha (divine spirit) or goddess of winds, storms and lightning. 'Shango': the powerful ruler deity, who wields a double-headed battle-axe and is worshipped through speaking (Bata) drums. And, lastly, a more homely name: 'Hattie', the deceptively endearing moniker of a devastating tropical cyclone in the 1961 Atlantic hurricane season. Hattie originated over the south-western Caribbean, and reached peak force as a Category 5 hurricane. But Nichols speaks to her with easy familiarity: a ready kinship and intimacy with her 'sweeping back-home cousin'.

Nichols asks these gods and kindred spirits: 'Tell me why you visit / an English coast?' It's just one of the many questions which run through the poem, capturing her bewilderment, confusion and a search for meaning. She's making sense of the intense, disorienting presence of the storm, and of her place in the world. There's a power in speaking these names aloud, the 'old tongues' awakening in the rolling hills of England, ancient beliefs and magics working in a new landscape.

Did you hesitate or falter at the phrase 'reaping havoc'? It's not the standard collocation: the familiar phrase, in British English, would be 'wreaking havoc'. But when Nichols describes the old spirits 'Reaping havoc / in new places', it's not a slip but a deliberate twist. Transposing 'wreak' to 'reap' is more ambivalent and unsettling. Rather than merely an image of violence or vengeance, the language suggests natural cycles and patterns: 'reap what you sow', 'reaping' the crop, bringing the harvest home. Are these ancient gods coming to harvest chaos, and gather in havoc? Perhaps, at the darkest edge of this metaphor, there's a hint that this might be a day of reckoning: the old spirits reaping the consequences of ancient wrongs and hurts. But, again, the poem is poised in ambiguity: fruitful havoc, a devastating harvest, the violence of the storm gathering meaning home.

In other writing, Nichols has recalled the 'cold morning on 3 November 1977' when she arrived at Heathrow Airport with her partner, the poet John Agard, and her young daughter. She remembers 'shivering in my stylish but light pantsuit on that frosty autumn morning'. The family lived in London for a few months before moving to Sussex: the rolling downland and open countryside where she lies awake, on that night in 1987, listening to the storm. Nichols reflects elsewhere on the disorientations and adaptations that came with migration to Britain: the need to adapt to English climate, customs and culture, and to change her 'calypso ways'.

Elements of Nichols' experience are shared by many others who travelled from across the British Empire or Commonwealth to Britain in the second half of the twentieth century, in a period of expanding migration and growing diversity. The arrival of the *Empire Windrush* in 1948 – a generation before Nichols' own migration – becomes a symbolic moment in the historical narrative, described by Nichols herself, in a 2018 interview with the magazine *Wasafiri*, as 'an important psychic milestone in post-war Caribbean migration to Britain'.

Before docking at the Port of Tilbury (for London), on the late evening of 21 June 1948, the *Empire Windrush*'s last port of call had been Kingston, Jamaica, in April. But the ship had also picked up passengers from Bermuda, Trinidad and Tampico, Mexico. The ship's records show that 802 passengers gave their last place of residence as somewhere in the Caribbean.

As the *Windrush* passengers embarked from the Caribbean, and disembarked in London, the 1948 British Nationality Act was working its way through parliament, to come into effect on 1 January 1949. Everyone born in the Anglophone Caribbean already held British subject status and the free right of entry to the UK. The act reinforced this status, and also enabled people from newly independent territories (including the British dominions) to be considered Commonwealth citizens. The act made 'provision for British nationality and for citizenship of the United Kingdom and Colonies', defining citizenship of the United Kingdom and the colonies as a single category: 'the expression "British subject" and the expression "Commonwealth citizen" shall have the same meaning'. Those first *Windrush* passengers, along with many others to follow from across the empire and Commonwealth, held exactly the same legal citizenship status as anyone else in Britain, legally indistinguishable from someone born in England. They saw themselves, rightly, as coming to the 'mother country', where they would belong.

We're familiar with black and white photos and grainy footage of those *Windrush* arrivals: hopeful, apprehensive and eager to make a new life. Many passengers on the *Windrush* were ex-servicemen who had fought for Britain in the Second World War. And the *Windrush* is traditionally represented as a male story. Partly, perhaps, that's because of that iconic Pathé newsreel, which shows only men, dapper in their suits, ties and trilbies, as the ship docks in London. The Trinidadian calypsonian Lord Kitchener (Aldwyn Roberts) features, too, singing 'London is the place for me', specially composed for the occasion.

But the 1,027 Windrush passengers were men, women (just over 300), and 86 children aged 12 and under. The sea arrival landing card completed by each passenger gives a glimpse into their lives and their journeys from Tilbury Docks, logging their onward destination and address. Ivy Horan, fifty-two, was headed for Clarence Gate Gardens, W1, where she hoped to find work in her occupation as a 'household domestic'. Phyllis and Ignatius Cruchley travelled on together to Carlisle Place, SW5, she to find work as a 'household domestic' and he to continue in the 'medical' profession. Anna Malcolm was set for Surrey, to find work in her career as a nurse.

Some onward addresses given are connected with employment, including Westminster Bank, Nestlé Milk Co. and the Colonial Office or War Office. Two hundred and eighty-six passengers – mostly men – were temporarily housed in the Deep-Level Shelter at Clapham South underground station, previously used as a bomb shelter during the Blitz. After three weeks, all had reportedly found alternative accommodation. Again, the photos show young men, smart in suits and hats, bunking, eating and socialising together.

Grace Nichols' poetry, a generation later, presents an important female perspective on twentieth-century migration narratives. Her poems centre stories of women's experience, influenced by the 1970s Women's Movement and second-wave feminism just as much as the politics of immigration and diaspora. In her collections *Fat Black Woman's Poems* and *Lazy Thoughts of a Lazy Woman*, female experiences come to the fore. The poems are reflective and challenging – but also funny, sexy, irreverent. 'The Fat Black Woman Goes Shopping' ends with the scathing, throwaway line 'Nothing much beyond size 14'. 'Wherever I Hang' reflects on coming 'to this place call England' and 'feeling like I in a dream'. 'I don't really know where I belaang', Nichols admits. But, she concludes: 'Wherever I hang me knickers – that's my home'. It's a playful, cheeky take on migration narratives (with a nod to Marvin Gaye).

'Hurricane Hits England', too, centres the female and feminine. Nichols draws to her 'Tropical Oya', the goddess of 'the Weather'. In that penultimate verse, we have another incantatory spiritual affirmation: 'I am aligning . . . ', 'I am following . . . ', 'I am riding . . . '. Through this mystical communion with the divine spirit, Nichols gathers power and energy. Out of disconnection, fracture and displacement, she becomes one with the goddess, here in the green hills of Sussex.

Out of the violence of the storm, ultimately, comes understanding and affirmation. In the fourth verse, there's that startling oxymoron of 'blinding illumination' – the force of two apparent opposites in violent collision. Perhaps the phrase calls to mind the more familiar collocation 'blind faith', often used to describe belief (and trust) in religion or authority without evidence or logical reason. But this is different: a blinding flash of epiphany in which everything is revealed and made clear – even if only for a split second. Again, this is imagery of paradox and ambivalence: lightning which blinds, but darkness (the night, clouds, power cuts) which brings revelation.

The layered imagery points us back, repeatedly, to memories of the Caribbean. Nichols asks 'What is the meaning of trees / falling heavy as whales'? The Sussex hills become, for a moment, a storm-lashed coast where mighty creatures are beached and lost. The trees' 'crusted roots' trigger another set of associations with migrant experience: identity, rootedness, belonging, the pain and rupture of being 'uprooted'. There are darker allusions, too. The fallen trees expose 'cratered graves': a disturbing confrontation with buried violence and loss. But Nichols exclaims, almost ecstatically, in that single-line verse: 'O why is my heart unchained?' The poem invokes the language of bondage, the weight of historical pain and slavery. Nichols is still asking questions, searching for meaning. But the storm gifts her with a sense of release, freedom and elation. A strange and wondrous benediction.

Wind recurs as a motif and metaphor throughout Nichols' poetry – some of which confronts the historical violence and horror of slavery directly. The collection *I Is a Long Memoried Woman* (1983, winner of the Commonwealth Poetry Prize), gives first-person voice to the story of an imagined enslaved Black African woman. It's a powerful, unflinching, visceral series of poems, which confronts bodily, emotional and spiritual violence and degradation. But the poems 'Blow Winds Blow' and 'Wind a Change' strikingly express resistance and rebellion, Black power and survival, hopes for justice and transformation.

A generation before Nichols' arrival in Britain, those *Windrush* passengers disembarked with a sense of possibility and optimism. Together with those who followed, they made major contributions to British society, communities and culture: from food to culture, language, arts, sports, business and economy. But, over the second half of the twentieth century, Britain becomes less welcoming.

Already, in November 1954, a House of Commons debate on 'Colonial Immigrants' includes the concern, expressed by Tom Iremonger, MP for Ilford North, that 'the way is open to thousands of "Dick Whittingtons"'. Henry Hopkinson, Minister of State in the Colonial Office, responds with an affirmation of the legal citizenship position.

As the law stands, any British subject from the Colonies is free to enter this country at any time as long as he can produce satisfactory evidence of his British status. That is not something we want to tamper with lightly. In a world in which restrictions on personal movement and immigration have increased we still take pride in the fact that a man can say *Civis Britannicus sum* whatever his colour may be, and we take pride in the fact that he wants and can come to the Mother country.

In January 1959, a memorandum for Cabinet by the Lord Chancellor raises a series of concerns around 'the problem of coloured immigration', including the 'large numbers of immigrants arriving in this country and their concentration in particular areas, with all the attendant social problems', and the 'criminal activities of a comparatively small number of these immigrants'.

Over the next twenty or so years, as the British Empire breaks up and nations achieve their independence, a series of laws comes into effect seeking to restrict citizenship and the right to entry and residence in the UK. Landmarks include the Commonwealth Immigrants Act, 1962; Commonwealth Immigrants Act, 1968; Immigration Act, 1971. Citizens and subjects from across the former empire are now redefined as 'immigrants', others, aliens. The law asserts tighter requirements on proving settled status, ancestral connections, on eligibility for citizenship. Then, the British Nationality Act, 1981, seeks 'to make fresh provision about citizenship and nationality, and to amend the Immigration Act 1971 as regards the right of abode in the United Kingdom'. Here, the basis for British nationality and citizenship contracts markedly. It's the end of imperial citizenship.

When Grace Nichols arrived in Britain in 1977, this process of tightening citizenship and immigration law was already underway. Questions of belonging are fraught and precarious, as the legal system repeatedly changes the status of migrants, potentially pulling their sense of identity out from under them. There's a clear line from this series of later twentieth-century legal interventions to Theresa May's 'hostile environment' (2012): the aim to make Britain a difficult and challenging place for (in her words) 'illegal immigrants'. Out of this context came the so-called Windrush Scandal (more accurately, the Home Office Scandal), breaking onto the political agenda in 2018, in which people with Commonwealth migrant background or ancestry had been denied citizenship, refused benefits and medical care, threatened with deportation, and in some cases deported from Britain. Many of these people belonged to the *Windrush* generation: they had come to Britain from colonies in the Caribbean that had long been under British jurisdiction. While most came as British subjects, under the terms of the British Nationality Act, theirs had been a long history of British subjecthood under the 1914 British National and Status of Aliens Act and the even earlier, long-established principle in English common law of *jus soli* ('right of the soil'). The scandal had a devastating impact on communities and on individuals – an unknown number of whom never received compensation, redress or apology.

In October 2023, the image of the hurricane was mobilised again – in a very different, more combative and divisive way – by the then-Home Secretary, Suella Braverman. Stoking ongoing anxieties about global migration to Britain, she spoke of a 'hurricane' of mass migration ready to make landfall. 'The wind of change that carried my own parents across the globe in the twentieth century was a mere gust compared [with] the hurricane that is coming,' she said. Braverman uses the metaphor of the hurricane in stark, desolating contrast to Nichols' poem. Where, for Nichols, the hurricane is a complex and multi-layered image, suggesting difference, but also contact and affinity across the globe, for Braverman, it is weaponised as a cipher for danger and destruction: a dehumanised force of nature ready to crash down, senselessly, upon the nation.

Let's move back to Nichols' words. In the last verse of the poem, Nichols expresses her realisation that the buffeting, blinding storm is a 'sweet mystery, / come to break the frozen lake in me'. Perhaps there's a hint, here, of that cold November day, back in 1977, when she arrived in London. That unaccustomed northern hemisphere chill paradoxically unfrozen and thawed by the power of the storm. A sense of release and freedom. And now the trees are interior, not just crashing down on the hillsides around Nichols' home. The storm is 'shaking the foundations of the very trees / within me': rocking and jolting her sense of identity and belonging, but bringing new insight and new possibilities. Nichols' Caribbean heritage comes magically alive in an English landscape. The storm stirs together both her Guyanese and British selves.

Grounded in real, individual experience of the Great Storm, that night of 15–16 October 1987, 'Hurricane Hits England' opens up a metaphor which connects us with stories of migration and belonging across the second half of the twentieth century and beyond. *Windrush*, winds of change, identity, welcome and exclusion, Black resistance and hope. The poem gives a glimpse into the new multicultural era of modern Britain: the vibrant hybrid identities and diverse communities being forged over decades.

Always poised in-between, ambivalent, Nichols' poem captures a hybrid emotional condition. She expresses a sense of loss and fracture with lands and ancestry left far away, and unanswered questions about roots and belonging. But, in the last line of her poem, Nichols responds to the message of the storm: this strange annunciation brought by divine harbingers from across the globe, just as isobars race across the weather map and winds rush over oceans. Everything is connected, joined. 'The earth is the earth is the earth.'

25.

Green

'The Groundsman' by Zaffar Kunial
(2022)

On 6 July 2016, a fortnight after the UK European Union member-ship referendum (23 June), Tory leadership hopeful Andrea Leadsom gave a speech to the Conservative Party. She pledged to steer the country to the 'sunlit uplands' of Brexit: a phrase which has stuck around in the political lexicon – as much in satire and irony as in the idealistic rhetoric of Brexiteers. The first uses of the phrase go back to the nineteenth century, but Leadsom, of course, was invok-ing Churchill: specifically his 'Their finest hour' speech of 1940, which looked ahead to the distant prospect of peace and freedom after defeat of the Nazis and victory in Europe. It's no accident that Churchill's vision of a peaceful future draws on pastoral imagery: his 'sunlit uplands' and 'island home' dovetail with the 'green and pleasant land' and 'sceptred isle' (with that familiar slippage between England and the whole island) of more than a thousand years of iconographic tradition.

What is England, now? Commentators point to a nation at a moment of self-doubt and crisis, in search of its present identity and future role in the world. Yet, across this book, we have seen repeated moments of doubt, catastrophe and reinvention in England's past. Is there anything distinctive or uniquely perilous about today? And what is England's history, now? Pride and nostalgia, as well as reck-oning, discomfort and conflict. A front line in the so-called 'culture wars'; a lightning rod for political controversies around identities, moral obligations and responsibilities. Where now for the 'green and pleasant land' of English imaginaries and poetic traditions? Shaped over centuries, and still invoked by politicians, artists and visionaries – are we reaching the edge of the map for England's picture of itself and kinship with its past?

Our last poem is a looking back: over memory, history, poetry, England. Through the poem, this chapter looks back, too: over English history, over the 1,300 years covered in this book, and over the place of poetry in making narratives and imaginaries of England. This last poem opens up questions about what we do with history, now, and how intimate, reflective encounters with the past – and with poetry – might help us write other future Englands into being.

Zaffar Kunial's poem 'The Groundsman', from his 2022 collection *England's Green*, imagines a small, cherished plot of land: pleasant, carefully bordered and tended. It's a cricket field, and Kunial is in character as the groundsman – now retired – speaking as he walks around its overgrown boundary, in the full, heady verdure of summer. But this little bounded piece of earth isn't just a cricket field, with its pristine pitch and clipped grass. Through Kunial's deliberate choice of words and imagery, it becomes much more. England. A page in a book. A single day in the continuing run of history.

> Since I retired, despite my runny hay fever
> I love this long grass, gone to seed, green ears
> left for ages that whisper to each other:
> blue flax – a flagpoled can – a ragwort's wires –
> foxglove spikes – shirty poppies – Queen Anne's lace –
> a breeze with a beardy face – a crow feather –
> a dotty cabbage white in a groundless shiver –
> the alive among the dead in the fine chaos
>
> of day. Its authorless sway of height and depth.
> The charged haze its own kind of light brigade.
> Rubbing my eyes I think of old work, each pitch
> or playing field that blurs now into one flat grief –
> grass shades that cross like ghosts, re-chalking lines
> over decades where others have gone. Life

is wider than its page. And days are a cut field, clipped and made
to run on.

Each word in this poem is tended as meticulously as a cricket
square. Take the first line, with its playful, whimsical cricket puns.
The groundsman is 'retired' – apparently he's stepped down from
his job maintaining the field – but of course we can't help thinking
of batters retiring from an innings. His hay fever is 'runny' – the
streaming eyes and nose which herald an English summer for so
many – but also an echo of the 'runs' of a match. From the start, per-
haps, the poem also invites us to think about the affinities between
groundsman and poet, each carefully tending and trimming their
allotted plot. Kunial's longstanding job as a verse writer for Hall-
mark seems pertinent: a career spent pruning the perfect words for
each little square of card.

Born in Birmingham, and today living in Yorkshire, Zaffar Kuni-
al's mother was English and his father from Kashmir. Kunial's poems
reflect his interest in ideas of England, Englishness, migration and
identity, as well as a deep love of the natural world (in 2014 he was
Poet in Residence at the Wordsworth Trust, Grasmere, connecting
him to that Romantic English pastoral tradition). And also: cricket.
Growing up near Edgbaston, the game was a major part of Kunial's
childhood, and continues to be a passion. His 2019 poetry pamphlet,
Six, brings together – you guessed it – six of his poems about cricket.
'The Groundsman' follows that lifelong fascination.

From the first line, the poem is looking back. 'Since I retired':
we join the groundsman at a moment of transition; a shift or
change in perspective and point of view. The tone is elegiac,
tender, poignant – but the poem offers up something more chal-
lenging than mere nostalgia. The 'long grass, gone to seed' evokes
the tall, lush drifts of grasses in high summer, but also hints at
something neglected, overgrown, even run to ruin. The 'green
ears' 'whisper to each other' – a sense of the groundsman eaves-
dropping as the rustling grasses tell their stories. The language is
disarmingly casual and conversational, but 'left for ages' has a dual

meaning. What scale of time are we looking at here? The weeks since summer began, since this boundary was mowed and tidied? Or eras and epochs in history? 'Ages' is a double exposure, a clue that the poem might be asking us to look further than this little patch of ground.

What does the groundsman see in this dense, luxuriant tangle of summer greenery? In the next few lines, the poem glances at a series of details: deft and quick, connected just by dashes. But there's more than first meets the eye. This green thicket is teeming with history, as well as nature. The chosen details point us beyond the flora and fauna of an English summer to histories of power, ambition, pride, aggression and loss. It's a bravura sweep across time, as light as skimming your fingers through summer grasses.

Blue flax: the summer perennial studded with masses of delicate blue flowers, from the family *Linaceae* – flax or linseed. The name transports us to the origins of the Industrial Revolution in England: the great mills of the Midlands and the north of England, noisy with the new technology of the water-powered spinning frame, processing yarn and cloth from (white) flax. Picture Ditherington Flax Mill in Shrewsbury (built 1797): the world's first iron-framed building, five storeys tall, humming with engines. Or Temple Works in Holbeck, Leeds, built between 1836 and 1840 in the Egyptian Revival style for the industrialist John Marshall, to house a 240-horsepower double-beam engine in what was, at the time, the largest single room in the world. Wealth, ambition and confidence – but also labour, inequality, misery. Cotton may have gained supremacy in the nineteenth century, but linen production was the first textiles boom of the machine age. Flax – the raw commodity in this mass production – changed the English economy, its towns and cities, for ever.

Next, 'a flagpoled can'. We could read this as a whimsical take on medieval pageantry or patriotic pride: a discarded drink can bobbing at the top of a stalk. Or is it about hooliganism and hate? Flags attract curious angst and controversy in contemporary English culture, with particular discomfort and ambivalence around England's national flag – the red St George's Cross – itself. A survey by think tank British Future in 2012 found that 24 per cent of English people considered the English flag to be racist, compared with just 10 per cent of Scots and 7 per cent of Welsh for their national flags. Far Right groups have tried to co-opt the St George's Cross for their own ends, even as it still flies on genteel country churches and is worn with pride by the national sports teams. When Keir Starmer walked into Downing Street as the United Kingdom's new Prime Minister, on Friday 5 July 2024, the carefully stage-managed crowds of supporters waved the Union Flag, the Scottish Saltire and Welsh Red Dragon – but the St George's Cross of England was conspicuous by its absence. England flags did appear a few weeks later, in the UEFA European Football Championship – and then, horrifyingly, in the racist and violent English riots of summer 2024. The poem doesn't make a judgement on the flag, either way. It gives us the image and lets us make up our own minds.

What else? A 'ragwort's wires' add more colour, the stunning yellow flowers abundant in this thriving grassy ecosystem, But it's divisive, too: the plant is regarded by some as invasive and can be poisonous to horses and cattle. In 2004 the Department for Environment, Food and Rural Affairs published a Code of Practice on how to prevent its spread; King Charles, while still Prince of Wales, repeatedly lobbied Natural England to tackle this 'injurious weed'. Even our green and pleasant countryside can be a battleground. The 'foxglove spikes' are splendid, their tall spires hung with purple flowers. But the wording is uneasy. Do we think of heads on spikes and the schoolbook lore of premodern power, punishment and violence? After wires and spikes, the poppies may have us thinking of war – specifically the Great War and the poppies which grew rapidly over the blasted ground. But 'shirty poppies'? Perhaps it's a nod to the revolutionaries and reformers – especially those leaning to the left or 'red' – and their role as agitators and disruptors, taking on the establishment and the status quo throughout English history.

'Queen Anne's lace' is a grand name but an utterly commonplace plant: that familiar, spectacular froth of white which bursts across English hedges and meadows every May. Kunial could have used

one of its other names – like 'cow parsley' – and the choice is sig-
nificant, playing with the language of royalty and history. Where
might the associations take us? Queen Anne reigned at the time of
the Acts of Union (ratified 1 May 1707), transforming her from Queen
of England, Scotland and Ireland to Queen of Great Britain and Ire-
land. A crucial moment for identities and polities within these islands,
as maps of power and sovereignty were redrawn. But how does the
union hold, today? The 2016 Brexit referendum exposed different
needs and priorities across the UK nations, following swiftly on the
marginal result of the Scottish Independence vote in 2014. Political
campaigns for secession and independence continue. The union, and
England's privileged place within it, seems more precarious than ever.

Each of these moments of history, glimpsed through the tangled
green of summer grasses, could be debated and contested. The
list-like form of these lines means the poem doesn't interpret or
explain – it doesn't take a stance – but hands the meaning over to
us. History, more than ever before, is a site of dispute and conflict
in England today, as in so many other countries in the developed,
industrialised world, reckoning with their pasts and torn between
increasingly polarised political standpoints. What – and whose – is
English history, now?

In our news media, it's often the act of pulling down statues
which is conflated with the process of confronting difficult histories.
England's most well-known case has probably been the dismant-
ling of the statue of Bristol-born merchant and slave trader – and
civic philanthropist – Edward Colston in 2020, as part of the global
Black Lives Matter movement. Toppled from its podium, daubed
in paint and rolled into the murky waters of Bristol Harbour, the
statue became a powerful symbol of the violence and exploitation
underpinning the city's wealth – as well as a site of fierce argument
about how we should memorialise uncomfortable pasts. Now part
of the permanent collection of Bristol's M Shed museum – in its
defaced state – the statue tells a fuller and more complex story, about
Colston's life and career, about his legacy in Bristol, and about con-
temporary debates around history, commemoration and reparations.

Eye-catching front-page photos of toppled statues aside, it's that fuller story which has been the objective of historians and heritage practitioners in recent years. Opening up and enlarging our histories, drawing in new evidence, and including more diverse voices – as this book has aimed to do, in its choice of twenty-five poems and those who get to tell our national story. Work by organisations such as the National Trust, for example, has expanded our understanding of the cherished landscapes and country houses of England, making room for the realities of global inter-connections, slavery, extractive industrial and economic processes – as well as the rich and colourful stories of lives beyond those of the privileged few.

In his leader's speech to the Conservative Party Conference in October 2021, then-Prime Minister Boris Johnson pointed to perceived threats to our national (wider UK as well as English) history, asserting that 'we attack and deny history at our peril'. 'They really do want to rewrite our national story', he told the conference (the sinister 'they' of his speech never explicitly identified); 'we really are at risk of a kind of know-nothing cancel culture iconoclasm'. But the process of reckoning with our difficult pasts is about doing *more* history, not cancelling or erasing: the painstaking work of researchers excavating evidence which has been long buried, pushing through silences, or asking questions which have been too often ignored. It's not, as Johnson claimed, comparable to 'a celebrity trying furtively to change his entry in Wikipedia'. History is, and always has been, a process of rewriting, expanding, deepening and bettering our understanding of the past. Kunial's poem speaks at a moment in which the very process of making history is under attack.

History is never just in the past: it's live and dynamic today. Surveying the overgrown cricket field boundary, the groundsman sees 'the alive among the dead in the fine chaos / of day'. It's the rich biodiversity of an English meadow. But it's also the crowded, densely inter-connected ecosystem of place and history: now and then, past and present entangled in a kind of cultural biome. The description of this heady abundance spills over into the second part of the poem.

And now we're focusing on the drift of the tall summer grasses: the 'authorless sway of height and depth'. Again, the words whimsically remind us that we're inside a poem: the beauty of the hedgerow – unlike carefully crafted verse – needs no author. 'Sway' conveys the rippling of the grasses in the breeze. But the word is used, perhaps unexpectedly, as a noun rather than a verb ('to sway'). *Sway* as a noun might be more familiar from its use in phrases like 'hold sway' or 'give sway'. What happens if we pause and pay attention?

Monday, 19 September 2022. The state funeral of Her Majesty Queen Elizabeth II is taking place in Westminster Abbey, London. The first hymn nears its end: 'The Day Thou Gavest, Lord, Is Ended', with words by John Ellerton (1826–93), to the familiar setting 'St Clement'. These are well-loved, comforting words, sung at evensongs and funerals around England and beyond, year after year. But this, of course, is also a great Victorian hymn of empire, sung for generations across a world map painted colonial pink and governed under the British Crown. It speaks of a Christian world on which the sun never sets:

> As o'er each continent and island
> the dawn leads on another day,
> the voice of prayer is never silent,
> nor dies the strain of praise away.

As sun sets upon the singers, it rises in the east ('The sun that bids us rest is waking / our brethren 'neath the western sky'), where 'fresh lips' sing God's praise. The imagery is implicitly of mission and conversion, as well as community across geography. The hymn imagines heaven itself as an empire – made in the image of that pink-tinted map – but one which 'shall never / like earth's proud empires, pass away'. And then the last line of the hymn is ringing out, as it looks to the eternal growth and power of God's kingdom, the final word resounding through the Abbey: 'till all thy creatures own thy sway'.

Sway as a noun: not a word we encounter much, but we heard it here. 'The Groundsman' was published in Kunial's collection *England's Green* just days after Queen Elizabeth's funeral. What meaning does the word take on, in the context of these resonances and echoes? Power, dominion, influence: the connotations of 'sway' reverberated through Elizabeth II's funeral and the national soul-searching surrounding her passing. She had reigned through the decline of the British Empire, the transition from the pink map of imperial subjects and possessions to the Commonwealth, the waning in global power and standing of the United Kingdom. What now for England's 'sway'? What, now, is the power and influence of the United Kingdom? Kunial's poem transplants the language of imperial pomp and power to the dominion of weeds in an over-grown summer thicket. He leaves us to ask our own questions.

In the second part of the poem, we continue to see nature, history and poetry all simultaneously overlaid together. You spotted it, of course, that reference to Tennyson: 'The charged haze its own kind of light brigade'. It's Kunial's characteristic wit and whimsy again, *almost* coupling together – but not quite – to make up 'The Charge of the Light Brigade'. We're viewing nature through the lens of poetry and history here, just as much as we're seeing history through nature. The poem's not speaking about war, but rather the hazy, pollen-heavy, mote-laden light around the thicket. Or is it? The groundsman rubs his eyes. That nuisance hay fever again, or something else? A sudden grief?

The cricket field now, all too easily, slips into imagery for the violence and conflict in England's history: 'pitch' becomes an attack, assault; the 'playing field' that old euphemism for a battlefield, the schoolboy training (as we saw in the young Charles Dodgson's poem in Chapter 18) for military service to empire and nation. Grief is as 'flat' and relentless as the painstakingly levelled terrain of the ground. The grass 'shades' are both their flickering shadows and the haunting of 'ghosts'. In the context of this language of war, violence and loss, the image of 're-chalking lines' becomes much more than the work of a groundsman marking out a sports pitch. There's perhaps a particular allusion to British imperial history here: the process of carving up territories and redrawing borders, sometimes seemingly as facile as chalking lines on a map.

And there may perhaps be a personal resonance here for Kunial, too, with his Kashmiri heritage. Ghosts of Partition: the dissolution of the British Raj and creation of the two independent states of India and Pakistan in 1947. Partition forced the migration of between 14 and 18 million people; deaths through violence and starvation remain only partially documented, but perhaps around another million: lives destroyed with lines drawn as easily as chalk on a cricket field. Kashmir itself remains the most fiercely disputed of the regions partitioned in 1947 and continues to be a flashpoint for Indo–Pakistani tensions. Despite strained relations between India and Pakistan throughout their modern histories, cricket is one of the few fields in which the two countries meet on relatively amicable terms. Indeed, the resumption of sporting ties in 1978, after a long period in which they had been suspended for political reasons, led to talk of 'cricket diplomacy'. Perhaps there are hints here of how the cricket green might be a symbol of healing in a fractured world. Or perhaps we think of the infamous 'cricket test' (also known as the 'Tebbit test'), posed by Tory politician Norman Tebbit in 1990. 'A large proportion of Britain's Asian population fail to pass the cricket test', Tebbit claimed in a newspaper interview. 'Which side do they cheer for? It's an interesting test. Are you still harking back to where you came from or where you are?' Tebbit retracted his comments in 2018, saying that 'race isn't an issue like it used to be' in sport. But the cricket green is a space where debates about race, immigration, multiculturalism and Englishness have played out for decades.

Were you expecting a sonnet? Here, the poem's time would be up, the full fourteen-line length complete. But it goes on – another of Kunial's games with the reader.

> . . . Life
>
> is wider than its page. And days are a cut field, clipped and made
> to run on.

It's a trick, a visual pun. The poem itself spills over; life doesn't fit neatly on the page. It's a clever bit of word play: the grass of a cricket field and the pages of a book are both 'cut' or 'clipped'. Days, too, are neatly trimmed and bounded, in our calendars, diaries and history books. But they escape their confines. The cricket pitch is made to 'run / on' – and (another pun) so are days, running on beyond the edges of pages, lines and poems. 'The Groundsman' is a poem about England, but the whimsy of its ending nimbly side-steps jingoism, judgement, or coercive nostalgia. Zaffar Kunial may seem like a neat 'Z' to end our list of poems. But history, he reminds us, doesn't end. It keeps going.

'The Groundsman' is rooted in a knowing, proud, sceptical and playful engagement with the pastoral tradition of English poetry – reflected in the title of the Kunial volume in which it's published: *England's Green*. It's in conversation with Bede, Shakespeare, Blake, Thomas and so many others, thinking with that green imagery and those powerful emblems of English identity, harvested out of the fields and hillsides of the country. England as verdant, pleasant, temperate and moderate; a land of mildness and clemency, not extremes; a green and generative earth, which brings forth flourishing and fruitfulness. In 'The Groundsman', Kunial, and the imagined character of the groundsman himself, connect with the past through England's green: its nature, wildlife, plants and flowers.

Throughout this book, we've seen imagery of England's natural world feature prominently in poems which, over time, have helped shape a sense of national tradition and identity. Birdsong has unfurled through these pages: the two-note call of the cuckoo celebrated in the medieval song 'Sumer Is Icumen In' (Chapter 5), or the misty, elegiac song of 'all the birds / Of Oxfordshire and Gloucestershire' in Edward Thomas's precious moment at Adlestrop, on the eve of the Great War (Chapter 20). And so much greenery: the exuberant springtime of Chaucer's pilgrims, as they ride through 'April, with his sweet showers' on their pilgrimage to Canterbury (Chapter 6), or the delightful landscape of the great country estate, so well established in the cultural imagination that it can be parodied and teased by Mary Leapor in 'Crumble-Hall' (Chapter 14). The flower-carpeted garden where the dreamer, grieving for his lost daughter, lays his head in *Pearl* (Chapter 7); the 'blessed plot' of the Edenic island in Shakespeare's *Richard II* (Chapter 11); and even those strange Green Children who climb out of the earth itself in the twelfth-century English civil war (Chapter 4). But the future of England's green and pleasant land is precarious.

The climate is changing: England is warming, with hotter summers and more intense and devastating rainfall events. Sea levels are rising. Plants in the UK now flower around a month earlier than they did hundreds of years ago, because of global heating. The rich, balanced ecosystem of Kunial's poem – with plants, insects and animals all flourishing together in a pattern of familiar seasonality – is at enormous risk.

Imagine a future in which we no longer hear the birdsong which connects us to these poems, lived experiences and moments in the past. No more cuckoos – currently on the 'Red' conservation list – to share with the thirteenth-century singers of 'Sumer Is Icumen In'. An April hotter, drier and out of step with the flowers and green shoots of Chaucer's *Canterbury Tales*. Even the salt-marshes at Maldon, where Byrhtnoth fought the Vikings and forged a sense of English homeland and heroism, are threatened by climate change and rising sea levels (though conservation efforts are underway). With these unprecedented threats to our natural environments, we also stand to lose intimacies and affinities with others who have marvelled at the beauty and wonder of our places, who have stood steeped in England's green, for hundreds of years.

We're not the first to fear or grieve such loss. In the mid-eighteenth century, Mary Leapor worries for the beautiful woods and groves around Edgcote House, as the owner – her employer – plans his 'modern' programme of landscaping and remodelling (Chapter 14). She foresees a future which is 'ravag'd' and 'barren': a landscape deceptively green, but sterile and artificial, robbed of nature and the creatures and spirits which so long inhabited it. Today, ironically, these very parklands and estates, elegantly laid out by garden designers across the country, are themselves folded into cherished ideals of the English countryside. (News that the planned High Speed 2 rail route would cut through the grounds of Edgcote House, just by its ornamental lake, was met with outrage by campaigners.) England changes over time – from common ground to enclosure, from wild forests to grazed hillsides – and some losses are already forgotten in our hallowed imagery of 'pleasant pastures' and gentle, docile green.

Now, perhaps, the imagery of Anna Laetitia Barbauld's satirical poem *Eighteen Hundred and Eleven* (published 1812; Chapter 16) reads differently. She looks ahead to an imagined – threatened – future in which England has lost its global power and dominance. London is a ruin, the Thames overgrown with reeds and sedge, nature creeping back to reclaim the land. Rather than a cautionary fable of loss and decay, we might welcome Barbauld's vision now as a radical rewilding, a regreening of a weary and sullied land. The prospect is poignantly beautiful, even achingly alluring. A re-enchantment of the land, with nature allowed to breathe again: to hold sway.

In a possible future without our 'green and pleasant land', what are the stories we'll tell about ourselves? What other imaginaries will we build; what other emblems of Englishness will we make? What will be irrevocably lost? Or will we succeed in saving England's green before it's too late? And what other voices might contribute to new poetics of England and Englishness, in another twenty-five poems, over another 1300 years of our country's history?

Questions of what's next for England – its place within the union, in Europe and the world; its internal identities and inequalities, its sense of purpose and values for the future: these are for the politicians and strategists, if they'll listen and learn. But questions of how we *imagine* England – what it is, what it was, what it could be – these, as we've seen throughout this book, are for the poets. Setting these twenty-five poems in their own historical moments allows us to see something of how the nation has dreamed itself into existence: how images of England have been shaped, celebrated, troubled and contested over centuries, by voices of power and authority, as well as by those writing from the margins, the rebels, doubters and visionaries. Through poetry, we discover radical empathy with distant lives in other Englands, familiar and unfamiliar, across time – as well as, perhaps, an ethical challenge to commit to that same audacious empathy in our own world today. Through poetry, we witness how imagination can reach beyond essays and arguments, beyond policy and manifestos, towards glimpses of the country we might share together in future.

Suggested Reading

This suggested reading points to key sources and references for each chapter, and gives ideas for further exploration. It includes a variety of material, ranging from sources mostly available in specialist libraries to readily available books, and texts accessible online. For further background on people mentioned throughout, see the *Oxford Dictionary of National Biography*, available as an online resource in many libraries. Starred items include editions (and sometimes translations, where relevant) of the chapter headline poems. Most of the headline poems are also readily available online.

Chapter 1: Beginnings:
Cædmon's Hymn (around 730)

*Bede's Ecclesiastical History of the English People, ed. Bertram Colgrave and R. A. B. Mynors, trans. Bertram Colgrave (Clarendon Press, 1969)

John Blair, *The Anglo-Saxon Age: A Very Short Introduction* (Oxford University Press, 2000)

Catherine A. M. Clarke, *Literary Landscapes and the Idea of England, c.700–1400* (Boydell Press, 2006)

Margaret Lindsay Faull, 'The Semantic Development of Old English *wealh*', *Leeds Studies in English*, New Series 8 (1975), pp. 20–44

Helen Gittos, 'Sutton Hoo and Syria: The Anglo-Saxons Who Served in the Byzantine Army?', *English Historical Review* CXXXIX, No. 601 (2024), pp. 1323–1358

Susan Oosthuizen, *The Emergence of the English: Rethinking the Evidence* (Arc Humanities Press, 2019)

Chapter 2: Vikings:
Extract from The Battle of Maldon *(around 1000)*

The Battle of Maldon, ed. Donald Scragg (Manchester University Press, 1981)
The Battle of Maldon, AD 991, ed. Donald Scragg (Blackwell, 1991)
J. R. R. Tolkien, *The Battle of Maldon:* together with *The Homecoming of Beorhtnoth*, ed. Peter Grybauskus (HarperCollins, 2023)
The Anglo-Saxon Chronicle, ed. and trans. Michael Swanton (Weidenfeld and Nicolson, 1997)

Chapter 3: Conquest and Resistance:
'The Death of King William' from
the Peterborough Chronicle *(around 1087)*

The Anglo-Saxon Chronicle, ed. and trans. Michael Swanton (Weidenfeld and Nicolson, 1997)
The Anglo-Saxon Chronicle: A Collaborative Edition, vol. 7, *MS. E*, ed. Susan Irvine (D. S. Brewer, 2004)
Stephen Baxter and C.P. Lewis, 'Domesday Book and the Transformation of English Landed Society, 1066–1086', Anglo-Saxon England 46 (2017), 343–403
Leonie Hicks, *A Short History of the Normans* (Bloomsbury Academic, 2020)
Elaine Treharne, *Living through Conquest: The Politics of Early English, 1020–1220* (Oxford University Press, 2012)
William of Newburgh, *The History of English Affairs*, Book I, ed. and trans. P. G. Walsh and M. J. Kennedy (Aris & Phillips, 1988)

Chapter 4: Anarchy: The Land Torn Apart:
'Who Will Give Me a Fountain of Tears'
by Henry of Huntingdon *(around 1146)*

*Henry of Huntingdon, *Historia Anglorum*, ed. Diana Greenway (Oxford University Press, 1996)

Suggested Reading

Catherine A. M. Clarke, 'Writing Civil War in Henry of Huntingdon's *Historia Anglorum*', *Anglo-Norman Studies*, vol. XXXI: *Proceedings of the Battle Conference 2008*, ed. C. P. Lewis (D. S Brewer, 2009), pp. 31–48

Jeffrey Jerome Cohen, 'Green Children from Another World, or the Archipelago in England', in *Cultural Diversity in the British Middle Ages: Archipelago, Island, England*, ed. Jeffrey Jerome Cohen (Palgrave Macmillan, 2008), pp. 75–94

William of Newburgh, *The History of English Affairs*, Book I, ed. and trans. P. G. Walsh and M. J. Kennedy (Aris & Phillips, 1988)

Chapter 5: Mice, Monks and 'Merry England': 'Sumer Is Icumen In' (around 1260)

*Helen Deeming, 'An English Monastic Miscellany: The Reading Manuscript of *Sumer Is Icumen In*', in *Manuscripts and Medieval Song: Inscription, Performance, Context*, ed. H. Deeming and E. E. Leach (Cambridge University Press, 2015), pp. 116–40

Johan Huizinga, *The Waning of the Middle Ages* (Dover Publications, 1999, and other editions; first published 1919 and first published in English 1924)

Andrew Taylor, *Textual Situations: Three Medieval Manuscripts and Their Readers* (University of Pennsylvania Press, 2002)

Chapter 6: What Women Want: Extract from 'The Wife of Bath's Tale' by Geoffrey Chaucer (probably 1390s)

*Geoffrey Chaucer, *The Wife of Bath's Prologue and Tale*, ed. James Winney (Cambridge University Press, first published 1966)

Middle English Lyrics, ed. Maxwell S. Luria and Richard L. Hoffman (W. W. Norton & Company, 1974), available online

Euan Roger and Sebastian Sobecki, *Geoffrey Chaucer and Cecily Chaumpaigne: Rethinking the Record* (The National Archives blog post, 2022), available online

The Case of Geoffrey Chaucer and Cecily Chaumpaigne: New Evidence, Special Issue, ed. Sebastian Sobecki and Euan Roger, *The Chaucer Review* 57:4 (2002)

Marion Turner, *The Wife of Bath: A Biography* (Princeton University Press, 2023)

Chapter 7: Love and Loss in a Time of Plague: *Extract from* Pearl *(around 1390)*

The Poems of the 'Pearl' Manuscript, ed. Malcolm Andrew and Ronald Waldron (Exeter University Press, 2007, and other editions)

*Simon Armitage, *Pearl* (Faber & Faber, 2016)

David K. Coley, *Death and the Pearl Maiden: Plague, Poetry, England* (Ohio State University Press, 2019)

Pandemic Disease in the Medieval World: Rethinking the Black Death, ed. Monica H. Green (Arc Humanities Press, 2015)

The Black Death, ed. and trans. Rosemary Horrox (Manchester University Press, 1994)

Leslie Lockett, *Anglo-Saxon Psychologies in the Vernacular and Latin Traditions* (University of Toronto Press, 2011)

Chapter 8: Once More unto the Breach: *Neighbours and Adversaries: 'Agincourt Carol' (1415)*

*Helen Deeming, 'The sources and origin of the "Agincourt Carol"', *Early Music* 35:1, 2007, pp. 23–36

Adam Chapman, 'The King's Welshmen: Welsh Involvement in the Expeditionary Army of 1415', *Journal of Medieval Military History* 9 (2011), pp. 41–64

Adam Chapman, 'Welsh Archers at Agincourt: Myth and Reality', *The Historian: The Magazine of the Historical Association* 127 (2015), pp. 12–16

Anne Curry, *Agincourt: A New History* (The History Press, 2015)

R. R. Davies, *The Revolt of Owain Glyndŵr* (Oxford University Press, 1995)

Chapter 9: Anne Boleyn and All That:
'Whoso List to Hunt' by Thomas Wyatt (around 1520s)

*Thomas Wyatt, *The Complete Poems*, ed. R. Rebholz (Penguin, 1978)

Kenneth Muir, *Life and Letters of Sir Thomas Wyatt* (Liverpool University Press, 1963)

George Puttenham, *The Art of English Poesy*, ed. Frank Whigham and Wayne A. Rebhorn (Cornell University Press, 2007)

Stephanie Russo, 'The Poet and the Queen: Thomas Wyatt and Anne Boleyn in Historical Biofiction', *a/b: Auto/Biography Studies* 36:1 (2021), pp. 65–91

Greg Walker, *Writing under Tyranny: English Literature and the Henrician Reformation* (Oxford University Press, 2005)

Chapter 10: Words for Burning:
'The Ballad Which Anne Askew Made and
Sang When She Was in Newgate' by Anne Askew (1546)

The Examinations of Anne Askew, ed. Elaine V. Beilin (Oxford University Press, 1996)

Kimberley Anne Coles, 'The Death of the Author (and the Appropriation of Her Text): The Case of Anne Askew's "Examinations"', *Modern Philology* 99 (2002), pp. 515–39

Theresa D. Kemp, 'Translating (Anne) Askew: The Textual Remains of a Sixteenth-Century Heretic and Saint', *Renaissance Quarterly* 52:4 (1999), pp. 1021–45

Diane Watt, *Secretaries of God: Women Prophets in Late Medieval and Early Modern England* (D. S. Brewer, 1997)

Chapter 11: Poetry, Prophecy and the Island: 'This England' (John of Gaunt's Speech) from Richard II by William Shakespeare (around 1595)

*William Shakespeare, *King Richard II*, ed. Charles R. Forker (Arden Shakespeare, Third Series) (Bloomsbury, 2002)

Jonathan Bate, 'Was Shakespeare an Essex Man?', *Proceedings of the British Academy* 162 (2009), pp. 1–28

R. R. Davies, *The First English Empire: Power and Identities in the British Isles 1093–1343* (Oxford University Press, 2002)

Dillian Gordon, 'A New Discovery in the Wilton Diptych', *Burlington Magazine* 134, no. 1075 (1992), pp. 662–7

Willy Maley, ' "This Sceptred Isle": Shakespeare and the British Problem', in *Nation, State and Empire in English Renaissance Literature* (Palgrave Macmillan, 2013), pp. 7–29

Chapter 12: The Arse-End of England: 'Bum-fodder, or, Waste-paper, Proper to Wipe the Nation's RUMP with, or Your Own' attributed to Alexander Brome (1660)

*'Bum-fodder', in *Rump, or, An exact collection of the choycest poems and songs relating to the late times by the most eminent wits from anno 1639 to anno 1661*, available online

Alice Hunt, *Republic: Britain's Revolutionary Decade, 1649–1660* (Faber & Faber, 2024)

Ronald Hutton, *The British Republic 1649–1660* (Palgrave Macmillan, 1990)

Mark S. R. Jenner, 'The Roasting of the Rump: Scatology and the Body Politic in Restoration England', *Past & Present* 177:1 (2002), pp. 84–120

Patrick Little, 'Oliver the Red-nosed Protector: Cromwell's Physiognomy Revisited' (History of Parliament blog post, 2021), available online

Angela McShane, 'Drink, Song and Politics in Early Modern England', *Popular Music* 35:2 (2016), pp. 166–90

The Diary of Samuel Pepys, available online

Chapter 13: Out of the Ashes:
Making the Metropolis: Extract from
Annus Mirabilis *by John Dryden (1667)*

*John Dryden, A Critical Edition of the Major Works, edited by Keith Walker (Oxford University Press, 1987)

Vanessa Harding, 'City, Capital and Metropolis: The Changing Shape of Seventeenth-Century London', in *Imagining Early Modern London: Perceptions and Portrayals of the City from Stow to Strype, 1598–1720*, ed. J. F. Merritt (Cambridge University Press, 2001), pp. 117–43

Mark Jenner, 'The Politics of London Air: John Evelyn's "Fumifugium" and the Restoration', *The Historical Journal* 38:3 (1995), pp. 535–51

Derek Keene, 'Ideas of the Metropolis', *Historical Research* 84 (2011), pp. 379–98

John Stow, *A Survey of London. Reprinted from the Text of 1603*, ed. C. L. Kingsford (Clarendon Press, 1908), available online at British History Online

The Diary of Samuel Pepys, available online

Chapter 14: Below Stairs in the Country House:
Extract from 'Crumble-Hall' by Mary Leapor (around 1745)

The Works of Mary Leapor, ed. Richard Greene and Ann Messenger (Oxford University Press, 2003)

The Country House Poem: A Cabinet of Seventeenth-Century Estate Poems and Related Items, ed. Alastair Fowler (Edinburgh University Press, 1994)

Corinne Fowler, *Green Unpleasant Land: Creative Responses to Rural England's Colonial Connections* (Peepal Tree Press, 2020)

Richard Greene, *Mary Leapor: A Study in Eighteenth-Century Women's Poetry* (Oxford University Press, 1993)

Slavery and the British Country House, ed. Madge Dresser and Andrew Hann (English Heritage, 2013)

Chapter 15: From Africa to New England to England: A Voice for Freedom: 'To the Right Honourable William, Earl of Dartmouth' by Phillis Wheatley (1772)

*The Writings of Phillis Wheatley, ed. Vincent Carretta (Oxford University Press, 2019)

Vincent Caretta, *Phillis Wheatley: Biography of a Genius in Bondage* (University of Georgia Press, 2011)

Critical Essays on Phillis Wheatley, ed. William H. Robinson (G. K. Hall, 1982)

Simon P. Newman, *Freedom Seekers: Escaping from Slavery in Restoration London* (University of London Press, 2022)

Runaway Slaves in Britain: Bondage, Freedom and Race in the Eighteenth Century, database available online

David Waldstreicher, *The Odyssey of Phillis Wheatley: A Poet's Journeys through American Slavery and Independence* (Farrar, Straus and Giroux, 2023)

Chapter 16: Contemplation of the Dust: England in Ruins: Extract from Eighteen Hundred and Eleven by Anna Laetitia Barbauld (1812)

*The Collected Works of Anna Letitia Barbauld, ed. William McCarthy, vol. 1: *The Poems, Revised* (Oxford Scholarly Editions Online, 2020)

Emma Clery, *Eighteen Hundred and Eleven: Poetry, Protest and Economic Crisis* (Cambridge University Press, 2017)

Dick Wakefield, *Anna Laetitia Barbauld: A Biography* (Open Gate Press, 2001)

Chapter 17: Under the Wheels of Progress: Extract from 'The Cry of the Children' by Elizabeth Barrett Browning (1842)

**Selected Poems of Elizabeth Barrett Browning*, ed. Margaret Forster (Chatto & Windus, 1988)

Emma Griffin, *A Short History of the British Industrial Revolution* (Palgrave, 2010)

Henry Morley, 'Ground in the Mill', *Household Words* IX, Magazine No. 213, 22 April 1854, pp. 224–7, available online

Rebecca Stott and Simon Avery, *Elizabeth Barrett Browning* (Routledge, 2014)

Royal Commission of Inquiry into Children's Employment (1842), available online

Chapter 18: You'll Be a Man, My Son: 'Rules and Regulations' by Lewis Carroll (Charles Lutwidge Dodgson) (1845)

*Lewis Carroll, *Useful and Instructive Poetry* (Geoffrey Bles, 1954)

Thomas Arnold, *Sermons Preached in the Chapel of Rugby School* (Longmans, Green and Co., 1874), available online

Stuart Dodgson Collingwood, *The Life and Letters of Lewis Carroll* (The Century Company, 1899 and later editions), available online

Anthony Fletcher, *Growing Up in England: The Experience of Childhood, 1600–1914* (Yale University Press, 2008)

M. Daphne Kutzer, *Empire's Children: Empire and Imperialism in Classic British Children's Books* (Garland Publishing, 2000)

Manliness and Morality: Middle-class Masculinity in Britain and America, 1800–1940, ed. J. A. Mangan and James Walvin (Manchester University Press, 1987)

Jackie Wullschläger, *Inventing Wonderland: The Lives and Fantasies of Lewis Carroll, Edward Lear, J. M. Barrie, Kenneth Grahame and A. A. Milne* (Methuen, 1995)

Chapter 19: Queen Victoria's Book:
Science, Nature and Faith: Extract from
In Memoriam A.H.H. *by Alfred, Lord Tennyson (1850)*

*Alfred, Lord Tennyson, *In Memoriam: Authoritative Text: Criticism*, ed. Erik Gray (W. W. Norton, 2004)

The Journals of Queen Victoria, available online

Richard Owen, *Report on British Fossil Reptiles* (Richard and John E. Taylor, London, 1841), available online

William Paley, *Natural Theology or Evidences of the Existence and Attributes of the Deity* (R. Faulder, London, 1802), available online

Frank Miller Turner, *Between Science and Religion: The Reaction to Scientific Naturalism in Late Victorian England* (Yale University Press, 1974)

Chapter 20: *The History of a Moment:*
'Adlestrop' by Edward Thomas (1917)

*Edward Thomas, *Selected Poems and Prose*, ed. David Wright, with a foreword by Robert Macfarlane (Penguin, 2013)

Edward Thomas: Prose Writings: A Selected Edition, vol. II: *England and Wales*, ed. Guy Cuthbertson and Lucy Newlyn (Oxford University Press, 2011)

Edward Thomas: Prose Writings: A Selected Edition, vol. V: *Critical Studies: Swinburne and Pater*, ed. Francis O'Gorman (Oxford University Press, 2017)

Edward Thomas: Selected Letters, ed. R. George Thomas (Oxford University Press, 1995)

Jean Moorcroft Wilson, *Edward Thomas: From Adlestrop to Arras: A Biography* (Bloomsbury Continuum, 2015)

Chapter 21: Modernity, Mourning and the Shadow of War: 'Funeral Blues' by W. H. Auden (1936 and 1937)

★W. H. Auden, *Tell Me the Truth about Love: Ten Poems* (Faber & Faber, 1994)

★W. H. Auden and Christopher Isherwood, *The Ascent of F6: A Tragedy in Two Acts* (Faber, 1937)

Abbie Garrington, 'What Does a Modernist Mountain Mean? Auden and Isherwood's *The Ascent of F6*', *Modernism Reloaded* 55:2 (2013), pp. 26–49

John Stevenson and Chris Cook, *The Slump: Britain in the Great Depression* (Routledge, 2013, and other editions)

Matthew Worley, 'Communism and Fascism in 1920s and 1930s Britain', in *W. H. Auden in Context*, ed. Tony Sharpe (Cambridge University Press, 2013), pp. 141–9

Chapter 22: Poetry after Auschwitz: 'September Song' by Geoffrey Hill (1968)

★Geoffrey Hill, *Selected Poems* (Penguin, 2006)

Nella Last's War: The Second World War Diaries of 'Housewife, 49', ed. Richard Broad and Suzie Fleming (Profile, 2006)

Alan Garner, 'The Edge of the Ceiling', in *The Voice That Thunders: Essays and Lectures* (Harvill Press, 1997), pp. 3–18

Tony Kushner, 'The Holocaust in the British Imagination: The Official Mind and beyond, 1945 to the Present', *Holocaust Studies* 23:3 (2017), pp. 364–84

Anthony Rowland and Robert Eaglestone, 'Introduction: Holocaust Poetry', *Critical Survey* 20:2 (Special Issue: *Holocaust Poetry*) (2008), pp. 1–6

Britain and the Second World War: A Social History, ed. Harold L. Smith (Manchester University Press, 1996)

Chapter 23: North–South Divide:
'England's Glory' by Fleur Adcock (1986)

*Fleur Adcock, *The Incident Book* (Oxford University Press, 1986)

Martin Adeney and John Lloyd, *The Miners' Strike, 1984–5: Loss without Limit* (Routledge, 2022; first published 1986)

British Political Speech, database available online

George Orwell, *The Road to Wigan Pier* (Penguin, 1989, and other editions)

David Smith, *North and South: Britain's Economic, Social and Political Divide* (Penguin, 1994)

Chapter 24: Winds of Change:
'Hurricane Hits England' by Grace Nichols (1996)

*Grace Nichols, *Sunris* (Virago, 1996)

Hannah Lowe, 'Inside the Frame: Women Writers and the Windrush Legacy. Interviews with Grace Nichols, Karen McCarthy Woolf and Jay Bernard', *Wasafiri* 33:2 (2018), pp. 3–9

Grace Nichols, *The Fat Black Woman's Poems* (Virago, 1984)

Grace Nichols, *Lazy Thoughts of a Lazy Woman* (Virago, 1989)

Grace Nichols, 'So I Pick Up Me New-World-Self', in *Liminal Spaces: Migration and Women of the Guyanese Diaspora*, ed. Grace Aneiza Ali (OpenBook Publishers, 2020), available online, pp. 123–34

Ian Sanjay Patel, *We're Here Because You Were There: Immigration and the End of Empire* (Verso, 2021)

Windrush: Arrival 1948 Passenger List, available online

The Windrush Scandal in a Transnational and Commonwealth Context: project website available online

Suggested Reading

Chapter 25: Green:
'The Groundsman' by Zaffar Kunial (2022)

*Zaffar Kunial, *England's Green* (Faber & Faber, 2022)

Ulf Büntgen and others, 'Plants in the UK Flower a Month Earlier under Recent Warming', *Proceedings of the Royal Society B (Biological Sciences)* 289 (2022), pp. 1–9

Stuart Jeffries, 'Patriot Games: How Toxic Is the England Flag Today?', *The Guardian*, 26 November, 2014, available online

Order of Service for the State Funeral of Her Majesty the Queen (2022), available online

UK Climate Projections (UKCP) from the Met Office (2018; Version 4, August 2022), available online

Acknowledgements

I started thinking about the project which would become this book in the spring of 2020. In the midst of Coronavirus lockdowns and stay-at-home restrictions, the prospect of travelling through poetry – of spending time in the company of other people, in different places and historical moments – was magical. Since then, this book has benefitted from the expertise, wisdom and generosity of many friends and colleagues. I'd like to thank all my colleagues at the Institute of Historical Research (IHR) and across the School of Advanced Study, University of London, for your support and encouragement. Special thanks go to the library teams in the IHR and Senate House Library, where I've undertaken so much reading and research for this project. Thank you to my former colleagues in the English Department at the University of Southampton, who helped to shape much of the thinking you'll find here. Costa Coffee in Upton, Dorset, kept me in an unstinting supply of chocolate tiffin on weekend writing sessions, while my daughter played in youth orchestra and chamber music groups nearby. Of course, my debts of gratitude go much further back than these last years, to all the wonderful teachers and mentors who first led me into the discovery of English literature and history – you know who you are.

In particular, I'd like to thank Philip Carter, Adam Chapman, Emma Clery, Justin Colson, Juanita Cox, Anne Curry, Matthew Davies, Leonie Hicks, Sue Horth, Alice Hunt, John McGavin, Philip Murphy, Marianne O'Doherty, Anna Reeve, Laura Varnam, and Diane Watt, who have read chapters, offered advice and feedback, and lifted my morale on the odd occasion when it was needed.

Thank you to Donald Futers (formerly of Penguin Press) for believing in the book, and to the excellent people I've worked with at Penguin: my editor, Simon Winder and also Kim Walker, the publicity team led by Thi Dinh, my publicist Pen Vogler and her colleague Lotte Hall, marketer Shauna Lacy, Olivia Kumar, Ingrid Matts, Nile Faure-Bryan, Ruth Pietroni and many others. Having Edward Bettison illustrate the book has been a dream for this long-term fan. Thank you to the art department at Penguin and especially designer Isabelle De Cat for the beautiful cover. Thanks to Louisa Watson for conversations in the margins.

Finally, thanks to people without whom this book wouldn't exist. I still can't quite believe my luck in having the brilliant Gordon Wise as my agent. Thank you for all the super-smart questions and insights, for championing my work, and for helping me navigate (little) bumps in the road with humour as well as complete confidence. Big thanks also to Elliot Prior for all your support and expertise. To my colleague, IHR Director Claire Langhamer, I am more grateful than I can say. Thank you, Claire, for everything you've done to help bring this book to life. Working with you has simply been a huge gift.

Thank you to my family, especially Ellen and Thomas for your patience and love, and for brownies, *Beano* jokes, beach hut days and all those visits to museums and castles. And thank you to my mum and dad, who were there every step of the way and read every chapter first. I dedicate this book, with love, to you.

Copyright Information

Cover

Text

The following pages are for any of your own poem choices that you would like to add to this book.